D1067530

THE EQUIVOCAL VIRTUE

MRS. OLIPHANT
Undated photograph by [H.L.] Mendelssohn

Reproduced by permission of the Bodleian Library, Oxford University

THE

EQUIVOCAL VIRTUE

*Mrs. Oliphant and the Victorian
Literary Market Place*

By

Vineta and Robert A. Colby

ARCHON BOOKS
1966

Library of Congress Catalog Card Number: 66–12770
Printed in The United States of America

"It has been my fate in a long life of production
to be credited chiefly with the equivocal virtue
of industry, a quality so excellent in morals, so
little satisfactory in art."

—Mrs. Oliphant, Preface to
The Heir Presumptive and the Heir Apparent (1892)

Contents

Abbreviations

A & L. *The Autobiography and Letters of Mrs. M. O. W. Oliphant.* Arranged and Edited by Mrs. Harry Coghill. Edinburgh and London: William Blackwood and Sons, 1899. (All quotations in the text are from this edition of the *Autobiography* unless otherwise identified.)

Annals. *Annals of a Publishing House: William Blackwood and His Sons.* 3 vols. (Vols. I and II by Mrs. Oliphant, Vol. III by Mrs. Gerald Porter) Edinburgh and London: William Blackwood and Sons, 1897–1898.

Blackwood MSS. Correspondence of William Blackwood and Sons, on file in the National Library of Scotland, Edinburgh.

Isbister MSS. Correspondence of William Isbister, on file in the Parrish Collection, Princeton University.

Macmillan MSS. Correspondence of Macmillan and Company, on file at Macmillan and Company, Ltd., St. Martin's Street, London, W. C. 2.

Maga. *Blackwood's Edinburgh Magazine.*

Preface

The task of finding and collecting, not to mention reading, the works of a writer as prolific as Mrs. Oliphant is formidable. Henry James once remarked of her periodical journalism alone that she practiced it on such an inordinate scale "that her biographer, if there is to be one, will have no small task in the mere drafting of lists of her contributions to magazines and journals in general and to 'Blackwood' in particular." Happily, thanks to the efforts of Mrs. Oliphant's cousin, Mrs. Harry Coghill, a list of her contributions to *Blackwood's Magazine* over a forty-six year period and another list of her published books are included in Mrs. Oliphant's *Autobiography and Letters* (1899). But such lists are merely road maps. Locating the material is another problem.

There is no collected edition of Mrs. Oliphant's writings. The richest source of her printed books is the British Museum. We have also found much material in the New York Public Library, the Library of Congress, the Bodleian Library, and the Cambridge University Library. We believe we have read, with varying degrees of attention and interest, every known published work of Mrs. Oliphant's—a testimony to endurance rather than achievement.

The primary sources for materials on Mrs. Oliphant's life are her posthumously published *Autobiography and Letters* and a large number of her letters to various publishers. The *Autobiography and Letters,* edited by Mrs. Coghill, suffers the faults of many similar Victorian personal histories—inaccuracy in matters of names and dates, exasperating omission of details, and teasing

reticence. (". . . whole correspondences which would have been
so valuable have been destroyed," Mrs. Coghill writes. "One
series of letters . . . is too intimate to furnish much of general
interest.") Far more valuable, though necessarily fragmentary,
usually undated, and frequently illegible, are Mrs. Oliphant's unpublished letters to her publishers. We are indebted to William
Blackwood & Sons, Ltd., Edinburgh, and to The Trustees of the
National Library of Scotland for permission to use the Blackwood
correspondence; to Macmillan and Company, Ltd., for allowing
us to read a number of her letters in their offices in London; and
to the Parrish Collection at Princeton University which has forty-
nine of her letters to William Isbister, publisher of *Good Words.*
Wherever possible we have let Mrs. Oliphant speak for herself.
In quoting from her letters—all of them hurriedly and carelessly
written—we have added only sufficient punctuation to clarify the
reading.

No attempt is made here at a complete bibliography. In our
Chronology of Mrs. Oliphant's Principal Works we have simply
made some additions and corrections to Mrs. Coghill's list. Our
primary object has been to give an idea of Mrs. Oliphant's contribution to Victorian literature and to relate it to the work of
some of her contemporaries, as well as to the age for which it
was written.

Introduction

Margaret Oliphant Wilson Oliphant (1828–1897), or Mrs. Oliphant as she came to be known, was a born writer. One of her early novels, *The Athelings, or The Three Gifts* (1857), is concerned with the fortunes of three children, each endowed by nature in a different way. It is surely herself she was depicting in the daughter named Agnes, whose peculiar gift was "that strange faculty of expression which is as independent of education, knowledge, or culture as any wandering angel." So Mrs. Oliphant recognized that she must have been a special child "to whom Providence had given, almost her sole dower, that gift of speech which is so often withheld from those who have the fullest and highest opportunity for its exercise." This gift was to be her blessing and her curse. Such was her ironical destiny that of the some 125 books that issued from her fertile pen, few brought her great material reward, fewer still gave her any deep satisfaction, and none secured her lasting fame.

Mrs. Oliphant wrote herself into *The Athelings* as the imaginative daughter Agnes when she herself was at the beginning of her career, ripe with promise. All too soon that natural facility with words which made her the pride of her humble Scotch family and flattered her youthful vanity had to be turned to the humdrum problems of bread, board, and bairns. From her early and short-lived marriage on, she rarely knew either the leisure or the joy of real creation. A succession of unfortunate family circumstances forced upon her shoulders ever-increasing economic burdens which surely would have proved insuperable to a woman of less courage and resource. Added to her financial burden was the spiritual burden brought on by a series of family deaths that left her in her last years a lonely and disconsolate old woman, having survived even the two sons for whom she had labored so hard to provide. But so resilient a spirit did she have that in a dark moment she could echo a refrain from her native literature: "Werena my heart licht I wad dee."

Scotch sagacity and Scotch second sight, two faculties she retained even though she lived all her adult life in England, jostled together in Mrs. Oliphant's temperament and in her writing. The first enlivened that rural English community she called Carlingford, a district once as well known to readers as Barsetshire; the second cast over the familiar scene the strange light from the Land of the Unseen. Her literary country also took in the Scotland of history and her childhood memory, the Liverpool of her girlhood, London where she moved as a young wife, Italy and France where she ventured on her many travels, and Windsor where she settled. The enormous list of her writings is virtually a summary of popular Victorian genres, but it is to the Chronicles of Carlingford and the Stories of the Seen and the Unseen that we turn along with her *Autobiography* for the qualities of mind which are uniquely hers.

What most accommodates the present-day reader to Mrs. Oliphant's work is a certain urbanity of attitude she reflects towards some of the sanctities of popular Victorian fiction. An ingrained canniness, for one thing, preserved her from that sentimentality which was a constitutional defect of even some of the best of her contemporaries. This "Scotchness," together with early widowhood and the responsibilities it entailed, instilled in her a particularly tough-minded attitude towards such household gods as love, courtship, marriage and family life. For related reasons, the best of her religious fiction is pious without being pietistic. Her many sorrows made her well aware of the difficulties that attend religious faith, so that her Stories of the Seen and the Unseen are generally astringent rather than unctuous. The travel forced upon her by family and professional necessity gave her, moreover, an unusually cosmopolitan outlook, for all her conventionality. At the same time her extensive reading in the line of duty enlarged her religious sympathies and kept her mind awake, making her something of an apostle of culture to the magazine reading public. Mrs. Oliphant claims our respect, therefore, as one who was very much of the Victorian Age and yet, as she called herself in a *Maga* series, a "Looker-on" sufficiently detached to be critical of it.

While her literary career proved in many ways unrewarding and disappointing and although she was, in her typical fashion, cynical as to her accomplishments, one cannot say that it brought no pleasure. Certainly she took pride in her industry. In fact, despite frequent protestations of her own to the contrary, she earned a substantial livelihood—though never enough to suit her extravagant habits—in a precarious profession, virtually the only one open at this time to a gifted, energetic woman of ordinary family and little formal education. Above all, literature conferred upon her, as it had upon Dickens, social status. It brought her into touch with many of the leading writers and intellectuals of the day; it made possible Eton and Oxford educations for her sons; and she was the favorite novelist of her neighbor at Windsor, Queen Victoria.

Nevertheless, by the time Mrs. Oliphant put down her pen, which was not until almost the last day of her life, she was quite glad to be quit of this world. "I have worked a hole in my right forefinger—with the pen, I suppose!" she wrote to her publisher William Blackwood in 1896, the year before she died. The pity was that she felt she had little else to show for all her quill-driving. It was her supreme misfortune to have outlived not only all her loved ones, but her reputation, her creative energies, and, so she believed, her usefulness. She felt herself being superseded by younger, fresher talents, and was dimly aware of a new public with new interests which she lacked the ability and inclination to satisfy. She went to her grave convinced that she had long since had her day. The esteem in which she was held at her death, to judge by obituary notices, rather belies her gloomy assessment of herself, but it is true that such prestige as she still enjoyed at the end of the 1890's was quickly swept away in the wave of anti-Victorianism which came with the turn of the century and destroyed so many once flourishing reputations. Unlike a number of her contemporaries, however, she has not been swept back by the new tide. An out-of-print Everyman edition and a few stray anthology pieces may occasionally bring her name to the attention of twentieth-century readers, but most of the vast output that made her easily the most prolific writer of the nineteenth century is scattered to the winds or buried in the stacks of the British Museum.

Mrs. Oliphant predicted that she would be forgotten by the next generation, and perhaps her eclipse is a Dantean justice for one who wrote too fast and too much. Yet for some half a dozen novels that can hold their own with the best of Trollope and Mrs. Gaskell, for a *nouvelle* of imperishable beauty, for several shorter tales of piercing poignancy, and for a few works of non-fiction that reveal a fine, if over-taxed, mind, she may one day earn a reprieve from oblivion. Meanwhile, to go back over her career is to recall one of the richest and liveliest periods of our literary history. For the author it was, to echo one of the greatest of them, the best of times and the worst of times. This was a period of such close rapport of novelist with publisher, critic, and reader as the literary world has not known before or since. It saw the rise and decline of the three-decker, the heydey of serial publication, the emergence of new outlets for the writer's wares, the swelling of his audience—all of which made for the triple tyranny of middle-class reader, publisher, and circulating library and transformed the genteel profession of letters into a bustling literary market place. Mrs. Oliphant emerged, developed, and lived out her life in the midst of this ferment, and in many ways her career epitomizes the Victorian Age of English Literature, whose historian indeed she eventually became.

Let me be done with this—I wonder if I will ever have time to put a few autobiographical bits down before I die. I am in very little danger of having my life written, and that is all the better in this point of view—for what could be said of me? George Eliot and George Sand make me half inclined to cry over my poor little unappreciated self—"Many love me (*i.e.,* in a sort of way), but by none am I enough beloved." These two bigger women did things which I have never felt the least temptation to do—but how very much more enjoyment they seem to have got out of their life, how much more praise and homage and honour! I would not buy their fame with these disadvantages, but I do feel very small, very obscure, beside them, rather a failure all round, never securing any strong affection, and throughout my life, though I have had all the usual experiences of women, never impressing anybody,—what a droll little complaint!—why should I? I acknowledge frankly that there is nothing in me—a fat, little, commonplace woman, rather tongue-tied—to impress any one; and yet there is a sort of whimsical injury in it which makes me sorry for myself.

Autobiography

Chapter I

Beginnings

The Victorian novelist often showed a curious indifference to the pride of authorship. He may have been so inclined by simple modesty, by a reluctance to having his name connected with "lighter" literature, by fear of invasion of his privacy, or by practical business considerations. Some novelists of the period indeed were so prolific that they used pseudonyms or published anonymously to avoid flooding the market with their own work. For Mrs. Oliphant literature was primarily a commodity—a product sold in the market place to provide the income she needed for her endless and overwhelming family responsibilities. It is not surprising, therefore, that she took little interest in claiming personal credit for her work. Her novels, once her reputation was established, were usually published under her name, but in their first appearances in serial form they were for the most part unsigned. The bulk of her non-fiction contributions to *Blackwood's Edinburgh Magazine (Maga)*—more than two hundred critical articles and essays—was unsigned, the exceptions being a few poems and obituary articles initialled "M. O. W. O." From time to time she expressed strongly her wish that a work should remain anonymous. "No *name* please—not even initials. This I particularly desire in respect of this article and trust you will be good enough to secure that it shall be *quite anonymous*," she wrote with vigorous underlining to Alexander Macmillan in 1863. She was horrified when Richard Holt Hutton, co-editor of the *Spectator*, recognized her style and identified her as author of *A Son of the Soil*, then running in *Macmillan's Magazine*, and was only grad-

3

ually reconciling herself to it a year later as the novel was being prepared for publication in book form: "You will understand, I am sure, that I have not changed my opinion about putting my name to it. In this case, however, the want of a name can do no possible harm. Since people have decided it to be mine let them have their own way, but we need not give them any definite information on the subject." [1]

Yet for all this diffidence about acknowledging authorship, Mrs. Oliphant was not without pride both in her work and in her family name. She was an Oliphant twice over—by her mother, born Margaret Oliphant, and by her husband, who was also her cousin, Francis Wilson Oliphant. Her characteristic signature was M. O. W. Oliphant, and her name most often appears on the title pages as simply Mrs. Oliphant. Occasionally she signed herself Margaret Oliphant W. Oliphant, but after her marriage she never used her maiden name Wilson beyond the initial. Although she dismissed the Wilson side of her heritage rather lightly, she took some pains to explore the Oliphant genealogy. It is an old but modest family history. The name is of Norman origin and takes a variety of forms—Olifard, Olyfard, Oliver, Holiforth, Olyfant. Its first appearance in Scottish records is with Baron David de Olifard who accompanied Kind David I of Scotland to the siege of Winchester in 1142. Another Oliphant, Sir William of Aberdalgy in Forfarshire, defended Stirling Castle against the English. His son married Elizabeth, an illegitimate daughter of The Bruce, thus enabling future Oliphants to claim proudly that they had Good King Robert's blood in their veins. The Oliphants next appear in Fifeshire, with their family seat at Kellie Castle—peace-loving people, loyal to their Scottish kings, "very satisfactory in the point of view of the domestic virtues," Mrs. Oliphant writes of them, "but not, perhaps, indicative of much greatness." Kellie Castle was lost to the family in the middle of the seventeenth century, not in glorious battle but through simple indifference and apathy. Mrs. Oliphant told the story in "The Heirs of Kellie"—the old laird Sir Walter dying without children, stubbornly refusing to name his much younger sister, a mere girl, his heir; her hopeless struggle to claim her inheritance; its passing to Lord Oliphant who was in London in service of King James I; his preoccupation with other cares;

and the eventual sale of the castle to another family. The family ramifications are, inevitably, complicated. Mrs. Oliphant dismisses them briefly: "I am grieved to say that none of the many branches of the family have done anything very remarkable in life." [2]

It was perhaps the very idea of failure and disappointment that lent the Oliphant name a certain romantic charm. Mrs. Oliphant's mother raised her with a sense of belonging to "an old, chivalrous, impoverished race." If her own branch of the family was nothing "to brag of," to use her candid phrase, it was nevertheless a pretty delusion to which her mother clung stubbornly. The Wilson side of the family boasted no long history but also offered no delusions. Mrs. Oliphant gives them only the briefest notice in her *Autobiography*. Not until 1851, when she was already a rising young novelist visiting Edinburgh with her mother, did she meet two distinguished second cousins—George Wilson (1818–1859), the chemist and religious writer who held a chair of technology at the University of Edinburgh, and his brother Daniel (later Sir Daniel) Wilson (1816–1892), an archeologist and educator who became a professor of English literature and history at the University of Toronto and later its president. Their sister Jeanie married Mrs. Oliphant's brother Frank. The Wilsons, however, played no important role in Mrs. Oliphant's life. Her indifference to them is largely the result of the shadowy, unhappy presence of Francis Wilson, her father, a man treated so passingly in the *Autobiography* that the reader is left totally ignorant of his personality, his achievements, or his fate: "My father is a dim figure in all that phantasmagoria. I had to be very quiet in the evenings when he was at home, not to disturb him; and he took no particular notice of me or of any of us. My mother was all in all."

It had often been observed by critics of Mrs. Oliphant's fiction that it is woman-dominated, that her male characters are poorly realized, weak and ineffectual. Like any generalization, the statement is only partly true, but it is certain that Mrs. Oliphant repeatedly characterizes women as strong physically and mentally, shouldering the burdens imposed upon them by feckless fathers, brothers, and husbands. The parallels with her own life—dependent brothers, improvident invalid husband, disappointing invalid sons—are too striking to be ignored. And the dreary cycle begins

not with her father but goes back to her maternal grandfather—
"a prodigal and I fear a profligate," she wrote, who had abandoned
his wife and family to the charity of relatives.

Francis Wilson was neither a prodigal nor a profligate, but
neither was he in any way, apparently, significant. Mrs. Oliphant
is vague even about his occupation, recalling only that he worked
for a while in Liverpool in the Customhouse taking affidavits. He
supported his family adequately but not generously. It was a
modest, lower middle class household in which the mother did
her own housework; on weekends the elder son walked six miles
home from his work in town; and little Margaret herself smuggled
in precious letters arriving on the Glasgow-Liverpool steamer in
order to save the postage.[3] In family crises it was the mother who
acted, not the father. He remains so much on the periphery of
Mrs. Oliphant's consciousness that she neglects even to mention in
the *Autobiography* what finally became of him. There is only the
hint that after her mother's death he went off by himself some-
where. We know that he was alive as late as 1855 because in a
letter to Blackwood she asks that a copy of *Maga* be sent to her
father at Mrs. Garland's, Castle Street, Burntisland. "He has established himself there for the winter and finds it not very easy to
get books."[4]

Her father was nothing, but her mother, as she says, was "all
in all." She dominates the first pages of the *Autobiography;* her
presence dominates many of her daughter's novels. The mother,
as Mrs. Oliphant came to recognize in later life, had just those
characteristics which she noted in herself—industriousness, wit, a
sharp tongue, and a quick temper. There was also a strong physical
resemblance—fresh complexion, large brown eyes (Mrs. Oliphant
called them "the Oliphant eyes, which in their kind were not to
be despised, brown, flowing, and liquid, full of laughter and
light"), prominent upper teeth, a tendency toward premature
greying. Both mother and daughter were obsessively maternal.
Both knew the agony of losing children and of watching children
grow up into wasted and doomed adulthood.

Margaret was the child of her mother's old age. She was born
April 4, 1828, some years after her two older brothers, Francis
(Frank) and William (Willie) and after an interval during which

three other children had been born and had died. As the youngest, an only daughter and a bright and pretty child, she was a favorite. The sturdy Scots mother was not demonstrative, however. There was no caressing, no petting, no calling of sweet names. It was a lonely childhood: "I was never at a dance till after my marriage, never went out, never saw anybody at home." The father was anti-social and discouraged visitors. His work necessitated several family moves—first from her birthplace of Wallyford, a little village near Musselburgh, in sight of Edinburgh; then Lasswade, where her first recollections begin, another village on the Edinburgh road; then, when she was six, to Glasgow, a move which demanded a painful separation between the mother and her sons; and, when she was about ten, to Liverpool, and finally, about 1849, to its suburb Birkenhead, where they lived until Margaret's marriage in 1852.

Mrs. Oliphant's memories of her childhood are fragmentary. There is no reconstruction of the past, only glimpses of a quiet, sheltered household, with a mother uneducated but widely read (so fond of quoting Pope that the children called her "Popish") and fervently liberal in politics ("radical and democratic and the highest of artistocrats all in one"), and two lively and affectionate brothers. Margaret was a sensitive child given to introspection and day-dreaming. There is no evidence that she had any formal education, though she probably attended a local school. She could read by the age of six, winning the admiration of her fellow-travellers on a canal boat journey from Edinburgh to Glasgow with her accomplishment. Only a year or two later she dismayed the proprietor of the local circulating library by clamoring for the next installment of Lytton's *Ernest Maltravers*. "The old lady was first amazed and then shocked that so small a reader should be so eager for such a book, and discoursed to me most seriously on the subject, ending the lecture by bringing forth *Fatherless Fanny,* an improving work of the period. All being fish that came to my net, I devoured *Fatherless Fanny* without being less eager for the other works." She read enormously, but she records little else of that early reading—Madame Cottin's *Elizabeth,* Miss Mitford's *Our Village,* in which the idyllic country pictures were a comfort and delight to the child growing up in Liverpool, and of course

Lytton and Scott.[5] Beyond that is only conjecture. Her solid grounding in Scottish history and tradition strongly suggests the influence of Burns, John Galt, and certainly the literary physician David Macbeth Moir (whose pen name was "Delta"), a family friend who attended Margaret when she burned her arm in a childhood accident.

Literature was the family's relaxation and their pleasure. In the same casual and off-hand manner in which she read, Mrs. Oliphant began to write. Nursing her mother through an illness, she scribbled away at a novel to divert herself. She read what she wrote to the devoted family—the proud mother, the admiring older brother Frank. They encouraged her, and she wrote more, sitting at the family table in the evening, "with everything going on as if I had been making a shirt instead of writing a book," looking up from her work to take part in the family conversation, writing in that quick careless scrawl which was to plague her printers and publishers in later years. The easy flow of language, the quick, inventive mind, the capacity for work under the most distracting conditions were gifts that came to her early. It was all perhaps too easy and facile, as she recognized, somewhat bitterly, years later in her *Autobiography:*

> When people comment upon the number of books I have written, and I say that I am so far from being proud of that fact that I should like at least half of them forgotten, they stare— and yet it is quite true; and even here I could no more go solemnly into them, and tell why I had done this or that, than I could fly. They are my work, which I like in the doing, which is my natural way of occupying myself, though they are never so good as I meant them to be. And when I have said that, I have said all that is in me to say.

At eighteen or nineteen, however, writing was merely a delightful game. Half a century later as Mrs. Oliphant reviewed her career she could scarcely remember those first attempts. They did not seem to count in the overwhelming mass of fiction she produced. The first *published* novel she chose to acknowledge was *Passages in the Life of Mrs. Margaret Maitland of Sunnyside* (1849). She called that novel "my first production," though her autobiography makes it clear that she had written at least two other novels before it. The first little book, the one she wrote at sixteen during her mother's illness, she later turned over to her improvident brother Willie to publish "on his own account" (*Christian Melville,* 1856). The second, an ambitious three-volume affair, she burned some years later. She wrote, or had a hand in the writing of, two or three other novels; there is the testimony of her proud mother in a letter in 1852 describing the success of her daughter's novel *Katie Stewart,* which had been published anonymously: "The reason Mr. Blackwood gave for not saying who the author was, was that it might be good for her to have an anonymous reputation,—honest man, he little knew of 'John Drayton' and his neighbour." To this the editor of the *Autobiography,* Mrs. Coghill, added an explanatory footnote: "Novels published anonymously for the benefit of her brother William, which some ingenious critics have supposed to be written by him."[6]

Her brother Willie was the first of a long line of relatives who were to benefit from Mrs. Oliphant's industry—"My poor, good, tender-hearted, simple-minded Willie." She wrote these words years later, when her brother was an old man dying in Rome. He had been the black sheep of the family, a good boy with a fatal flaw. "Poor Willie! the handsomest, brightest of us all, with eyes that ran over with fun and laughter—and the hair we used to say he had to poll, like Absalom, so many times a year. Alas!" With typical Victorian reticence she never named the flaw, but it is obvious enough. Willie drank. Although he struggled valiantly against the habit, his life story, scanty in detail as it is, is the usual pathetic record of the confirmed alcoholic. He had been born in about 1819. He tried his hand at various occupations before he began to study for the ministry. He had been a clerk for some time in various businesses in Liverpool and had probably studied briefly at the University of Glasgow. His life is altogether a dismal record of failures and setbacks. He was at home in Liverpool idle a good deal of the time, yet not completely lost. The family's hopes for him rose and fell feverishly. In the early 1840's there was unemployment and hardship among the many Scottish engineers and their families in Liverpool. The Wilson family, united for once, rallied to the help of their fellow countrymen. Mr. Wilson was treasurer of a church-sponsored relief fund. Brother Frank, until then indifferent to religion, delighted his mother by plunging into church work. And Willie dashed about energetically distributing food and coal to the needy. There was another flurry of hope in the family when he set off to London to study for the ministry at the English Presbyterian College. Alone in London, however, Willie began to weaken, "fallen once more into his old vice and debt and misery," Mrs. Oliphant writes. It is a telling comment on the power of the women in the family that young Margaret, then only in her early twenties, was sent alone to London for three months to look after her erring brother and bring him into line again. She did her job zealously: "I was a little dragon watching over him with remorseless anxiety." She steered him along a strict and narrow course, never let him out of her sight except to attend his lectures, saw to it that he studied and paid his bills and at last completed his training.

Willie was ordained minister at Etal, a little village in the border country of Northumberland, October 24, 1850, and his sister bolstered his perhaps flagging courage with a vigorous and militant poem composed on the eve of the ceremony, "The Christian Knight's Vigil." With a refrain that echoes prophetically "Watch thine arms!" she urged him to brave and manful labor in the ministry, and Willie set out upon his career with high hopes. He spent a little less than two years at Etal. For part of that time at least he made a creditable record. There he wrote a novel, *Mathew Paxton* (1854). It is a story closely modeled upon the life of the community, in which local figures actually appear, and it won for Willie the title "The Literary Priest." He preached well and was popular with his congregation. But his "weakness" inevitably appeared, causing the inevitable gossip:

> On one occasion, being present at a baptism, and it being the custom to partake of the hospitality of the family, one of the friends having drunk to the health of the inmates put a peppermint lozenge in his mouth. When Mr. Wilson asked him why he did so, "Oh," said the man, "to put away the smell." "Oh," said Mr. Wilson, "I put away the smell by taking another glass."[7]

When the gossip reached the Berwick Presbytery, a member was sent to Etal to review matters. Before he arrived, Willie took flight.

This time it was his mother who came to the rescue, traveling north alone, and finally and hopelessly bringing her ruined son home to Birkenhead. Mrs. Oliphant's account of the remainder of Willie's story is brief—the painful reunion of the family (from which the father was characteristically absent), the long months of wretched idleness in which Willie sat home reading novels and smoking, his only work the occasional copying out of his sister's manuscripts, and the real horror of the situation—the fact that he seemed quite content in this existence. At last, some time in the early 1860's, Willie settled in Rome where he did odd jobs for the photographer Robert Macpherson but remained dependent upon his sister for financial support. She saw him very rarely. His sad history closes with an appeal from Mrs. Oliphant in a letter to her publisher Blackwood, May 18, 1885, for a loan of £200: "I have some immediate claims which I cannot provide for. . . . My poor brother, for whom I have long been in anxiety, is dying in Rome of a most painful and dreadful malady which has necessitated repeated and very costly as well as painful operations." Blackwood sent a check the next day, and we hear no more of Willie.[8]

Mrs. Oliphant shut Willie out of her life early, but the charming, ne'er-do-well alcoholic brother slips into her fiction over and over again. The image is unmistakably Willie, and the situation invariably duplicates the pathetic story she tells in the *Autobiography*. Within a year after Willie came home from Etal, the hopes of the family crushed, she published a novel, *Harry Muir: A Story of Scottish Life* (1853), in which the central character is a sweet and well-meaning young man whose weakness for drink almost ruins his family. Only his providential death in an accident and the tireless spirit of a strong-minded older sister save his wife and children from destitution. In this undistinguished and otherwise quite uninteresting novel, Mrs. Oliphant begins the process of exorcising the spirit of Willie from her conscience:

> When others praised the gay wit, the happy temper, the quick intelligence, those to whom he was dearest could only say, poor Harry! for the good and pleasant gifts he had made the bitterness of their grief only the deeper. Their pride in him aggravated their shame. Darkest and saddest of all domestic calamities, these women, to whom he was so very dear, could not *trust* the man

in whom all their hopes and wishes centered. He had not lost their affection—*it* seemed only the more surely to yearn over and cling to him, for his faults—but he had lost their confidence.

She continued to draw Willie—sometimes in light, almost comic, fashion, sometimes in tearful melodrama. In *The Doctor's Family* (1863) the hero is prevented from marrying because of his responsibilities to a drunken brother and his family. Here again it is a woman—the pretty young sister of the drunkard's wife—who shoulders the burden until, fortunately, he is killed in an accident (the second instance, one might note, of Mrs. Oliphant's unconscious will to brother-murder), leaving his widow, his sister-in-law, and the hero free for a happy ending. What is most remarkable here is the portrait of the wastrel brother which actually duplicates the portrait of Willie in the *Autobiography,* smoking and reading novels in total, happy idleness:

> The skeleton is not in a cupboard. It is in an upstairs room, comfortable enough, but heated, close, unwholesome—a place from which, even when the window is open, the fresh air seems shut out. There is no fresh air nor current of life in this stifling place. There is a fire, though it is not cold—a sofa near the fire— a sickening heavy smell of abiding tobacco—not light whiffs of smoke as accompany a man's labours, but a dead pall of idle heavy vapor; and in the midst of all a man stretched lazily on a sofa, with his pipe laid on the table beside him, and a book in his soft, boneless, nerveless hands. A large man, interpenetrated with smoke and idleness and a certain dreary sodden dissipation, heated yet unexcited, reading a novel he has read half a dozen times before.

Still another such brother appears in *The Perpetual Curate* (1864), although here, unmarried and independently wealthy, he victimizes no one and actually has a certain perverse charm. Nevertheless he is a lazy, unethical scoundrel and his first appearance sets him off in sharp contrast to his upright clergyman brother who is the hero of the book:

> He was in a dressing-gown with his shirt open at the throat, and his languid frame extended in perfect repose to catch the refreshment of the breeze. Clouds of languid smoke, which were too far out of the way to feel the draught between the windows, curled over him; he had a cigar in one hand, which he had just taken

from his lips, and with which he was faintly waving off a big night-moth which had been attracted by the lights; and a French novel, unmistakable in its paper cover, had closed upon the other. Altogether a more languid figure never lay at rest in undisturbed possession of the most legitimate retirement.

There are still other such unfortunate brothers—one in *The Days of My Life* (1857) who sits home in idleness with cigars and brandy while his sister and clergyman brother (named William, incidentally) support him; another, a promising young student in *A Son of the Soil* (1866), plans to study for the ministry until his life is wrecked by his fatal weakness.

Willie was a problem and a burden most of his life, but he did have his moments of enterprise. One of these was in 1849 when, a student in London, he took the manuscript of his sister's novel *Passages in the Life of Mrs. Margaret Maitland* to the publishing firm of Colburn. Whether he did so at her urging or out of brotherly pride in her accomplishments is unknown, but the news of its acceptance surprised and delighted her.

The future was suddenly full of promise for the young novelist. She went to London to watch over Willie, but also to meet her publisher and to receive proudly the sum of £150 for the book.

I remember walking along the street with delightful elation, thinking that, after all, I was worth something—and not to be hustled about. I remember, too, getting the first review of my book in the twilight of a wintry dark afternoon, and reading it by the firelight—always half-amused at the thought that it was *me* who was being thus discussed in the newspapers.

She saw her first play, *Twelfth Night,* with a disillusioning fat Viola played by Mrs. Charles Kean, and visited the National Gallery for the first time—again curiously disappointed, her sheltered provincial background leaving her completely unprepared for the appreciation of art. "I can't tell what I expected to see—something that never was on sea or shore. My ideal of absolute ignorance was far too high-flown, I suppose, for anything human. I was horribly disappointed, and dropped down from untold heights of imagination to a reality I could not understand." She also met her first society—her artist-cousin Frank (Francis) Oliphant whom she married three years later, his brother Tom, young Gerardine Bate, niece of the literary lady Mrs. Jameson. (Gerardine or Geddie, as she was called, was about to marry Frank Oliphant's friend Robert Macpherson.) Altogether it was a very modest social debut.

Her literary debut was equally modest, although the simple little book *Mrs. Margaret Maitland* caused something of a stir at the time of its publication and remained a popular novel for at least the next two decades. Mrs. Oliphant herself wondered about the reasons for its success and offered as good an explanation as any: "I cannot think why the book succeeded so well. When I read it over some years after I felt nothing but shame at its foolish little polemics and opinions. I suppose there must have been some breath of youth and sincerity in it which touched people, and there had been no Scotch stories for a long time."[9]

The mature and sophisticated novelist who wrote those words had good reason to question the success of her first published novel. She had been twenty when she wrote it—with no formal education, with a narrow and constricted family background and little or no experience of life. She had never been to London or travelled abroad; her memories of Scotland were kept alive only by her mother's stories of their old home; she lived in the drab industrial city of Liverpool and rarely even saw the countryside. This first novel, in fact all the novels written before 1860, reflects these deficiencies only too well. They are a series of experiments in various genres. There are regional novels exploiting the Scottish scene—*Margaret Maitland* (1849), *Merkland: A Story of Scottish Life* (1851), *Memoirs and Resolutions of Adam Graeme of Mossgray* (1852), *Harry Muir: A Story of Scottish Life* (1853), *Lilliesleaf: Conclusion of Margaret Maitland* (1855), *The Laird of Norlaw* (1858). There are historical novels—*Caleb Field* (1851), *Katie Stewart* (1853), *Magdalen Hepburn* (1854). There are domestic romances—*The Quiet Heart* (1854), *Zaidee* (1856), *The Days of My Life* (1857), *The Athelings, or The Three Gifts* (1857), *Lucy Crofton* (1860). There are "issue" novels—the issue specifically being the position of women—*Orphans: A Chapter in Life* (1858) and, to a lesser degree, the above-mentioned *Merkland*. In *Merkland,* incidentally, she also experimented tentatively with the genre of the sensation novel, introducing a murder mystery into her plot. And finally there were some miscellaneous efforts—one in children's (more precisely young girls') literature, *Agnes Hopetoun's Schools and Holidays* (1859), and another in non-fiction evangelistic prose, *Sundays* (1858).

As experiments these books have some interest. Their intrinsic merits are few. Only the demands of the fiction market of the 1850's, the ever-increasing clamor for novels at once entertaining and highly moral, can account for her early success, the fact that eminent publishers like Blackwood's seized upon her work and that critics received it favorably. With the exception of some regional humor and local color in the Scottish novels, these books strike the modern reader as totally undistinguished.[10] The qualities which enliven so much of her later fiction—satire, sophistication, cynical humor—are totally lacking. The early novels are the work of a period of trial and error, experimentation and rejection. Though she must have known at first hand every type of fiction produced in the 1850's, the young novelist was careful to work only in those genres in which she was at home or which she could master by a reasonable amount of study. Thus, familiar as she was with the novels of Lytton and Mrs. Gore, she steered clear of the society novel. When she very rarely introduced characters of the upper classes she kept a careful distance from them. She never described a contemporary European scene until she had been to the Continent. Germany, which she visited on her wedding journey, is introduced briefly in *Zaidee* and *Days of My Life;* but France and Italy, the scenes of many of her later stories, are never used. As the range of her personal experience widened, so did her settings and the range of her characters. She began with characters closest to home—warm-hearted Scotch matrons, simple country folk, innocent home-loving heroines, Liverpool clerks. With her marriage and move to London the horizon widened—artists, writers, well-to-do business people. But each step forward was tentative. Indeed, there is little evidence of steady progress in the work of this first decade of her career, either in technique or conception, and *Margaret Maitland,* the earliest book, is certainly the best of them.

As Mrs. Oliphant suggested, the success of her first novel may be explained in part at least by its "youth and sincerity" and in part by the fact that there was a market for Scotch stories. These were the appeals of the book to the formidable critic Francis Jeffrey who, only a few weeks before his death, wrote an enthusiastic letter to the unknown author:

Edinburgh, 5th January 1850

I was captivated by 'Margaret Maitland' before the author came to *bribe* me by the gift of a copy and a too flattering letter— which I am now taking the chance of answering—though not trusted either with the name or address of the person to whom I must express my gratitude and admiration! Nothing half so true or so touching (in the delineation of Scottish character) has appeared since Galt published his 'Annals of the Parish'—and this is purer and deeper than Galt, and even more absolutely and simply true.

To be sure, Jeffrey was equally outspoken in his objections to the book. He found it overly long, "sensibly injured by the indifferent matter which has been admitted to bring it up to the standard of three volumes." But the general impression was favorable. He was touched by the book's naturalness, the keen and sympathetic observation of the Scottish character, and the sturdy moralizing.[11]

The novel is a first-person narrative by Margaret Maitland, a spinster, "a quiet woman of discreet years and small riches." Her father, brother, and nephew are all ministers in the Kirk of Scotland. She lives by the strictest religious principles, having once, before the action of the book begins, rejected a suitor whose principles were too lax. Remote and isolated as her life is, however, she becomes deeply involved in the lives of others—her brother and his family, her neighbors, and, most important, a distant relative, a little motherless girl, Grace Maitland, whom she adopts. Grace's experiences in claiming her inheritance from an unscrupulous father and her romance with Margaret Maitland's nephew provide the substance of the plot. There is a parallel romance between her niece and a wealthy and headstrong young man. (Their married life is the main subject of the sequel, *Lilliesleaf*.) The sentimental love episodes, the intrigue and villainy, are singularly slight and uninteresting; what holds the reader's attention primarily is the authentic Scottish background of the story.

The Scottish regional novel enjoyed wide popularity in the first third of the nineteenth century. For the English reader of the period Scotland had the charms of the remote, the half-civilized and the half-savage. He knew it best from the historical image Sir Walter Scott had created, in which outlaws and renegades probably stood out more prominently—for the reader at least—than the nobler souls like David and Jeanie Deans. In fact the popular conception of the Scotsman in the literature of this period was largely comic or grotesque. Susan Ferrier had satirized him; Galt had drawn him sympathetically but rather broadly in *Annals of the Parish;* and David Macbeth Moir had made him a farcical figure in *Mansie Wauch.* What Mrs. Oliphant offered was the more natural and homely domestic scene. Here is no Scotland of quaint and eccentric regional types, but of quite ordinary people who differ from their English cousins only in dialect and perhaps in their stricter observance of the Sabbath. Otherwise they are much the same as the rest of the world. While not ignoring their uniqueness as Scots, neither did she emphasize nor exaggerate their "Scotchness." Margaret Maitland is more pious and certainly more conservative than her southern counterparts might be, but essentially she is the universal matron, modelled slightly, Mrs. Oliphant tells us, upon her own mother.

The career of the young novelist, launched so modestly in 1849, did not really begin until 1851 when she made a trip to Edinburgh. There she met her Wilson relatives and, through them, Major William Blackwood, partner with his brother John in the publishing firm of William Blackwood and Sons. She was admitted to the inner sanctum, as it were, with an introduction by her old family friend Dr. Moir to the colorful and venerable John Wilson, who, under the pen name of "Christopher North," had enlivened the pages of *Maga* during the 1820's with his share of the satirical *Noctes Ambrosianae* (other contributors were Lockhart, Maginn, and Hogg). The young author was deeply impressed by the tall, gaunt old man—"a Norse demigod," she called him. Dr. Moir made some introductory remarks about her literary achievements and suggested that she should be warned against overwork. "No need of that," North said, "so long as she is young and happy work will do her no harm."[12]

These were only social meetings, but they marked the beginning of a long and productive connection. Although Mrs. Oliphant had many publishers and contributed to a literally countless number of periodicals, she was identified by her contemporaries and she identified herself primarily as a Blackwood's author. She took great pride in the association, and in spite of a few stormy passages between them over the years, it was on the whole a happy one for her. She was fully aware of and impressed by the prestige of the firm, its power in literary circles, and, not least, its staunchly Scottish roots. She had boldly but unsuccessfully submitted *Margaret Maitland* to them in 1849. During the next two years, as a published author with at least three novels to her credit and more under way, she gained in assurance. When she returned to Birkenhead from Edinburgh, she completed *Katie Stewart*. Her letter offering the story to the firm is in the files of the Blackwood correspondence and rather charmingly reveals the canny business sense of the young writer:

> 24 Kenyon Terrace
> Birkenhead, 26 November
> [1851]
>
> Sir,
> I am just now engaged upon a story which I should be pleased to publish in your Magazine if you had space for or were inclined to accept it. It will be no longer than one octavo volume, perhaps scarcely so much as one volume of 'The Caxtons' [Bulwer's novel, then running serially in the magazine]. The story is a true one, a bit of family history, illustrating the rural life of Fife in the middle of the last century, and the rebellion of '45 passes over the scene though it does nothing more.
> I see that it is not your custom to make Bulwer's fine novel your sole piece of fiction—and there are so many old kindlinesses of feeling connected with your Magazine that it would please me better to have this story appear in it than in the usual way.
> At the same time I should not think it right to do this at a pecuniary loss. Will you then be good enough to tell me whether it would suit you to accept my MS and what are the terms on which you generally treat this class of contributions.
>
> M. O. Wilson[13]

On January 16, 1852 she sent the manuscript, and on February 4 the Blackwoods accepted it, though with some criticism of its "want of incident." She asked for £200 but indicated a willingness to discuss terms if that sum were unsuitable. Evidently it was, for a week later she wrote to accept the offer of £100, "and when you have ascertained how your one-volume edition sells, if it is sufficiently successful, I shall not scruple then to accept the additional fifty."[14] She received the galley proofs of *Katie Stewart* on May 4, 1852, her wedding day.

Few writers have said so little and yet so much about their personal lives as Mrs. Oliphant. There is remarkable candor in the *Autobiography,* which she intended for posthumous publication, but also an infuriating reticence. She freely described her brother's weakness; she frankly admitted her disappointment in her sons' failures to establish themselves professionally; she gratuitously informed us of conflict between her mother and her husband; and she openly accused her husband of irresponsibility in dragging her and their children to Italy on what he knew would be a fatal expedition for himself. Yet nowhere did she give any inkling of what it was that first attracted her to him, of why she abruptly changed her mind and agreed to marry him after she had refused him, or of whether she loved him. On these matters, apparently, Victorian modesty sealed her lips. It is not difficult to sketch in most of the details from the outline she left in the *Autobiography* and in her letters, but such work remains only conjecture and has from time to time produced rather dubious conclusions.[15]

One must assume that the marriage was a love match. There was too much family friction and too little advantage on either side for it to have been an "arranged" marriage. One may also safely conclude that it was neither critical unhappiness at home nor desperate fear of spinsterhood that forced her into it. Her parents moved to London to be near her after the marriage, so no escape was involved, and her successful writing career, combined with her natural reserve and independence and the fact that she was only twenty-four, scarcely even by Victorian standards an old maid, preclude any possibility that it was a last-chance grab at matrimony. There seems no reason to doubt that Frank Oliphant was an attractive man, with some success as an artist behind him and a bright future ahead. He was sophisticated, well-travelled, cultivated, and had interesting if somewhat bohemian friends. As her cousin he had the advantages of familiarity and respectability; as an artist whom she had only recently met he had the charm of distance. What was more inevitable and more promising than that these two talented people should fall in love and marry? True, she had refused his first offer in 1849. But at that time, she explains in the *Autobiography*, "my mind had been preoccupied with Willie chiefly and a little with my book." When Oliphant turned up in Birkenhead to propose, she was "totally unprepared" and could answer only "an alarmed negative, the idea never having entered my mind." But, she continues, "in six months or so things changed. It is not a matter into which I can enter here."

The marriage was not an altogether happy one. For this a large measure of blame is surely external and circumstantial—financial difficulties, the deaths of two babies, Frank Oliphant's ill health and premature death. Part of the responsibility must be borne by Oliphant who was too self-absorbed, apparently, and perhaps not sufficiently gifted to succeed in either his family responsibilities or his work. But Mrs. Oliphant was equally at fault. Interestingly, she gives evidence of her own suspicions that in some ways she had failed her husband as much as he failed her. She never analyzed the marriage. She described it briefly in the *Autobiography* with a touching mixture of happiness and regret. Nowhere else, certainly not in her letters, does she do more than allude to it. Yet, as with so many other problems in her life, she dramatized it endlessly in her fiction, going back to the subject time and again relentlessly as if to work it out for herself, shaping and reshaping it in different but always thinly veiled fictitious disguises.

Mrs. Oliphant wrote in the *Autobiography* that only once in her life did she ever use "an actual bit of real life" in a book. This was a brief sketch of the painter George Lance who appears in the novel *Zaidee* as the jolly Mr. Steele. Her statement is simply not true.[16] She drew so literally and so constantly out of her personal experience that sometimes one almost squirms in embarrassment at the painful frankness and intimacy of some of her writing. The image of Willie as it appears and reappears in the novels was a relatively uncomplicated one. Francis Wilson Oliphant was a more complex personality, and her feelings toward him were more deeply involved and divided. As a result he figures more prominently in outline but often less distinctly in detail than does Willie. He was an artist, more probably of talent than of genius, and unlucky in his choice of artistic specialization. His memory survives in a brief entry in the *Dictionary of National Biography*, one slim volume that he wrote—*A Plea for Painted Glass, Being an Inquiry into its Nature, Characters, and Objects and its Claims as an Art* (Oxford, 1855)—and the record of having exhibited several paintings at showings of the Royal Academy. He was a Scotsman, though born in England at Newcastle-on-Tyne, August 31, 1818. He grew up in Edinburgh, studied at the Edinburgh Academy of Art, and, by his own account, "was practically trained from a child to glass painting." Coming thus early under the influence of the Gothic Revival in architecture, Oliphant steeped himself in ecclesiastical art. It was his bad luck that the revival was ephemeral and that by the time he reached professional maturity and should have been realizing success in his work the movement was already in decline. Nevertheless, during the 1840's he had had some encouragement. For eleven years he assisted Augustus Welby Pugin, a leader in the Gothic Revival, designing the figures for which the older artist did the ornamental decorations, and in 1846 Oliphant came to London to do the cartoons for the glass in the new House of Lords. He travelled extensively in Germany, France, Belgium, and Holland, studying church architecture and stained glass. He also had some success as a painter of large, ambitious "story" paintings of the type so popular in mid-century Victorian art. His painting of the interview between Richard II and John of Gaunt sold "for a tolerable price," his wife recalled.

Two years after his marriage Oliphant went into business for himself, setting up a studio where he could execute his own designs. Here he produced some windows for the ante-chapel of King's College, Cambridge, those for the chancel in Aylesbury Church, and the design and drawing for the east end of Ely Cathedral.[17] He started out on the venture hopefully enough. Though he preferred painting, glass work had the distinct advantage of offering a more steady and a larger income, provided, of course, there was a market for it and also provided the business was run efficiently. But Oliphant was not a business man. He had trouble managing

his workmen. His financial records were so chaotic that a businessman who examined them congratulated him "that his circumstances
permitted him to be so indifferent to profit." Furthermore, he had
a charming but, for a man in his position, unfortunate indifference
to making money, an open-handed and open-hearted artistic generosity which at times dismayed his wife. For example, when no
donor appeared for one of the windows he had designed for the
Aylesbury Church, Oliphant donated the window himself. At the
time, Mrs. Oliphant remarks, "it seemed the most natural and
pleasant thing in the world." When, shortly after, he died, leaving
his family penniless, the church made the window a memorial to
him—"a graceful act, which gave some forlorn pleasure to his
widow, then just returning with her little children to an altered
life at home."[18]

At no time did the studio provide the steady income which Oliphant needed for his family. This is not to suggest that he failed in
his responsibilities nor that his wife was forced to write, during the
early years of their marriage, simply to avoid starvation. But the
security of a regular income was lacking. Within the first year of
her marriage Mrs. Oliphant was writing to Blackwood for money:
"We are just now (my husband and I) reached to that tide in the
affairs of men, which I fancy must strain nerve and sinew in all
who have their own fortune to make, but I have no doubt that
your seasonable help is all we need to bring us over the crisis once
for all."[19]

Never in the forty-five years which remained to Mrs. Oliphant
was she brought over that crisis "once for all." Her financial needs
increased and multiplied endlessly. But in these early years there
was at least a cheerful, independent note to her appeals:

24 January [1853]

Now I find myself to have a present occasion for fifty pounds. If
'John Rintoul' seems to you suitable for the Magazine, and is
worth so much, may I ask you to send me that sum as soon as
you shall find it convenient. I don't put this value on my story—
because I am neither sure of its dimensions nor understand how
you are in the habit of doing with contributors of short articles,
but if you think the story worth as much to you as the sum I
have mentioned, it will be a matter of personal convenience to
me.[20]

Again, on July 22, 1854, she wrote: "It happens that just at the present time I am considerably in want of money." When Oliphant opened his studio the need became even more urgent:

n.d. [1854]

My husband has been engaged for some time lately in fitting up *ateliers* for the execution of works in the branch of art to which he has been gradually induced to devote himself, and in consequence our income has had a great many things to do which incomes in general do not have the burden of.

March 28 [1854]

I come immediately to matters of everyday prose. I should like very much if you would employ me in some miscellaneous work— reviews or essays of the lighter sort—by which I might make fifty pounds by the end of May.[21]

Oliphant himself sought the aid of the Blackwoods, at first indirectly through his wife and later directly. Just three months after their marriage he offered to illustrate his wife's novel *Katie Stewart*. Mrs. Oliphant proposed this to the Blackwoods with considerable delicacy: "I think Mr. Oliphant might not be disinclined to make sketches for some of the interior scenes himself." In October of the same year Oliphant applied to them directly, offering to do a half-dozen illustrations etched on copper or wood. The Blackwoods declined the offer and Mrs. Oliphant accepted their decision meekly: "I believe it is the wisest plan after all to leave 'Katie Stewart' unillustrated." But *Katie Stewart* was not left unillustrated.[22] The first edition appeared in 1853 with two engravings by J. Adams. The Oliphants could not resist a final thrust:

5 January [1853]

Katie Stewart's externals are very good, and it makes a pretty little volume—but I don't think it is improved by the illustrations. Mr. Oliphant has just been pointing out to me the contrast between them and the "Vicar of Wakefield" which he originally suggested as a kind of model—it is certainly very striking—and he begs me to desire of you very particularly that in case a second edition should be called for, these illustrations may be omitted. He thinks in comparison with the many fine things constantly produced, that the character is lowered and injured by them.[23]

The offending illustrations were not removed in the second edition of 1855.

In 1856 Oliphant appealed to the Blackwoods for their intercession in helping him to obtain a much desired appointment to design and execute new windows for Glasgow Cathedral. He wrote at least half a dozen letters that year to the Major and to John Blackwood. He described himself—with the self-boosting that is inevitable in letters of this sort—as having attained "a knowledge of my art equalled by few, indeed by any in Britain, nor do I fear any comparison with foreign artists . . . and certainly think I can advance as fair pretensions to the local Scotch commission as any of them can."[24] What he sought from the Blackwoods was a recommendation to the art collector and historian Sir William Stirling Maxwell of Keir, a member of the committee which would select the artist. The Blackwoods were evidently cooperative, at least to the extent of suggesting that he see Thackeray and get an introduction to Stirling through him. Whether Oliphant got the invitation we do not know. He did not get the commission. This was simply another disappointment—one in the long run affecting him less seriously than it did his wife.

In Mrs. Oliphant's fiction of this period there was beginning to arise a new image—the artist of talent and promise who is a failure in his work and consequently in his life. Years later she transferred this image to herself, seeing in her own lifetime of grinding industry only the reward of neglect and the disappointment of being passed over by newer and more popular writers. But not more than a year after her marriage she was already playing with the idea. In a story so personal that one wonders how she could have allowed her husband to read it, *The Quiet Heart* (published in *Maga* December 1853–May 1854; in book form in 1854), she introduced a heroine whose mother and fiancé are in open conflict. The heroine and her mother come down from their home in Scotland to London where the fiancé, on the basis of one successful book, has a promising career as a journalist. During the same year in which Mrs. Oliphant wrote this novel her parents moved to London and settled in a little house in Park Village near her, a step which she soon regretted: "Had the circumstances been different—had they stayed in Birkenhead and I gone alone with my husband to London—some unhappiness might have been spared. Who can tell? . . . Our house in Harrington Square was very near: it looked all happy enough but was not, for my husband and my mother did not get on." There was no serious rift, but there were irritations, clashes of personality—the outspoken, critical mother, proud of her talented young daughter, the equally proud and outspoken artist, a little contemptuous perhaps of his provincial in-laws, certainly resentful of his possessive mother-in-law.

The conflict in *The Quiet Heart* is rooted in precisely these delicate relationships. The mother, Mrs. Laurie, thinks the fiancé, Randall Home, proud and arrogant. He in turn is irritated and antagonized by everything she says. Menie, the daughter, is of course the victim of all this friction. She longs to intervene, to say from one to the other—" 'He means something else than he says; he is not cold-hearted nor insincere; you mistake Randall. . . . Do not speak so; you vex my mother; but she does not mean to be angry.' " At last the engagement is broken, though through no fault of Mrs. Laurie's. Menie returns to Scotland sorrowfully, presumably to spinsterhood. Here the plot takes an ironic twist. In the years that follow, Menie, who had shown some talent for art, becomes a successful illustrator. Home meanwhile is never able to match the success of his first book and rapidly sinks into failure. The novel ends five years later with Home, humble and contrite, returning to Menie and her mother: "Day by day, advancing steadily, the son drew farther in, to his domestic place. The mother gave her welcome heartily; the daughter, saying nothing, felt the more."

In 1853 it was perhaps only morbid day-dreaming for Mrs. Oliphant to imagine her husband a failure. He was young and had his future before him. Twenty years later, however, when he was but a memory, she could see her early suspicions only too sadly realized. Oliphant was dead and his work forgotten outside the family circle. In *At His Gates,* published in 1872, she introduced an artist and his wife and examined their relationship with extraordinary frankness. The artist is moderately successful; the family is happy and prosperous; but the wife is plagued by her lack of faith in him:

> Robert, good Robert, was not a success either, not such a man as she had hoped. She loved him sincerely, was grateful to him for his love, and his constant regard to her wishes. But yet in the depths of her heart,—no, not despised him, the expression is too strong,—but felt a minute shade of indignation mingled in her disappointment with him for not being a great genius. *Why* was he not a Raphael, a Titian?

She is painfully conscious of her failure in her duty towards him, yet she is unable to change, seeing herself sometimes as Lucrezia, the soul-destroying wife in Browning's "Andrea del Sarto," goading him into misery. After some disastrous financial speculations, the artist is ruined and disappears, presumably a suicide. For the next seven years his wife and daughter struggle in genteel poverty, until finally he is restored to his family. During his absence he has painted one great picture, the only achievement of his life. Nothing else he does ever comes up to it. Nevertheless, as a result of her long years of lonely widowhood, the wife is now content with his mediocrity: "She was satisfied; her craving for genius and fame had once been fed, almost to the cost of their lives, and now she was content to descend to the gentler, lower work—the work by which men earn their daily bread." This is the kind of adjustment to reality that Mrs. Oliphant could give her characters, but could not apparently make herself.

If it was not altogether a happy marriage, however, neither was it altogether unhappy. A favorite situation in Mrs. Oliphant's novels is the mental and emotional maturing of a young heroine through the experience of marriage. This process may be the result of stark tragedy—poverty, widowhood, the deaths of children—or it may be through gentler strokes of fate—the piling up of domestic and social responsibilities, the disenchantment as romantic love fades into married routine. Her own maturing was a product of both. On the less somber side there was the establishment of a home—a modest but genteel house at 6 Harrington Square in northwest London, then, as the family increased, a larger house at 7 Ulster Place. There was a wedding tour to Germany in the late summer of 1852,[25] and there was a modest, but to the shy and sheltered young Mrs. Oliphant, rather active social life. Her husband, who was more sociable than she, took her to parties, urged her to pay and receive calls, all of which she did in a reluctant, half-hearted fashion.

From the distant perspective of 1888 when she was writing her autobiography, a sophisticated woman who travelled in very high social circles indeed, the society of 1852 seemed "not of a very elevating kind," and she looked back at it with amusement and not a little scorn. To some degree it had been a disillusioning experience. She had expected to meet brilliant, profound, witty, successful people. Instead she met second-raters—good, kind people, artists and writers, but plainly mediocre. She sketched some of them sharply in the *Autobiography*: Mr. Stephen Watson Fullom, whom she had regarded as "an eminent literary man . . . He turned out a very small personage indeed, a solemn man, with a commonplace wife, people whom it was marvellous to think of as intellectual. He wrote a book called 'The Marvels of Science,' a dull piece of manufacture." And the Samuel Carter Halls, a literary couple of unflagging energy and awesome productivity (they wrote and edited, it has been estimated, more than five hundred volumes): "Mrs. Hall had retired upon the laurels got by one or two Irish novels, and was surrounded by her husband with the atmosphere of admiration, which was the right thing for a 'fair' writer. He took her very seriously, and she accepted the role, though without, I think, any particular setting up of her own standard." And Dinah Mulock (later Mrs. Craik), whose phenomenally successful *John Halifax, Gentleman* was yet to be written: "She was a tall young woman with a slim pliant figure, and eyes that had a way of fixing the eyes of her interlocutor in a manner which did not please my shy fastidiousness. It was embarrassing, as if she meant to read the other upon whom she gazed— a pretension which one resented. It was merely, no doubt, a fashion of what was the intense school of the time." And a "lion-hunting" American who wrote under the name "Grace Greenwood" (Mrs. Sara Jane Clarke Lippincott), whom Mrs. Oliphant remembered as being very patronizing to her and describing her as "a homely little Scotch woman" in a book. Actually Miss Greenwood was more flattering, for she wrote:

Of our party that day was the authoress of Margaret Maitland, of
Sunnyside—a fair Scotchwoman, not over twenty-two, a modest,
quiet, lovable person, who seems far from having made up her
mind to admit the fact of her own genius. Having wakened one
morning to find herself famous, she believes the world to be labor-
ing under some strange delusion, and counts herself an immensely
overrated little woman after all.[26]

There were others, sketched briefly—the badly crippled Frank
Smedley who wrote sporting novels about daring feats of strength
and athletics (*Frank Fairlegh, Harry Coverdale's Courtship,* and
so on); Mary Howitt and her husband and collaborator William,
famous as editors of miscellanies and authors of popular histories;
a playwright, George William Lovell (whose *The Wife's Secret*
struck Mrs. Oliphant when she saw a revival of it in the 1880's
as "one of the most conventional and unreal possible").

Fortunately, there were more satisfactions than society for Mrs.
Oliphant in these years. She was achieving modest success as an
author. The novels were uneven, to be sure, and the critical recep-
tion and sales in this period left something to be desired. But by
1854 she had the additional satisfaction, financial as well as
spiritual, of being a regular contributor of reviews and essays to
Blackwood's Magazine. For a girl in her mid-twenties a position
like this on a journal of such prestige as *Maga* was considerable.
The Blackwoods called her "Katie" for her first contribution to
their pages, *Katie Stewart,* and they relied on her for important
work. "If you're sure of [Sir Edward] Hamley, [Laurence]
Oliphant, and Katie for this month, we shall have a first-rate number," the Major wrote his brother. In February 1856 he visited
her in Ulster Place and reported: "They have a nice house off
Regent's Park at the head of Portland Place . . . a nice situation.
She was working away at Sydney Smith. . . . She did not think his
works correspond with his reputation; so he will be let down a peg
or two."[27] She spoke her mind freely in these early articles for
Maga and handled an amazing variety of subjects from art and
travel to theology and literature. For the Blackwoods the advantage lay primarily in the fact that she was intelligent, tractable,
and reliable. For Mrs. Oliphant the advantage was primarily a

steady income, but she was also getting a vast, perhaps scattered but certainly valuable education:

> I suppose I must have become by this time a sort of general utility woman in the Magazine, as I remember being called upon to write a short article on this [Warren's *Religion in Common Life*] at a moment's notice, which I did in the midst of a removal, with flying pen, in a room unoccupied as yet by anything but dust and rolled up carpets, where a table and an inkpot had been hurriedly set out for me. Never was trumpet blown under more disadvantageous circumstances.[28]

Her career was a source of pride and gratification as well as income in the early years of her marriage. The greatest source of whatever happiness she had, however, was her children. The bitterness she may have felt toward her husband was more than balanced in the total account by the fact that he had given her children. Motherhood was her passion. Any other human relationship, any intellectual pursuit, was secondary to it. "At my most ambitious of times I would rather my children had remembered me as their mother than in any other way."

The first baby was a daughter, Margaret (Maggie), born May 21, 1853. A year and a day later, on May 22, 1854, a second daughter, Marjorie, was born,[29] but almost simultaneously with the arrival of this child came Mrs. Oliphant's mother's fatal illness. Mrs. Wilson lived through a long and painful summer and died in September 1854, leaving the daughter who had nursed her faithfully with a guilty sense of relief that the ordeal was over. In February 1855 the baby Marjorie died, and Francis Oliphant wrote to the Blackwoods for his wife: "Our poor little darling left us as we feared, about half past three, yesterday afternoon. Mrs. Oliphant would beg as a favour that her article on Chas. Dickens which was to have appeared in the Magazine for March might now be arranged for April."[30] The shock of the child's death was perhaps no greater for Mrs. Oliphant than the realization of how much more this grieved her than had her mother's death: "My dearest mother, who had been everything to me all my life, and to whom I was everything; the companion, friend, counsellor, minstrel, story-teller, with whom I had never wanted for constant interest, entertainment, and fellowship,—did not give me, when she died, a pang so deep as the loss of the little helpless baby, eight months old . . . at that moment her loss was nothing to me in comparison with the loss of my little child." There was a further blow to be endured, the death of another baby who lived but one day. For a while it seemed as if Mrs. Oliphant's healthy constitution would give way, but comfort came quickly in the form of a fine, strong son. Cyril, called throughout his childhood "Tiddy" from his baby mispronunciation of his name, was born on a Sunday, November 16, 1856, between galley proofs and press deadlines. On November 18 Frank Oliphant sent some of his wife's galleys back to John Blackwood, writing happily that "both are doing very well indeed—how well my wife is getting on you may guess when I tell you she corrected the enclosed today, with the consent of her nurse and without effort to herself."[31]

The three years that followed were filled with work and domestic felicity. Money was short, Oliphant's business was precarious, and, although his wife's writings had a market, she was receiving warnings from all sides against over-producing.[32] Nevertheless, because her children were thriving, she lived in a kind of euphoria which no other concerns could really disturb. She reproduces most vividly in the *Autobiography* not the great dramatic incidents of her life, but the inconsequential glimpses of utter, though momentary, contentment—a quiet evening of sewing at home, the children asleep: "It was light enough with the lamplight outside for all I wanted. I can see it now, the glimmer of the outside lights, the room dark, the faint reflection in the glasses, and my heart full of joy and peace—for what?—for nothing—that there was no harm anywhere, the children well above stairs and their father below." Not even the first symptoms of her husband's tuberculosis seriously alarmed her. She was concerned, but only in a fitful, erratic way— so serene in her little domestic world that she could not really believe that anything could upset it. She had gone to Scotland with the children on a holiday and then in sudden panic, as if suspecting that she had deserted him, she telegraphed her husband in London. He reassured her. Indeed, the burden of her bitterness against him was the fact that he always reassured her and took even the most serious of matters in his light, easy way.

By the end of 1858 it was apparent, perhaps to everyone but his wife, that Oliphant was gravely ill. He consulted a Harley Street specialist and came away cheerfully to tell her that the report was excellent—a brief rest in Italy and he would be fit again. He lied only to shield her; yet when after his death his friend Robert Macpherson told her of the deception, she could not forgive her husband: "I was angry and wounded beyond measure and would not believe that my Frank had deceived me, or told another what he did not tell to me. Neither do I think he would have gone away, to expose me with my little children to so awful a trial in a foreign place had this been the case." The Italian journey was a nightmare from start to finish. They set out in January 1859 with almost no money. Their only prospects of getting any were in Mrs. Oliphant's hands. She had engaged, before they left, to contribute articles to *Maga,* for which she would receive a stipend of £60 quarterly. Oliphant, who had never been to Italy, now quickly turned into a helpless, querulous invalid. This left the entire burden on his wife who at that time could speak neither French nor Italian, was totally inexperienced in travel, and was preoccupied with two children, aged five and two. Her only help was a loyal and sturdy nursemaid, Jane, "a finely developed, strong, large substantial tower of a woman." Before the year ended there was still another baby to provide for. Inevitably her resentment toward her husband grew—not to the point of destroying her love for him, for now that he was ill and needed care he was like a child. He was "poor Frank," huddled miserably in blankets against the bone-chilling damp of a Florentine winter, wretchedly contemplating the failure of his career, looking about him, when he was well enough to go out, at great paintings and coming home in despair. "His feeling was not the *anch' io pittore,* but the other far less cheerful sense of what wonders had been done, and how far he was from being able to come within a hundred miles (as he thought) of what he saw." She was a conscientious wife, a good nurse, a faithful companion. But also, like most young and bloomingly healthy people in the presence of illness, she was curiously obtuse to the real suffering of her husband. Years later she recognized her failing: "No doubt illness had much to do with this depression, which I, all sanguine and sure that he could do what he would, were he but well, could not sympathize in,—almost, I fear, felt to be a weakness."

The experiences of the Italian journey are reflected in two novels, both written five or six years after it took place—*Agnes* and *A Son of the Soil.* The heroine of *Agnes,* a poor and humble but beautiful girl, marries a young man who is far above her socially. Disinherited by his snobbish family, they live abroad because life is cheaper on the continent. Gradually Agnes begins to detect signs of moral weakness in her husband. He is not vicious or cruel, but simply weak, and she judges him guilty with what seems to her (and apparently to Mrs. Oliphant) complete fairness:

> For it is true that a wonderful disenchantment had already come to Agnes—such a disenchantment as any sentimental young woman, brought up upon novels and fine feelings, would regard either as the occasion of utter despair, and the most summary death by heartbreak which was possible, or else as a release from all obligations towards the man who had disappointed her so sorely. She was no longer able to admire Roger, however much she tried, nor to look up to him, nor even to trust him much. She was aware that his ideas of right and wrong were confused, and his impulses very often anything but just ones; and when any emergency occurred, Agnes was very far from being confident that her husband would not utterly break down in it; and yet, withal, she had not ceased to love him, and stand by him with all her might, which wonderful problem of humanity is one very little discussed in works of imagination.

He dies and leaves her helpless and penniless with three young children, giving little thought before he dies to the enormity of the burden he has put upon her.

Perhaps the most intimate personal insight in *Agnes* is a scene in which the heroine, in Florence during the first year of her marriage, sees Albertinelli's painting, "The Visitation." She is pregnant, a stranger in a foreign land, and totally cut off from all close female companionship: "She stood in a trance of interest regarding the divine mystery of nature which linked these two women; Mary, with her secret in her heart—Elizabeth, with a look that divined and asked, and replied, all in a moment. The young spectator too might have her secret, but for her there was no Elizabeth." In the

Autobiography Mrs. Oliphant described her own feelings toward this same painting:

> I for my part used to stray into one small room in the Pitti, I think, where at that time the great picture of the Visitation—Albertinelli's—hung alone. By that time I knew that another baby was coming, and it seemed to do me good to go and look at these two women, the tender old Elizabeth, and Mary with all the awe of her coming motherhood upon her. I had little thought of all that was to happen to me before my child came, but I had no woman to go to, to be comforted—except these two.

Another intimate picture of the Oliphants in Italy is drawn in *A Son of the Soil*. The hero, who has been ill, goes to Italy to convalesce. On his way he meets Arthur Meredith, dying of tuberculosis, and his sheltered young sister. All settle in Frascati—where the Oliphants lived from July through September 1859 and where at last it became apparent to Mrs. Oliphant that her husband was dying; they were there in summer, her characters are there in winter. Mrs. Oliphant simply transferred to the novel her own recollections of the bitter cold of their first months in Florence. She described their first horrified entrance into the cold, damp rooms: "The tired travellers turned toward the fire as the only possible gleam of consolation"—Meredith bundled in blankets leaning over the fire, and the general disillusion of the travellers. The dying man Meredith is not Frank Oliphant. He is a religious fanatic, morbidly preoccupied with thoughts of death and salvation as Oliphant never was. When Frank Oliphant learned that his case was hopeless, his comment was, "Well, if it is so, that is no reason why we should be miserable." Nevertheless they share one characteristic—a selfish indifference to the fate of the helpless women they have brought to Italy. The idealistic young hero of the novel comments: " 'He would never have brought his sister here if he had had anyone to leave her with—that is, if he believed, as he says, that he was going to die.' " To this his older and wiser friend replies:

> "And I cannot say I am satisfied, for that matter, that he brought his sister here for want of somebody to leave her with; she's a kind of property that he would na like to leave behind. He was

not thinking of *her* when they started, but of himsel'; nor can I
see that his mind's awakening to any thought of her even now. .
. . I'm not blaming the poor dying lad. It's hard upon a man if
he cannot be permitted to take some bit female creature that
belongs to him as far as the grave's mouth. She maun find her
way back from there the best way she can."

The Oliphants were trying to live on the £20 a month which
the Blackwoods sent them—not a large sum, though living was
cheap in Italy in 1859. Finances were perhaps the least of Mrs.
Oliphant's worries. But there was a considerable problem related
to finances, and that was the fact that she had not been successful
with the articles she had contracted to do for *Maga*. She wrote
faithfully—critical articles, stories, travel sketches. Blackwood's,
however, did not publish everything she sent. Only four pieces by
her appeared in 1859, a sharp drop from her normal number of
contributions, usually at least one article a month. The firm continued to send money, but Mrs. Oliphant sensed that this was an
act of charity. Her appeals for help began within a month after
their arrival in Florence. The journey to Italy had cost more than
she had calculated upon—"and I shall be very glad if you could
give me the price of two miscellaneous articles which I shall send
you within the next two months." On March 21 she asked them to
send the next payment quickly—"one feels a little nervous at leaving oneself short in a strange place and the return of post takes so
much time at such a distance." A month later she wrote:

> I am afraid you will think it rather selfish of me to continue
> sending you papers and asking money when your hands are so
> full of material. And indeed I do not find it easy to justify myself
> to myself. But as I have depended upon this and made all my
> calculations upon it, I can only trust that some of your other
> contributors may take a holiday shortly at this busy time.[33]

By May 20 she was seriously alarmed at the failure of her work:

> One thing however gives me a little anxiety. I came here in the
> idea of being able to keep my contributions to the Magazine to
> our mutual satisfaction. As you think the 'Week in Florence'
> unsuitable in the meantime I feel a little unsettled in this im-
> portant particular. . . . I should like very much if you would

tell me what you would prefer me to do. You have always treated
me with so much consideration and kindness that I have no
hesitation in saying with perfect plainness that your support is
at present very necessary to me.

Pride had to bow to financial needs. "I feel extremely uneasy and
troubled to think that while you have felt able to use so few of my
papers I am under the necessity of continuing to ask you for
money," she wrote on June 25.[34] She continued to ask, and they
continued to send money. By November 1859, when Frank Oliphant was dead, she was hundreds of pounds in their debt and
could soothe her conscience only with repeated promises to "make
it up" with work.

For all its anguish, the Italian journey was not without lighter
moments. The Oliphants had settled in Florence in mid-winter, in
sunless rooms on the Via Maggio. With the coming of warmer
weather Frank's health seemed to improve a little. His wife was
caught up in the enchantment and excitement of the city—the
Italian struggle for independence, the unfurling of the new Italian
flag. They made a few friends too in the English colony, but were
disappointed to learn that the Brownings, to whom they had letters of introduction, had already left Florence for Rome.[35] Just
as they were beginning to feel settled and comfortable in Florence
Oliphant decided that they should move on to Rome. Although
Mrs. Oliphant vigorously opposed the plan, citing the dangers to
the children of fever and the heat of a Roman summer, Oliphant
insisted and reluctantly she consented. On April 25 she wrote to
John Blackwood that they were making the move because the
weather in Florence did not agree with her husband, and "there
are few artistic facilities, art being extinct here except in the shape
of copying."[36] This was of course a feeble echo of her husband's
decision, pure rationalization, as she suspected even at the time
and recognized before the year ended. For what really drew Oliphant to Rome was his friend Robert Macpherson, and at the
heart of Mrs. Oliphant's reluctance to go was her dislike of Macpherson.[37]

Mrs. Macpherson, however, the former Gerardine (Geddie)
Bate, niece of Mrs. Jameson, became one of Mrs. Oliphant's
closest friends. She had married her big, burly Scots husband in

1849, when she was eighteen. They led a colorful, bohemian life together. Because of failing eyesight he had to give up his career as a painter. He turned with energy and enterprise to the pioneer work of photography, sold photographs of Roman scenes for five shillings apiece, and wrote an earnest little guidebook on the sculpture in the Vatican (*Vatican Sculptures, Selected and Arranged in the Order in Which They Are Found in The Galleries,* London, 1863). But in characteristic bohemian fashion he never could provide a secure income for his family. He died in 1873, leaving his widow only debts and two children. Less talented than Mrs. Oliphant, she did what she could to support her family—gave English lessons, wrote some hack journalism and a book about her aunt, *Memoirs of the Life of Anna Jameson* (London, 1878). Worn out with rheumatism, heart disease, and overwork, she died, May 24, 1878, before the book was published. Mrs. Oliphant saw the book through the press and wrote a touching memoir of her in the preface.

In the long run, Mrs. Oliphant later conceded, her husband had been right to move to Rome. Nothing could either save or damage his health by now and at least he had the small comfort of knowing that they were among friends. The Macphersons were openhearted and jolly. Oliphant responded well to his association with them. His wife held back with a chilly stiffness typical of her in those days. Nevertheless, she admitted that thanks to the Macphersons there were good times as well as bad in this last summer of her husband's life. For three weeks in June the two families shared a cottage in the quaint old village of Nettuno. Although she was sensitive to the beauties of the place, Mrs. Oliphant was disturbed by "certain difficulties for such humble particulars as meat and potatoes," and, she concluded in a letter to Blackwood, "I fear I am too prosy and too old for the delights of an Italian life."[38]

There were even a few happy days during the three months which followed in Frascati, but by the end of summer the doctors gave up all hope for Oliphant. The family moved back to Rome on October 1, where Mrs. Oliphant nursed her husband through his last days. On October 8 she wrote to Blackwood:

I have been obliged to suspend work for some weeks past in consequence of the illness of my husband, which has taken a much more serious and alarming form during the past month. I am at present kept close to his sick-room in very anxious and trembling condition as his weakness is very great and the doctor not very encouraging. In these circumstances I can only ask you as a matter of kindness to make the usual remittance of £60 trusting both that you may have found my later papers acceptable and that I may shortly be able to go on as I had intended with further contributions. . . . I know your kindness and I trust you will not think I am trespassing too far upon it in asking what I do. I am entirely disabled for the moment, in great anxiety and trouble and among strangers, and I can only ask you to stand by me in what may be the most trying time in my life, in the hope of soon being able to make up the material part of your kind aid.

Oliphant died early in November. There were loyal friends in England. As soon as the news of his death reached them, John Blackwood sent a loan of £200; Henry Blackett, who had published most of Mrs. Oliphant's novels during the 1850's, offered to come to Rome himself to bring her back; her husband's sister, Mrs. Murdoch, came out to be with her. Meanwhile she awaited the birth of her baby and planned for all contingencies, including her own death. "My debt to you," she wrote to Blackwood on December 1,

is now very large. If I live I will repay as much as is possible in money as soon as I get the necessary business done in London and the rest in work with the least delay and the best skill I have. If on the other hand I should not live, enough will be left nearly if not altogether to discharge this. . . . I have left full directions with my brother in respect to the means and liabilities which I will leave behind me, and he will have instructions to place all my literary remains in your hands. In such a case late precedents make me hope that perhaps a pension might be got for my children.[39]

On December 12 she gave birth to a son, christened Francis Romano, afterwards always called Cecco in the family. Two months later, in February 1860, Mrs. Oliphant, her three children, little Willie Macpherson whom she was taking home to his aunt, and faithful Jane returned to England.

Chapter II

Chronicler of Carlingford

In mid-February 1860 Mrs. Oliphant was thirty-one. Her responsibilities and liabilities included three young children, a dependent alcoholic brother, a lease on a house in London which she could not afford to live in, and a debt of about £1,000, most of it owed to the Blackwoods. Her assets were only her energy, her courage, and her writing talent. The one close relative left in England was her brother Frank Wilson, now married and living in Birkenhead, and on him and his family she descended with her children. It was an emergency measure, fraught with danger, as she readily recognized: "It is a perilous business when one is very sorry for oneself, and the sight of happy people is apt, when one's wounds are fresh, to make the consciousness keener." In March she sent John Blackwood a check for £100, probably out of her husband's insurance, "as a very small installment towards the repaying of the great debt I owe you. I had hoped to have sent more, but I find so many things to do, more than I reckoned on."[1] Every effort met with disappointment and frustration. She asked Blackwood to apply for a royal pension at Hampton Court for her. The application was refused: "Many thanks for your kind exertions in the matter of Hampton Court," she wrote to him on March 23: "I am sorry her Majesty does not think it worth while to exert her royal bounty on my behalf; but I had not placed my hopes very high."[2]

What was more alarming, however, was the fact that her writing was proving so unsuccessful. The Blackwoods had stood by her loyally during the unhappy Italian journey, but they did not publish the papers she sent them. Unless they accepted her work, she had no prospect either of wiping out her debt or of providing the income she now needed to support her family. There are gaps in her record of publication for these years. Although she was writing steadily, not a line of hers appeared in *Maga* from December 1859 to May 1860. Her fiction had fallen off sadly both in quantity and in quality. In 1859 appeared only an insignificant book for little girl readers, *Agnes Hopetoun's Schools and Holidays;* in 1860 a slight romance, not much more than an expanded short story, *Lucy Crofton;* and in 1861 a gloomy three-decker, *The House on the Moor,* and a quite undistinguished travelogue-romance that ran for four installments in *Maga,* "The Romance of Agostini." Only this from a writer who in the 1850's had produced almost two novels a year and scores of critical articles. At this point in her life, when she needed money so desperately, the well of her invention was running dry. Her pride suffered equally. On April 27 she wrote Blackwood that she hoped he was not publishing her articles unless he found them worthy—a somewhat gratuitous observation since he was not at that time publishing anything of hers. "And I should much prefer being in your debt with the hope of making up my deficiencies honestly if slowly than to feel that you benevolently put papers to my credit which you can't satisfactorily use."[3]

To help her work off the debt, Blackwood offered a project of a quite different nature from anything she had done before—a translation from the French of the ambitious work in progress of the Count de Montalembert, *Les Moines d'Occident depuis Saint Benoît jusqu'à Saint Bernard.* It was a rather extraordinary undertaking. Only a little more than a year before, when Mrs. Oliphant had set off with her husband for the Continent, her French was, she admitted, "of the most limited description." She had had opportunity in her travels to improve it somewhat, but hardly to the extent of translating a book of this magnitude. It is not surprising, therefore, that her initial efforts met with Montalembert's disapproval. She began work in July 1860, when she was living at a summer cottage at Elie in Fife. "I think it very likely you won't like the execution," she wrote to Blackwood, "and pray don't hesitate in the least to say so, for I am not vain of my French . . .

But I beg you will not feel any delicacy in saying, if you think so, that the translation is too bad for using. I am quite prepared to believe as much."

Blackwood submitted the translation to Montalembert who did indeed find fault with it, so much fault that the publisher suggested that Mrs. Oliphant get a French teacher. She accepted Blackwood's criticism with good grace and offered to turn over the second volume to another translator. Montalembert's criticism, however, she received less meekly. Some of his corrections, she protested, were "mere substitutions of one word for another, not always (with humility) to the improvement of the sound." Nevertheless, she was in no position to be overly sensitive. She worked away steadily and before the end of the year she had won the author's complete approval. Then she could be magnanimous. She wrote Blackwood that he might tell Montalembert "that I was never in the least affronted by his strictures but on the contrary extremely glad for them, since they have so greatly increased the pains taken later in the revise and will, I trust, make the work much more satisfactory."[4]

In the long run the Montalembert translation proved a success, a work which engaged Mrs. Oliphant completely and introduced her to a vast new area of religious and philosophical thought that profoundly influenced her life and work. In the summer and autumn of 1860, however, it did little to relieve her anxiety about the future. The letters to Blackwood with their appeals for money once more take on a note of urgency—"I have troubled you so often after this same fashion that I am afraid that all my apologies look stereotyped. Pray excuse and be good to me as you always are." That winter she moved to Edinburgh, apparently in order to be near her publisher, and took a house in Fettes Row within easy walking distance of the Blackwood offices in George Street. It was a severe winter, bleak and terrible for her. Years later she vividly recollected her desperate situation, telling the story of what was the turning point of her career in two places, the *Autobiography* and *Annals of a Publishing House,* relishing and understandably romanticizing a little that painful afternoon when she went to the Blackwood offices to offer the brothers a novel to pay off her debt:

They shook their heads of course, and thought it would not be possible to take such a story,—both very kind and truly sorry for me, I have no doubt. I think I see their figures now against the light standing up, John with his shoulders hunched up, the Major with his soldierly air, and myself all blackness and whiteness in my widow's dress, taking leave of them as if it didn't matter, and oh! so much afraid that they would see the tears in my eyes. I went home to my little ones, running to the door to meet me with 'flichterin' noise and glee'; and that night, as soon as I had got them all to bed, I sat down and wrote a story which I think was something about a lawyer . . . and which formed the first of the Carlingford series,—a series pretty well forgotten now, which made a considerable stir at the time, and *almost* made me one of the popularities of literature. *Almost,* never quite, though "Salem Chapel" really went very near it, I believe. I sat up nearly all night in a passion of composition, stirred to the very bottom of my mind. The story was successful, and my fortune, comparatively speaking, was made.

The story, "The Executor" (published in *Maga,* May 1861) did not signal any meteoric rise in fame and fortune. *Salem Chapel* was not published in book form until 1863 (it began running serially in *Maga* in February 1862), and the most remunerative of the Carlingford series, *The Perpetual Curate,* came a year later. But with "The Executor" and the two short stories of Carlingford which followed it—"The Rector" (*Maga,* September 1861) and "The Doctor" (*Maga,* October 1861–January 1862, published in book form by Blackwood as *The Rector, and The Doctor's Family,* 3 volumes, 1863), Mrs. Oliphant found her place as a writer. There was no sudden flash of inspiration. The stories were simply the culmination of a gradual development and maturing of her talent. She knew her own strength now. She had acquired a calm confidence in herself and in her work.

Mrs. Oliphant's Carlingford, like Barchester and Middlemarch, is a country of the mind. It lacks the breadth and depth of Middlemarch and the minute particularity of Barchester. On the one hand it is not, as is George Eliot's imagined community, a microcosm, a universalization of the whole pattern of Victorian provincial life. On the other, neither does it have a local habitation, as

Trollope's community had in Salisbury, nor its precise geographical detail. It would be impossible to draw a map of Carlingford and difficult to illustrate the scenes and characters of the Carlingford novels. Yet the scenes are described with sufficient vividness so that Carlingford emerges as a place with an identity of its own. It is a pleasant, sleepy little town, far enough from London to be free of its pressures yet close enough for its inhabitants to run up in a short rail journey whenever the plot demands it. The two principal streets are Grange Lane, where the more affluent and distinguished citizens live, and Grove Street, at the unfashionable end of which is Salem Chapel where the Dissenters, "none above the rank of a greengrocer or milkman," worship. There is also George Street, the modest business district, and far back of town Wharfside, a slum district, which most respectable Carlingforders carefully ignore.

At the top of the social hierarchy in Carlingford are the inhabitants of Grange Lane—the beautiful Lady Western, who serves as a kind of queen of local society in *Salem Chapel* but then disappears from the series; Lady Richmond, who graces parties with her presence but has no function in the novels otherwise; prosperous Dr. Marjoribanks and his splendid "managing" daughter Lucilla; and the Wodehouse family, consisting of Mr. Wodehouse, a widower, and his two daughters—the elder a fading spinster, and the pretty younger Lucy. Then of course there is the clergy of the Establishment who serve this section of town—Mr. Bury, so dangerously Low ("profoundly low—lost in the deepest abysses of Evangelicalism") that he has driven half his congregation to the Chapel of St. Roque, "the very topmost pinnacle of Anglicanism," on the fashionable north side of town, where the handsome young Perpetual Curate Frank Wentworth holds forth. Mr. Bury is succeeded briefly by the shy, scholarly Mr. Proctor, formerly Fellow of All Souls. He in turn is followed by Dr. Morgan, a crisply efficient clergyman of unchallengeably High principles, but unfortunately a victim of a hot temper and delicate conscience. Other characters weave in and out of this small circle—the society entertained by Miss Marjoribanks at her Thursday evenings, the ambitious young medical Dr. Ryder, the artistic but impoverished Lake sisters. The dramatis personae are actually few, and their relationships are far less complex than those of the parallel social set in Trollope's Barsetshire series. There are no aristocrats save the widowed Lady Western, whose title has been won through marriage. This is a bourgeois society even at its highest level.

Its lower half consists largely of substantial tradesmen and their families. Dissenters who worship at Salem Chapel. "Greengrocers, dealers in cheese and bacon, milkmen, with some dressmakers of inferior pretensions, and teachers of day-schools of similar humble character, formed the *elite* of the congregation." This group is dominated by Mr. Tozer, Carlingford's prosperous butterman and senior deacon of the Chapel. He is a blunt, blustering, self-important man, determined to do right and usually succeeding, though his methods are crude and clumsy. He is one of Mrs. Oliphant's best characters, possessed of a vulgar charm both amusing and at times touching.[5] There is less charm but a certain hearty appeal in his pink and blooming daughter Phoebe and his earnest, humorless wife, and in some of the other tradesmen and their families. The most interesting figure among the Dissenting clergymen is the sensitive and intelligent Arthur Vincent, the hero of *Salem Chapel.* He serves his congregation for only six months, his proud spirit rebelling against their bourgeois dictatorship. Vincent is succeeded by the far more pliable young Mr. Beecher,[6] who marries Phoebe Tozer and moves on to new triumphs in a wealthy London congregation. Their daughter, the heroine of *Phoebe, Junior,* returns to Carlingford some years later, but with the exception of the Tozers the characters are all new. The series ends here.

Seven works of fiction comprise the Chronicles of Carlingford. Three, *The Executor, The Rector,* and *The Doctor's Family,* are long short stories. Indeed, *The Executor* and *The Doctor's Family* may claim to be part of the series only because they are set in Carlingford, but they form no real part of the Carlingford scheme. The longer novels are two which center mainly on clerical life, *Salem Chapel* (1863) and *The Perpetual Curate* (1864) with clergymen as their leading characters, and two which center mainly on social life in the community, *Miss Marjoribanks* (1866) and *Phoebe, Junior* (1876), with young women as their leading characters. With the exception of the last-named novel, they were

all written within the five years 1861 to 1866, a period crowded
with other literary activity (including two serious long novels,
Agnes and *A Son of the Soil,* the biography of Edward Irving, the
translation of Montalembert's *Monks of the West,* and a flood of
contributions to *Maga* and other periodicals), with travel, personal
triumph and tragedy. All, with the exception of *Phoebe, Junior,*
were published by Blackwood, first serially in *Maga* and subsequently in book form. They were written in haste—from the first
all-night vigil in which Mrs. Oliphant dashed off *The Executor*
through the witty installments of *Miss Marjoribanks,* which she
wrote during the months of restless travel in Europe in 1864 following the sudden death of her daughter Maggie. Haste of composition is apparent everywhere—repetition, minor inaccuracies of
detail, looseness and diffuseness of structure, clumsy padding and
stretching. Nevertheless, with all their faults the Carlingford novels
reveal Mrs. Oliphant at her best. They are lively, clever, humorous, sharply observed. At times they rise to social comedy worthy
of comparison with Trollope's. In their more serious aspects they
treat of family life and religious vocation with dignity and insight.

Carlingford brought Mrs. Oliphant her first fame as a novelist,
a success which she never again equalled. The series also brought
her her first real fortune, including the magnificent sum of £1,500
for *The Perpetual Curate,* the largest amount she ever received
for one novel. Written—as almost everything of hers was written
—under the dictates of dire financial necessity, they were "pot-
boilers" in as close to a literal meaning of the phrase as is possible.
After Blackwood late in 1861 accepted with hearty approval *The
Doctor's Family,* she put the case to him bluntly.

> But I should like to go on with a succession of others under the
> main title Chronicles of Carlingford, if it so pleases you. Perhaps
> three or four of equal length with this, and I should be glad to
> know whether you would like it, and whether, if you did like it,
> you would be disposed to make a kind of arrangement with me
> to the ease of my mind and partial lightment of my anxieties. I
> have not very ambitious thoughts upon the subject, knowing that
> my other books have not done much upon republication and that
> it is doubtful whether you would think it worth your while to
> try the experiment with them. But some portion as the following
> has occurred to me. Supposing you to be disposed to receive from

me a series of these stories going over a twelvemonth, would you mind, instead of putting them to my credit month by month, to give me two hundred and fifty or three hundred pounds for the year long of them? a hundred of it to go to the repaying of my debts to you and the rest to be open to me to draw upon? If you felt disposed to make such an arrangement, it would be a relief to me, as my settling down [she had just moved to Ealing] has been attended not only by its own expenses but by the necessary settlement of old burdens which were waiting for me, and I shall want some money at Christmas more than I see my way to otherwise.[7]

Obviously, then, all the longer novels of the series were written with an eye to the literary market. If they were to make money, they must be modelled upon novels which were making money. To Mrs. Oliphant's credit, with the single exception of *Salem Chapel's* dismal melodrama, she chose good models and studied them well. Far more important, while she worked in conventional styles and was inevitably (like all novelists including her superiors) influenced by contemporary styles and trends, the Chronicles of Carlingford are not imitative. She borrowed plot details occasionally as did others. She quite deliberately echoed Trollope when she subtitled *Phoebe, Junior* "A Last Chronicle of Carlingford." She was not, apparently, offended when a number of well-informed readers mistook her unsigned novels as they appeared in *Maga* for works by the eminent author of *Scenes of Clerical Life*.[8] But she worked with a sturdy independence of mind, developing in fiction at least one major theme uniquely hers and creating several characters—Tozer, Miss Marjoribanks, Phoebe Beecham—who have freshness and personalities quite their own.

The major theme which unites the three principal religious stories of the series is vocation for the priesthood. It is a subject so serious that one wonders at Mrs. Oliphant's daring to treat it at all. On closer examination one finds she was peculiarly well suited by background and by sympathy for the subject. Because of the popular success of *Salem Chapel* and the relative obscurity into which the other novels fell soon after their publication, it is generally assumed that the Carlingford series was about Dissenters and the Dissenting Church only. Mrs. Oliphant was not a Dissenter herself. Only *Salem Chapel* and *Phoebe, Junior* actually treat of the Dissenting movement. The Rector, in the story of that name, is a staunch member of the Church of England, as is the hero of *The Perpetual Curate;* and while some Low Church members figure amusingly in the latter novel, Dissent has no place in it. Indeed, it is the question of how High a man may go short of conversion to Roman Catholicism which is central in this work.

Still it is true that her picture of the Dissenting congregation of Salem Chapel was the great attraction of that novel for Victorian readers. This gave the book its ring of truth and of originality—an inside view of an independent congregation presented with candor and humor and with just enough snobbish condescension to appeal to a predominantly Church of England reading public for whom the popular image of the Dissenter was still a vulgar, hymn-singing tradesman.[9] As for Mrs. Oliphant's qualifications or lack of them, a woman who could write serious religious-historical novels like *Caleb Field* and *Magdalen Hepburn* while in her early twenties, who could learn French to translate Montalembert's history of early Christianity, and study theology to write a biography of Edward Irving, would hardly be discouraged by the prospect of describing a non-conformist religious movement peacefully pursuing its routine worship.[10] In addition her own religious background in the Scotch Free Kirk was excellent preparation for portraying Dissent, the structure of which was not unlike it:

> As a matter of fact I knew nothing about chapels, but took the sentiment and a few details from our old church in Liverpool, which was Free Church of Scotland, and where there were a few grocers and other such good folk whose ways with the minister were wonderful to behold. The saving grace of their Scotchness being withdrawn, they became still more wonderful as Dissenting deacons, and the truth of the picture was applauded to all the echoes.

What Mrs. Oliphant did not know at first hand about church life and administration she learned from research. Almost simultaneously with the writing of *Salem Chapel* she was completing a biography of the controversial Scottish clergyman Edward Irving. Nowhere in her sympathetic portrait of him was she more deeply stirred than in describing his removal from his pastorate by

his Presbytery. Her account rings with indignation at "these obscure Presbyters . . . homely old men, half farmers, half ministers
. . . without a single special qualification for deciding any question
which required clear heads and practised intelligence," who passed
judgment upon Irving and declared him unfit to preach in their
church. It was but a small step from Irving's rural Scotch village
of Annandale to the fictitious Carlingford, where "homely" groc-
ers and tradesmen who smell of bacon and cheese sit in judgment
upon their young minister. And it was only a slightly larger step
from the gifted and sensitive Irving, the spell-binding preacher,
to the gifted and sensitive hero of *Salem Chapel,* Arthur Vincent,
whose oratory doubles the number of seat-holders of his church
within six months and who can move his stolid bourgeois congregation to tears and applause by his eloquence. Both come to the
same resolution after stormy sessions with the heads of their
congregations—as Arthur Vincent expresses it: " 'If there is any
truth in the old phrase which calls a church a cure of souls, it is
certain that no cure of souls can be delegated to a preacher by
the souls themselves who are to be his care. . . . I am either servant,' " he tells them, " 'responsible to you, or God's servant, responsible to Him—which is it? I cannot tell; but no man can
serve two masters, as you know.' " And Irving, cast out by his
church, like Vincent turned his back upon it—not upon its laws
or its authority, but upon his "judges" and their judgment, "not
binding upon any man who was truly commissioned of God,
[which] thrust him more and more upon that isolated platform
of direct responsibility—to his Master, and not to anyone beneath."[11]

Irving was the divinely inspired clergyman, "born" to his work
and pursuing it, even after his church had repudiated him, to his
death. Mrs. Oliphant's fictitious clergymen lack the divine spark—
not because she was incapable of giving it to them, but because
she conceived them entirely differently. They are small men, not
weak perhaps but highly fallible. They are troubled by their con-
sciences (like Dr. Morgan), their sense of inadequacy in practical
situations (like Mr. Proctor in *The Rector*), their intellectual
pride and arrogance (like Arthur Vincent), their religious scruples
(like Gerald Wentworth who goes over to Catholicism in *The*

Perpetual Curate), or, in a much lighter key, their romantic problems (like the Perpetual Curate Frank Wentworth, or the Dissenting Mr. Northcote in *Phoebe, Junior*). Only the fanatics (like Low Church Mr. Bury), the vulgarians (like Mr. Beecher-Beecham), or the ignorant (like Mr. Tufton) lead relatively happy and uncomplicated lives. The others constantly question and examine themselves, testing their fitness for clerical office. It is interesting to observe how many of them fail to measure up to their own standards.

The Rector, the shortest of the Carlingford series and a fine story in its own right, is an excellent illustration of this kind of self-analysis on the part of a clergyman. Mr. Morley Proctor, a gentle, middle-aged bachelor, comes to his post in Carlingford after fifteen quiet years as a Fellow of All Souls. Faced with the practical demands of a congregation, he soon begins to doubt his fitness for the office. He is socially awkward and shy. When called to minister at the deathbed of a parishioner, he is helpless and tongue-tied. In contrast, his poised young curate Wentworth ("not half nor a quarter part so learned as he, but a world further on in that profession which they shared—the art of winning souls") knows how to say and do all the right things, leaving the older man painfully aware of his own inadequacies. The Rector preaches his sober, learned sermons to "a crowd of unsympathetic, uninterested faces." Defeated, not by an action of his congregation but by his own conscience, he resigns his post and returns to the academic life. Here, however, he is now curiously dissatisfied, remembering not only his failures but the parallel situation of the aging spinster Miss Wodehouse, who, like him, was helpless at the deathbed and had to defer to her brisk, efficient younger sister: "The good man had found out that secret of discontent which most men find out a great deal earlier than he. Something better, though it might be sadder, harder, more calamitous, was in this world. . . . When he went back to his dear cloisters, good Mr. Proctor felt that sting: a longing for the work he had rejected stirred in him—a wistful recollection of the sympathy he had not sought." Yet the story does not end on this gloomy note. Almost as an afterthought Mrs. Oliphant adds a hopeful last paragraph suggesting that Proctor will marry Miss Wodehouse (as he does in *The Perpetual Curate*) and return to the world.

In one sense *Salem Chapel* is an expansion of the theme treated so delicately and charmingly in *The Rector*. Mr. Vincent, many years younger and far more gifted for clerical life than Mr. Proctor, has nevertheless the same problem. He too comes to doubt his fitness for the office, at least as it is administered in his church, and in the end he too resigns with a keen sense of personal failure. Had Mrs. Oliphant explored and developed the idea at leisure, she would certainly have produced a better book. Unfortunately, she set out to write a best seller. More unfortunately, from the point of view of her literary reputation, she succeeded. Artistically it is a failure. Her interesting young hero becomes enmeshed in a crudely melodramatic plot almost totally obscuring the important issues of the book. The more perceptive of her contemporary readers recognized this failing immediately. *"Salem Chapel* consists of two different and incongruous parts—the plot of a sensation novel and a series of descriptions of the inner life of a dissenting congregation. The plot may be dismissed as not only bad but unnecessary," commented the *National Review* (January-April 1863). Even the *Spectator* (February 14, 1863), which predicted with more enthusiasm than accuracy that "This book will take a permanent place in English literature," confined its admiration to "that portion of it . . . which relates to Salem Chapel and its organisation" and recommended that in a new edition the "Mildmay melodrama" be "skilfully removed from the book by some neat surgical operation."

Mrs. Oliphant herself had been uneasy about the plot. "Enclosed is the third part of Salem Chapel," she wrote Blackwood. "I trust you won't think it too melodramatic." Her publisher was reading the novel in parts as she wrote them and commenting on the story as it went along. At times he appears to have been engrossed in it —"Much charmed to have made you anxious about Susan. I'll get her off yet," she writes to him.[12] In another encouraging letter he commented: "Bravo! This part of 'Salem' is splendid. You are winning the race." But he also apparently balked at the murky intrigue of the plot, for she writes in another letter:

I have cut short so far as I can the scene you object to. I see you don't like my villain. And I don't pretend to say I admire him myself. Feminine instinct suggests that villains should be painted so black as to deceive nobody—and I much fear we generally make them very impotent rascals as well. I mean to do the best I can—and perhaps he will grow upon you as we go on. I am charmed to think you are mystified about the lady—which is exactly the result I hoped to produce.[13]

Of course, melodramatic "shockers" were the fashion of the day. The public clamored for them. Mrs. Oliphant analyzed the trend shrewdly in an article "Sensation Novels" she wrote for *Maga* at the time *Salem Chapel* was running in it serially (May 1862). Attributing the vogue to the age itself, "in which we begin to feel the need of a new supply of shocks and wonders," she observed: "it is a fact that the well-known old stories of readers sitting up all night over a novel had begun to grow faint in the public recollection. Domestic histories however virtuous and charming, do not often attain that result. . . . Now a new fashion has been set to English novel writers." She traces this "new fashion" through its development in American fiction, specifically Hawthorne and Holmes ("here a Scarlet Letter and impish child of shame, there a snake-girl, horrible junction of reptile and woman")—and into British fiction with Lytton, Dickens, and its most successful prac- titioner, Wilkie Collins. Her good taste rebelled at the lurid hor- rors; her common sense objected to the grotesque fantasy, of some of this fiction. But in Collins' *The Woman in White* she found an almost ideal example of the genre. Here the effects of horror are achieved not through any supernatural agency but "by common human acts, performed by recognizable human agents, whose motives are never inscrutable, and whose line of conduct is always more or less consistent."

There can be no doubt that the intrigue of *Salem Chapel* was devised with *The Woman in White* in mind. No element of the fantastic enters into it, although the coincidences and improbabil- ities are so gross as to be almost fantastic. As in Collins' novel, the villainy for all its horrible threats comes to nothing. No one is killed—though there is attempted murder, abduction (with threats of seduction), concealed identities, and two victimized young women, one who is driven nearly mad, the other who is feeble-minded. But where Collins' plot holds the reader in breathless suspense, Mrs. Oliphant's simply confuses. The hero of *Salem Chapel*, Mr. Vincent, meets among his parishioners a mysterious needle-woman, Mrs. Hilyard, who is obviously of a higher social class though she lives in poverty and obscurity. Quite accidentally he overhears a conversation between her and the villainous Colonel Mildmay (shouted in an open courtyard for his convenience), which reveals that they were once married but now—for no given reason—hate each other bitterly. They have had a daughter whose mind has been affected in some mysterious way by the brutality of the father and whom Mrs. Hilyard keeps in hiding from him. Fearing now that he may find the daughter, Mrs. Hilyard asks Vincent to let her send the girl to his mother and sister who live in another town. In a misunderstanding caused by an unlucky crossing of letters, Vincent's mother is already on her way to Carlingford to seek her son's advice. His sister Susan has become engaged to a Mr. Fordham, about whom nobody knows anything, and the mother has just received an anonymous letter warning her against this marriage. By now the reader is two volumes ahead of the author, who plods on relentlessly to reveal at long last that Mr. Fordham is really Colonel Mildmay (the *real* Mr. Fordham, whose name he has taken, is a suitor of the beautiful Lady Western, whom Vincent hopelessly loves), that in the mother's absence the treacherous Colonel lures away both Susan and his feeble-minded daughter who has sought refuge with her, that Mr. Vincent pursues them frantically to the neglect of his duties at Salem Chapel, that Mrs. Hilyard shoots her husband; that Susan, now delirious with brain fever, is accused of the crime; and that, finally, though shot in the head, Mildmay recovers, absolves Susan of all guilt, nobly refusing to name his assailant to the police.

Another sensation novel from which Mrs. Oliphant drew both inspiration and actual plot detail was Mrs. Henry Wood's *East Lynne* (1861), one of the most phenomenally popular novels ever written. Mrs. Oliphant discussed *East Lynne* in her article on "Sensation Novels" with the respect it demands for its extraordinary popularity, but she was by no means impressed with its literary merits, calling it "a clever novel . . . which some inscrutable breath of popular liking has blown into momentary celebrity." She especially objected to the sympathetic portrait Mrs. Wood draws of the fallen woman: "Nothing can be more wrong and fatal than to represent the flames of vice as a purifying fiery ordeal, through which the penitent is to come elevated and sublime." In her own borrowing, she shunned the main plot of the novel in favor of some details in the subplot intrigue. The idea of the villain's confusing his pursuers by taking the name of another character (the Mildmay-Fordham business) seems to have been derived from the scoundrel Francis Levison in *East Lynne,* who performs his villainy under the name of Captain Thorn, another character in the novel. She owes an even greater debt to Mrs. Wood, however, for the origin of Tozer, her finest bit of characterization, who may well have been suggested by Mrs. Wood's minor character the prosperous Mr. Joe Jiffin, owner of a shop "in the cheese and ham and butter line." Behind his shop there is a comfortable parlor and upstairs a well-furnished drawing room. Mrs. Oliphant's Tozers similarly have a comfortable little parlor, "being on the same floor with the butter-shop, naturally . . . not without a reminiscence of the near vicinity of all those hams and cheeses," and they too entertain their guests in a drawing room above the shop.

Salem Chapel is not the only example in Mrs. Oliphant's work of a potentially good novel which is almost wrecked by the author's efforts to make it a best seller, but it is a particularly unfortunate example because there is so much in it both promising and original. Vincent, the hero, is finely conceived. He is the "unheroic" intellectual hero—self-centered, arrogant, insecure. Outside his pulpit and his study he is weak and ineffectual. He goes dashing off on well meaning but futile efforts to rescue his sister. He is forever five minutes too late or miles off in the wrong direction. Instead of being a comfort and support to his widowed mother—a typical Oliphant mother, weak and genteel but where her children are concerned a giantess of energy and strength—he withdraws into his own problems and ignores her. In matters of romance he also behaves foolishly and unheroically, falling madly in love with a woman socially superior but spiritually unworthy of him and suffering agonies of what he knows is hopeless passion.

The really valid issue of the novel is the character of this young

man, "well educated and enlightened according to his fashion . . .
yet so entirely unacquainted with any world but that contracted
one in which he had been brought up" (Ch. I), and the gradual
discovery he makes of his unfitness for his chosen profession. He
comes to Carlingford firm in his Dissenting principles and fired
with idealism, not without a trace of the egoism common to the
young: "All he wanted—all any man worthy of his post wanted—
was a spot of standing-ground, and an opportunity of making the
Truth—and himself—known." Almost immediately the fire is
dampened. He appears at Mr. Tozer's six o'clock tea party over
the butterman's shop with the fat and prosperous congregation
of tradesmen and their fat and overdressed wives. They patronize
him; they remind him that the minister is the servant of the flock;
they shock him with their vulgarity. When he turns to his predecessor in the office, the elderly Mr. Tufton, now retired, he finds a
foolish and commonplace old man whose spirit, whatever it had
been, has long since been beaten down by Salem Chapel life. Thus
from the outset the prospects are grim:

> Was he actually to live among these people for years—to have
> no other society—to circulate among their tea-parties and grow
> accustomed to their finery, and perhaps 'pay attention' to Phoebe
> Tozer; or, at least, suffer that young lady's attentions to him?
> And what would become of him at the end? To drop into a
> shuffling old gossip, like good old Mr. Tufton, seemed the best
> he could hope for; and who could wonder at the mild stupor of
> paralysis—disease not tragical, only drivelling—which was the
> last chapter of all?

The only light in the gloom is his wild infatuation for Lady
Western. She is gracious and cordial, but even before he discovers
that she loves another man, Vincent is only too sharply aware of
the social gulf between them. He tries to lose himself in work,
not the small business of the parish but in an ambitious course
of lectures on Church and State which is proposed by Tozer:
" 'Give us a coorse upon the anomalies, and that sort of thing—
the bishops in their palaces, and the fisherman as was the start of
it all; there's a deal to be done in that way.' " The lectures succeed. They shake Carlingford to its foundations. Vincent alone
recognizes the hollowness of this success. He moves his naive pro-

vincial audience "as a nursery story-teller perceives the rising sob
of her little hearers. When he saw it, he awoke as the same nursery
minstrel does sometimes, to feel how unreal was the sentiment in
his own breast which had produced this genuine feeling in others."
At this point in his journey toward self-discovery, Mrs. Oliphant
unfortunately plunges him into the intrigues of the plot. From time
to time as the novel proceeds, by bringing the minister into contact
with Tozer, who in his fumbling way tries to help and advise him,
she reminds the reader of Vincent's original dilemma. But not
until the final chapters, after his sister's problems have been
solved, does he meet this dilemma point-blank.

Mystified by scandal about his sister, buzzing with gossip about
his romance with Lady Western, but mainly offended because he
has neglected what they think is his duty, a group of his parishioners decide to censure him. They hold a meeting where sentiment goes badly against the minister until Tozer rises to defend
him. The speech is a little gem of homely wisdom and shrewdness.
He berates the offended parishioners for expecting their minister
to attend tea parties—"to go for to judge the pastor of a flock, not
by the dooty he does to his flock, but by the times he calls at one
house or another." And he reminds his audience of the fundamental weakness of the sect, saving Vincent from their censure
by making a telling thrust at their pride and vanity:

> "You mark what I say. It's what we're doing most places, us
> Dissenters: them as is talented and promisin', and can get a
> better living working for the world than working for the chapel,
> and won't give in to be worried about calling here and calling
> there—we're a driving of them out of the connection, that's what
> we're doing! . . . If the pastor don't make hisself agreeable, I
> can put up with that—I can; but I ain't a-going to see a clever
> young man drove away from Salem Chapel, and the sittings
> vacant, and the Chapel falling to ruin, and the Church folks a-
> laughing and a-jeering at us, not for all the deacons in the
> connection, nor any man in Carlingford. And this I say for
> myself and for all as stands by me!"

Thanks to Tozer's oratory, the parish heartily endorses Vincent.
But the approval comes too late. He has already decided to leave
Salem, to abandon the ministry altogether. How much this act is

the result of wounded pride because his congregation had turned upon him, or of a broken heart, because Lady Western has married another man, Mrs. Oliphant never makes clear. Certainly Vincent has been a victim of himself, his own weaknesses, as well as of his narrow-minded bourgeois parishioners. Not until he leaves the ministry—and this period she sums up only briefly in the final pages—does he really arrive at any understanding of himself. He drifts closer to the Established Church, as Mrs. Oliphant herself had done in her own life:

> It began to be popularly reported that a man so apt to hold opinions of his own, and so convinced of the dignity of his office, had best have been in the Church, where people knew no better. Such, perhaps, might have been the conclusion to which he came himself; but education and prejudice . . . stood invincible in the way. A Church of the Future—an ideal corporation, grand and primitive, yet not realised, but surely *real,* to be come at one day—shone before his eyes, as it shines before so many.

Meanwhile he goes into literature, founding a "new organ of public opinion," the *Philosophical Review*. The novel ends on a quiet note of reconciliation. For the troubled hero there is no rapturous union with the woman he loved, no triumphant professional success. His mother, his sister, and the feeble-minded Alice Mildmay, now apparently restored to normal mentality, come to live with him. There is a curious hint that some time in the future he will marry Alice. He is in better spirits, at peace with himself, and hopeful of the future, but the future remains only a vague promise.

The final installment of *Salem Chapel* was published in *Maga* in January 1863. In June of the same year the first installment of *The Perpetual Curate* appeared. Between those two dates *Salem Chapel* was published in book form, and its success was firmly established. As a result Mrs. Oliphant was in a far more advantageous position to bargain with John Blackwood than she had ever been before. "My feeling about this book," she wrote to him of the new novel, "is that if it extends to the three-volume length, and promises to be as successful as Salem, you should give me a thousand pounds clear for it independent of the Magazine, or else a share in the copyright." In October 1863 she called on her publisher in Edinburgh to discuss the matter. He was cautious and made no promises. "The great thing for you," he wrote on November 16, "is to make it as good as you can, and you may rely upon my doing the best I can for you." In June 1864 when the novel had almost finished its run in *Maga* and preparations were under way for book publication, Mrs. Oliphant repeated her request for £1,000. William Blackwood, then an assistant to his uncle John in the firm, was somewhat overwhelmed by her demand: "I think her letter will rather surprise," he wrote his uncle, "and her asking £1,000 for The Perpetual independent of Magazine payments is altogether out of the question." He suggested paying her £550 or £600 for a three-volume edition and leaving future arrangements on a contingent rate. It is a sign of Mrs. Oliphant's increasing confidence in herself that she was now ready to fight for her price. On October 25 she wrote John Blackwood from Paris: "It is common for people in my trade, as you know, to calculate the success of one work in a great degree by the success of the previous one, and having done tolerably well at one time to think themselves justified in expecting to do rather better the next."[14] It is also a sign that her confidence was well founded, since she got £1,500, £500 more than she had originally asked. Years later, writing in the *Autobiography,* she remembered with amusement David Stott, the bookseller, describing to her "the awe and horror" of Mr. Simpson, Blackwood's business manager, "at the prodigal price" paid for the book: "One could see old Simpson, pale, with the hair of his wig standing upon his head, remonstrating, and John Blackwood, magnanimous, head of the house of Blackwood, and feeling rather like a feudal suzerain, as he always did, declaring that the labourer was worthy of his hire."

The Perpetual Curate did not sell as well as its predecessor. It is, however, a far better novel. Whether at Blackwood's urging or in response to her own good taste, she avoided melodrama and the sensational. The story concerns the struggles of an upright young clergyman, Frank Wentworth, of rather "High" persuasion, to find a secure living in which he will not have to compromise his principles. The obstacles in his way are the community itself, full of gossip and misunderstanding, the enmity of his hot-tempered rector, Dr. Morgan, and his own rather divided and confused family. Mrs. Oliphant introduces a subplot which is potentially lurid (a mysterious bearded stranger, the disappearance of a young girl, for which the hero is blamed) but which actually proves to be comic. The bearded stranger is a disreputable but harmless scapegrace brother; the abducted girl is a silly young thing who fully deserves and enjoys the scandal she causes. This is the first of the Carlingford novels in which the parallel to the Barsetshire series is noticeable, although Mrs. Oliphant was not indebted to Trollope for specific details. Yet the novel has the happy insularity that is so characteristic of Trollope's clerical novels— the self-contained, snug world of the Established Church and the squirearchy: stubborn, outspoken older clergymen and their patient wives, strong-minded spinsters, oily and unctuous curates, stalwart but rather unworldly heroes, and dewy-eyed but commonsensical heroines. Into this mild and pleasant atmosphere, however, Mrs. Oliphant introduces one far more serious issue—a clergyman who becomes converted to Catholicism. She treats the subject with delicacy and sympathy. While it may seem at first glance a jarring note in the otherwise smooth harmony of the book, it in fact gives the novel greater depth and interest. The weakness of *The Perpetual Curate* is a characteristic failing in Mrs. Oliphant's fiction. It is too long. There is simply not enough incident to support its length. Where *Salem Chapel* suffered from an excess of incident, *The Perpetual Curate* suffers from a deficiency. But the fact that she manages to sustain the reader's interest even when nothing important is happening is a tribute to her skill. Making bricks without straw was becoming a habit with her.

To give some substance to her charming but insubstantial story, Mrs. Oliphant added what is not actually a subplot but simply a complication in the character of Gerald Wentworth, the convert to Rome. Originally her plan had been ambitious. On May 18, 1863 when she was working on the opening chapters of the novel, she wrote to Blackwood: "I think I have materials in my hands for a little exhibition of all the three parties in the Church. I mean my curate's brother to go over to Rome, and we will not be neglectful of the claims of Exeter Hall."[15] In the actual writing of the novel, however, she reduced her scope. The "claims of Exeter Hall" are represented humorously in the hero's aunt, Miss Leonora Wentworth, to whom "the very name of priest was an offence in its way," and who prefers the Dissenting services at Salem Chapel to her nephew's High services at St. Roque's. The claims of the Broad Church get very little attention. The Rector of Carlingford, Dr. Morgan, is presumably "Lower" than his curate, but his quarrel with Frank is on personal rather than religious grounds. It is the High Church which receives Mrs. Oliphant's chief attention. Her hero is devoted to his principles. Temptation cannot sway him: "for the Curate of St. Roque's was not only a fervent Anglican, but also an Englishman *sans reproche,* with all the sensitive, almost fantastic delicacy of honour which belongs to that development of humanity; and not for a dozen worlds would he have sacrificed a lily or a surplice on this particular Easter, when all his worldly hopes hung in the balance." Such thinking naturally makes him sympathetic to the dilemma faced by his brother Gerald, the Rector of Wentworth, who finds himself relentlessly drawn to Rome. Mrs. Oliphant and her characters are deeply sympathetic to him. Even iron-willed evangelical Aunt Leonora remarks: " 'Remember, I believe he is a good Christian all the same. It's very incomprehensible; but the fact is a man may be a very good Christian and have the least quantity of sense that is compatible with existence. I've seen it over and over again. Gerald's notions are idiocy to me,' said the sensible but candid woman, shrugging her shoulders; 'but I can't deny he's a good man for all that.' " Only scatter-brained Aunt Dora misses the point completely: " 'But it's so sad to see how he's led away . . . it's all owing to the bad advisers young men meet with at the universities; and how can it be otherwise as long as tutors and professors are chosen just for their learning, without any regard to their principles? What is Greek and Latin in comparison with a pious guide for the young?' "

Thus Mrs. Oliphant introduces the Oxford Movement. Gerald Wentworth is a man of sensitivity and intelligence. He has the fervor and the resolution of the born martyr. Part of his dilemma indeed is that the comfortable little world in which he lives has no place for martyrs. His struggle, Mrs. Oliphant writes, has been a history not unprecedented or unparalleled, such as has been told to the world before now by men who have gone through it in various shapes, with various amounts of sophistry and simplicity. But it is a different thing reading of such a conflict in a book, and hearing it from lips pallid with the meaning of the words they uttered, and a heart which was about to prove its sincerity by voluntary pangs more hard than death. . . . Gerald did not leave any room for argument or remonstrance; he told his brother how he had been led from one step to another, without any lingering touch of possibility in the narrative that he might be induced to retrace again that painful way. It was a path, once trod, never to be returned upon; and already he stood steadfast at the end, looking back mournfully, yet with a strange composure.[16]

With Gerald too the issue of the priesthood as a vocation is introduced. There is no such problem for his brother Frank whose suitability—mentally, morally, and spiritually—for his office is not for a moment in doubt. His smooth career is never seriously jeopardized, though it is disturbed temporarily by gossip and by economic problems. As an Anglican, Gerald, like his brother, is a priest. His dedication to the priesthood is as solemn as any tenet of his faith. In becoming a Roman Catholic, he reasons, he must continue to be a priest: " 'I have put my hand to the plough, and I cannot go back. If I am not a priest, I am nothing.' "

There is, however, a rather formidable obstacle in the way of his becoming a Catholic priest—namely a wife, Louisa, and five children (with another on the way). For Gerald their sacrifice is the tragic but inevitable price that he must pay. He faces the prospect of leaving his family nameless and all but destitute with the calm resignation of the martyr he longs to be. His fluttery wife quite understandably takes a different view. She is not very intelligent, and she treats her husband somewhat in the manner of a mother pampering a spoiled child. Let him have his whims, she cries, but let him remain in the Church: " 'He might have preached in six surplices if he liked. . . . Who would have minded? . . . Why should he leave Wentworth where he can do what he likes, and nobody will interfere with him? The Bishop is an old friend of my father's, and I am sure he never would say anything.' " Mrs. Oliphant balances her sympathy skilfully between the comic obtuseness of the wife and the tragic self-immolation of the husband. When Blackwood, reading the manuscript of the novel in parts, expressed his fears about the delicacy of the subject, she reassured him:

> Make yourself quite easy about Gerald and his wife. I never meant that he should succeed in getting free of her, but I am at present in expectation of the most definite information from headquarters, having appealed to a cardinal in Rome whom I had the honour of encountering while there, and who is a friend of the Macphersons. I mean to hold up the old medieval rule which I believe is still in force that the final consent of the wife makes the matter practicable, which happened to be particularly suited to my plan—but I have no intention finally of carrying out the sacrifice.[17]

Gerald eventually works out such a compromise. He joins the Roman Church, but renounces the priesthood. The price is a great one for him to pay. He sees it as almost a martyrdom. When Frank reminds him of his resolution that he would be a priest or nothing, Gerald replies with melancholy resignation: " 'I am content to be nothing, as the saints were. The fight has been hard enough, but I am not ashamed of the victory. When the law of the Church and the obedience of the saints ordain me to be nothing, I consent to it. There is nothing more to say.' " Yet Mrs. Oliphant does not leave him with a totally blank future. Gerald rediscovers his vocation in a kind of lay priesthood. Facing the scoundrel Tom Wodehouse, almost without thinking, "by instinct," he begins to preach to him. He advises him to leave his wicked associates: " 'Go now and leave them,' said the man who was a priest by nature. The light returned to his eye while he spoke; he was no longer passive, contemplating his own moral death; his natural office had come back to him unawares."

There is a good deal of fairly serious religious matter in *The Perpetual Curate* including a theological discussion between the two brothers which is a simplified but not oversimplified debate on the Oxford Movement—with Gerald clinging desperately to the "rock of authority" which Rome offers him, and Frank accepting the mysteries of existence, his own doubts and perplexities, as part of his fundamental faith.[18] But Mrs. Oliphant carefully keeps the balance between religion and social comedy. Unlike *Salem Chapel*,

The Perpetual Curate moves smoothly from one plane to another, its material thoroughly integrated. Frank Wentworth's father, the Squire, has made his personal transition and adjustment in the Church-State relationship with his sons: "The eldest the squire, the second the rector. That's my idea . . . of Church and State." Characters like the Squire enrich this novel with quiet but telling strokes of satire: "He was not a man of any intellect to speak of, nor did he pretend to it; but he had that glimmering of sense which keeps many a stupid man straight, and a certain amount of natural sensibility and consideration for other people's feeling which made persons who knew no better give Mr. Wentworth credit for tact, a quality unknown to him." Weighed down by the burdens of a large family, the poor old man looks to his son Frank for help. The eldest son and heir is an idle, unprincipled rascal. Gerald's religious dilemma exasperates him. He now has the problem of disposing of two younger and not very clever sons, and the only course he can see is to send them to Australia: "Cuthbert and Guy were arrows in the hand of the giant, but he had his quiver so full that the best thing he could do was to draw his bow and shoot them away into as distant and as fresh a sphere as possible."

Mrs. Oliphant's comedy in *The Perpetual Curate* is gentle and her satire mild. Even while she laughs at her characters and holds their weaknesses up to mockery, she treats them with sympathy. Nowhere is her method better illustrated than in her sketch of Dr. Morgan and his wife. They are middle aged but newly married, the victims of their own prudence which kept them waiting ten years until Dr. Morgan had an adequate income for marriage. Established at last in Carlingford, he has the nervous insecurity of a man who wants very badly to succeed. Furthermore, he has a Welsh temper which flares up in the face of Frank Wentworth's calm, assured control of the little congregation that is within Mr. Morgan's parish. His wife too has her problems. Sadly conscious that in those ten years of waiting she has lost not only her youthful beauty but also the intangible glow of romance, she sees her marriage in the sober, dim light of middle age. She bears patiently the minor irritations of her life—the hideous carpet left by their predecessor in the rectory, the unctuous gossipy curate Mr. Leeson who persistently invites himself to dinner, and, a little less patiently, the major one—her husband's violent prejudice against Frank Wentworth, whom she admires. Her husband's announcement to her that he wishes to resign from his post in Carlingford is bitter proof of her superior wisdom and of his own failure. But when he goes on to explain that he is arranging to have Wentworth put in his place, a gallant gesture and admission of his errors, her disillusionment turns to delight and admiration, and she bursts into tears:

> The excellent man was as entirely unconscious that he was being put up again at that moment with acclamations upon his pedestal, as that he had at a former time been violently displaced from it, and thrown into the category of broken idols. All this would have been as Sanscrit to the Rector of Carlingford; and the only resource he had was to make in his own mind certain half-pitying half-affectionate remarks upon the inexplicable weakness of women, and to pick up the stocking which his wife was darning, and finally to stroke her hair, which was still as pretty and soft and brown as it had been ten years ago. Under such circumstances a man does not object to feel himself on a platform of moral superiority. He even began to pet her a little, with a pleasant sense of forgiveness and forbearance. "You were perhaps a little cross, my love, but you don't think I am a man to be hard on you," said the Rector.

In January 1864, during the course of writing the second half of *The Perpetual Curate,* Mrs. Oliphant lost her daughter Maggie. There was a period of relative inactivity after the child's death, interrupted only by the work she was committed to—the completion of *The Perpetual Curate* for *Maga* and of *A Son of the Soil* for *Macmillan's Magazine.*[19] It is hard to believe that the witty novel *Miss Marjoribanks* was conceived during this period. Perhaps the answer lies simply in the extraordinary gift for work which never seemed to fail her even under the most painful circumstances. The original plan was for a short novel, but in the writing the book began to grow. She wrote to Blackwood early in 1865: "I send you with this the second number of 'Miss Marjoribanks' which I hope you will like. I am not quite sure myself that there is enough progress made, and I am afraid I am getting into a habit of over-minuteness. . . . I meant it to be only four or five numbers, but I have already put in too many details to make that possible, and it seems to suit my demon best to let it have its own way."[20] Several months later in sending him another number she remarked: "I feel a little too *fluent,* as if I had all run to words, as I suppose a preacher may feel after a long sermon—if indeed preachers ever do have any human or Christian compunctions on that subject."[21] In spite of this "fluency," *Miss Marjoribanks* was a difficult novel for Mrs. Oliphant to write. Blackwood nursed her along with praise, to which she responded with modesty but also with a degree of pride:

> Don't frighten me, please, about 'Miss Marjoribanks.' I will do the very best I can to content you, but you make me nervous when you talk about the first rank of novelists, &c.—nobody in the world cares whether I am first or sixth. I mean I have no one left who cares, and the world can do absolutely nothing for me except giving me a little more money which, Heaven knows, I spend easily enough as it is. But all the same, I will do my best, only please recognise the difference a little between a man who can take the good of his reputation, if he has any, and a poor soul who is concerned about nothing except the most domestic and limited concerns.[22]

The sense of personal loss, the hopelessness and despair from which she suffered at this time, make themselves felt even in the comedy of the novel. The gentle humor of *The Perpetual Curate,* the sympathy and compassion for human weakness, turn into chilling satire in *Miss Marjoribanks.* There are traces of the old tenderness now and then—for example, a sketch of a devoted elderly couple who, in spite of their devotion, get on each other's nerves: "thus the two old people kept watch upon each other, and noted, with a curious mixture of vexation and sympathy, each other's declining strength"; or in her admirably restrained but moving account of the death of gruff old Dr. Marjoribanks. But for the most part the satire is bitter and the feeling cold. Blackwood detected this about halfway through the novel, and Mrs. Oliphant acknowledged it, though she had a good defence:

As for what you say of hardness of tone, I am afraid it was scarcely to be avoided. I hate myself the cold-blooded school of novel-writing in which one works out a character without the slightest regard to whether it is good or bad, or whether it touches or revolts one's sympathies. But at the same time I have a weakness for Lucilla, and to bring a sudden change upon her character and break her down into tenderness would be like one of Dickens's maudlin repentences, when he makes Mr. Dombey *trinquer* with Captain Cuttle. Miss M. must be one and indivisible, and I feel pretty sure that my plan is right.[23]

Even as she approached the end of the novel, however, the writing became no easier. "As for 'Miss Marjoribanks,' " she wrote to Blackwood, "I am a little disgusted with her, and with novels in general." And this note is repeated in the covering letter with the concluding number: "Herewith I send you the last no. of Miss M. which has cost me an infinite deal of trouble, as you will partly perceive from the state of the MS, but it is not quite satisfactory yet."[24]

No doubt both Mrs. Oliphant and her publisher were plagued by the question of whether the novel was worth that "infinite deal of trouble." Blackwood apparently thought it was not. He offered her considerably less money than she had expected, and he received a stinging response:

I am, I confess, considerably disappointed by your letter about Miss Marjoribanks. Your way of speaking about it at the beginning was so very different that the downfall is all the more severe—and I cannot help feeling it all the more from what I hear on all sides of the prices received by my contemporaries. Miss Mulock (that was) has I believe larger prices even without the interposition of a magazine. Mrs. Norton, Mr. Blackett tells me, is to have £1,000 from Mr. Macmillan for the mere passage of her story through his Magazine, beside another thousand for the reprint, and they speak of ever so many thousands coming to Wilkie Collins for his present rubbish. . . . I never for an instant imagined that you were to offer me *less* than for the Perpetual Curate. I know you have no desire to place me at a disadvantage, but at the same time I think you must feel that if I, like others of my craft, had insisted upon a bargain at the time Miss M. commenced, it would have been concluded upon more liberal terms.

But the publisher was firm and Mrs. Oliphant had to accept his decision. Later that same year she had evidently forgiven him, but not forgotten. In writing to acknowledge a check and a letter in which he had complained of a toothache, she observed slyly: "Is this intended as compensation to my wounded feelings? See what it is to ill-use your authors. I *feel* that this toothache is judicial and hope like a true friend that it will be 'for your good.' "[25]

Miss Marjoribanks was thus a disappointment to its publisher and consequently to its author. Its Victorian readers too were disappointed, for the smug, self-centered, self-righteous heroine was not appealing or attractive enough to hold their interest through three volumes. The charms of the Carlingford series—those "inside" glimpses of church and home life—are lacking. In their place we find a relentlessly satirical character sketch of a female egoist. There is very little "charm" in the novel and almost none in its heroine. The satire wears thin when stretched to three volumes. There is, properly speaking, no plot, and only the most minimal character development. Yet the sharpness, the malice, the wit of the book are remarkable. In *Miss Marjoribanks* for the first time in her fiction the sophisticated, anti-sentimental, hard core of Mrs. Oliphant's personality asserts itself. Lucilla Marjoribanks is the spiritual grand-daughter of Jane Austen's Emma Woodhouse. She is a "managing" woman, running her widower father's household and the lives of all who come into her orbit. Like Emma, she tries to mould and manipulate people—with results that sometimes come perilously close to disaster for them. Like Emma, she is absolutely convinced of the rightness of her actions. The comparison ends there. Miss Marjoribanks lacks Emma's intelligence and sensitivity. Although she has her moments of self-doubt, she never comes to any real self-knowledge. She grows older and stouter in the ten-year span of the novel, but she never grows spiritually. At the end of the book she is the same person she was at the beginning. This is the essential humor of the book, but it is also its principal limitation.[26]

The comic conception of the novel is clever and ambitious. The form that Mrs. Oliphant was attempting here was mock domestic epic. Her inspiration may have been that best-selling *vade mecum* of the mid-nineteenth century, Arthur Helps' *Friends in Council* (the favorite reading, incidentally, of the head-mistress of the school Miss Marjoribanks attends). Helps opens his little essay "On the Art of Living with Others" with this challenge:

> The Iliad for war; the Odyssey for wandering: but where is the great domestic epic? Yet it is but commonplace to say, that passions may rage round a tea-table, which would not have misbecome men dashing at one another in war-chariots; and evolutions of patience and temper are performed at the fireside, worthy to be compared with the Retreat of the Ten Thousand. Men have worshipped some fantastic being for living alone in a wilderness; but social martyrdoms place no saints upon the calendar.

It is certainly in epic terms that Mrs. Oliphant tells her story: "One fytte of Lucilla's story is here ended. . . ." she writes at the beginning of Part III. When one of her suitors, Mr. Cavendish, is suspected of flirting with another girl and enters a room full of Miss Marjoribanks' loyal friends—"The Balaclava charge itself, in the face of all the guns, could have been nothing to the sensation of walking through that horrible naked space, through a crowd of reproachful men who were waiting for dinner." Or when Miss Marjoribanks herself makes a dramatic entrance before her guests: "Fifty eyes were upon Lucilla watching her conduct at that critical moment—fifty ears were on the strain to divine her sentiments in her voice, and to catch some intonation at least which should betray her consciousness of what was going on." And finally, when the news of her marriage to her cousin is announced in Grange Lane:

> there was first a dead pause of incredulity and amazement, and then such a commotion as could be compared to nothing except a sudden squall at sea. People who had been going peaceably on their way at one moment, thinking of nothing, were to be seen the next buffeted by the wind of Rumour and tossed about on the waves of Astonishment. To speak less metaphorically (but there are moments of emotion so overwhelming and unprecedented that they can be dealt with only in the language of metaphor), every household in Grange Lane, and at least half of the humbler houses in Grove Street, and a large portion of the other dwellings in Carlingford, were nearly as much agitated about Lucilla's marriage as if it had been a daughter of their own.

Miss Marjoribanks too has the ingenuousness and self-confidence of epic heroes. In her there is none of that modesty and self-questioning characteristic of weaker mortals: "She was possessed by nature of that kind of egotism or rather egoism, which is predestined to impress itself, by its perfect reality and good faith, upon the surrounding world . . . the calmest and most profound conviction that, when she discussed her own doings and plans and clevernesses, she was bringing forward the subject most interesting to her audience as well as to herself." Such conviction is eminently consoling to her as one by one her suitors succumb to other women's charms. At last, after ten years of being "out" in society, she marries her cousin Tom Marjoribanks, persuades him to buy a country estate, and sets out with him to "a new sphere . . . still near enough to Carlingford to keep a watchful eye upon society, and yet at the same time translated into a new world, where her influence might be of untold advantage, as Lucilla modestly said, to her fellow-creatures."

The portrait of Miss Marjoribanks has wit, freshness, and originality, but it lacks humanity. In 1876, when Mrs. Oliphant returned to Carlingford, she brought back with her a heroine who is Lucilla Marjoribanks reduced to human dimensions. This is Phoebe Junior, the blooming daughter of Phoebe Tozer who, back in *Salem Chapel,* had married the Dissenting minister Mr. Beecher (or Beecham, as he becomes in the later novel). She is the same self-possessed, marvellously assured and capable young woman, but she has been softened down and humanized into a thoroughly charming and believable character. *Miss Marjoribanks* was a broad joke which lost most of its effectiveness through exaggeration and repetition; *Phoebe, Junior* is a quiet witticism, delivered with subtlety and economy. Technically it is by far the best of the Carlingford novels. It has a well-constructed though by no means original plot. The action is swift. The characters are lively and interesting, and one at least, the Reverend Mr. May, is fairly complex. The intrigue is kept to a minimum, but what there is is handled skillfully. The novel, written a decade later than its predecessors in the Carlingford series, shows on every page the author's increased mastery of her craft.

One of the minor curiosities of publishing history is why Blackwood should have rejected this novel when he published so many that were inferior to it. The answer probably lies in the business policy described by Mrs. Oliphant of calculating the success of one work "in a great degree by the success of the previous one." The previous ones in this case—i. e., the Carlingford novels after *Salem Chapel*—had been disappointing to the publisher. They sold, they remained in print with new editions appearing from time to time, but they were not financial successes. In 1897 Mrs. Oliphant remarked of them: "These books, I fear, are no longer very well remembered by anyone."[27] Furthermore, Blackwood seems to have taken a generally unfavorable view of her fiction after about 1870. While the firm continued to publish vast quantities of her criticism and non-fiction, they were extremely reluctant to accept her novels. From 1870 until the year after her death they published only ten works of fiction (plus a few odd stories reprinted from *Maga* in *Tales from Blackwood*)—a fraction of the total of sixty-six she published during this period.[28] Hence, when she revived the Carlingford series in 1876, it was through another publisher, Hurst and Blackett.

In giving the new novel the subtitle "A Last Chronicle of Carlingford," she was deliberately echoing Trollope's *The Last Chronicle of Barset* (1867). And there are more than mere echoes of Trollope in *Phoebe, Junior*. One whole episode is lifted out of *The Warden* (1855). Young Reginald May, fresh from Oxford, with the dimmest economic prospects, is offered and under family pressure accepts a sinecure as chaplain to the Carlingford College, an ancient foundation which supports a few indigent old men. The post comes under sharp attack from the Dissenting minister, Mr. Northcote, who immediately seeks to make a great issue out of it —all of which of course harks back to Mr. Harding's difficulties with Tom Towers and the press. A less overt case, but certainly an example of unconscious, if not conscious, borrowing, is the main dramatic incident of the book—the curate Mr. May's poverty and his forging of Tozer's name to a promissory note—which recalls the charges, in this case unwarranted, against the much put upon Reverend Josiah Crawley in Trollope's *Last Chronicle*.

These borrowings concern only secondary issues in the novel, however. The lively social comedy is Mrs. Oliphant's creation exclusively. Into the narrow provincial world of Carlingford she introduces a breath of fresh London air with young Phoebe, who comes to visit her grandparents, the Tozers:

> "Do you live down this nice road? How pretty it is! how delightful these gardens must be in summer. I beg your pardon for calling it the country. It is so quiet and so nice, it seems the country to me."
>
> "Ah, to be sure; brought up in the London smoke," said Mr. Tozer. "I don't suppose, now, you see a bit of green earth from year's end to year's end? Very bad for the 'ealth, that is; but I can't say you look poorly on it. . . ."
>
> "Oh, we do get a little fresh air sometimes—in the parks, for instance," said Phoebe. She was somewhat piqued by the idea that she was supposed to live in London smoke.

Phoebe has had every advantage—German governess, music, languages, lectures at the ladies' colleges; and, at the same time, "she patronized Mr. Ruskin's theory that dancing, drawing, and cooking were three of the higher arts which ought to be studied by girls." Perhaps a further advantage has been that her doting parents, who have risen far above their humble origins, have shielded her from a knowledge of her background. She has met her tradesman grandfather on country holidays but has never before seen him in his proper surroundings. Therefore, when she comes to Carlingford, though her parents have made careful efforts to prepare her, Phoebe is somewhat dismayed to find that he "looked neither more nor less than what he was, an old shopkeeper, very decent and respectable, but a little shabby and greasy, like the men whose weekly bills she had been accustomed to pay for her mother. She felt an instant conviction that he would call her 'Ma'am,' if she went up to him, and think her one of the quality." Furthermore, she realizes with a shock that as a member of a Dissenting family who worship at Salem Chapel she is automatically excluded from the higher orders of Carlingford society. But like Miss Marjoribanks, Phoebe has sublime self-confidence and accepts the situation with good grace: "She knew very well by all her mother said, and by all the hesitations of both her parents, that she would have many disagreeable things to encounter in Carlingford, but she felt so sure that nothing could really humiliate *her*, or pull her down from her real eminence, that the knowledge conveyed no fears to her mind."

She hops neatly over the social barriers to make friends with the May family. Mr. May is curate of St. Roque's, one of the long line of underpaid, overburdened clergymen who struggle to maintain a genteel position in society on a poor man's income. But Mr. May's is an even unhappier condition than most, for he lacks the very Christian qualities which he preaches—humility and patience. He is intelligent, handsome, "of sufficiently good family and tolerably well connected. Yet he never got on, never made any real advance in life." Constantly in debt, careless of what little money he gets from time to time, rather inclined to bully his children, he is not a sympathetic figure. Nevertheless, Mrs. Oliphant treats him with considerable understanding and insight. When his financial affairs reach a crisis, he simply postpones disaster by forging Tozer's signature to a bank note. It is an act of weakness rather than of criminality, Mrs. Oliphant suggests, but there is no equivocating about his guilt or his ultimate punishment. The latter— thanks to Phoebe's intervention—is supplied not by the law but by his own conscience and is severe—a mental breakdown followed quickly by his death. This is the only serious note in the novel. Mrs. Oliphant disposes of it as swiftly and economically as she can. Otherwise the May family offers happier opportunities for her. It provides her, particularly, with a sweet and sentimental young heroine, Ursula, who is a foil to the anti-sentimental, practical Phoebe. Ursula's romance with Horace Northcote, the Dissenting minister, is tepid and innocuous. Similarly, Ursula's brother's infatuation for Phoebe—to which that young lady responds appreciatively but negatively—is simply the conventional matter of Victorian romance.

For Phoebe herself Mrs. Oliphant reserves a less conventional fate. She is one of a small number of refreshing Oliphant heroines who allow their reason rather than their emotions to rule them and who marry for money rather than for romantic love. When

Reginald May offers her his love, she is touched: "She cried, and her heart contracted with a real pang. He was very tender in his reverential homage, very romantic, a true lover. . . . Phoebe went in with a sense in her mind that perhaps she had never touched so close upon a higher kind of existence, and perhaps might never again have the opportunity." Phoebe has other plans, however, in the large but not very prepossessing person of Clarence Copperhead. Clarence is not bright; he has been sent down from his university; but he is a good-hearted fellow and the son of a millionaire. Mrs. Oliphant draws a devastating portrait of the vulgar Copperhead *père* who tyrannizes over all those around him because he knows that he can buy and sell them. Young Clarence is his father much softened and slightly sweetened. He has the same vulgar appreciation of money:

> He felt the power and beauty of money almost as much as his father did. What was there he could not buy with it?—the services of the most learned pundit in existence (for what was learning?) or the prettiest woman going to be his wife, if that was what he wanted. . . . He aired himself on the hearth rug with great satisfaction, giving now and then a glance to one of his long limbs to see that all was perfect in the *sit* of the garment that clothed it. He had been plowed, it is true, but that did not interfere much with his mental satisfaction; for, after all, scholarship was a thing cultivated chiefly by dons and prigs and poor men.

Phoebe is not entirely mercenary. What draws her essentially to Clarence is not money but a realization that here is a man she can mould and manage. She can free him of his weak-kneed dependence on his father. She can even send him to Parliament—where, she quickly recognizes, she will write his speeches for him:

> What was Phoebe to do? She did not dislike Clarence Copperhead, and it was no horror for her to think of marrying him. She had felt for years that this might be on the cards, and there were a great many things in it which demanded consideration. He was not very wise, nor a man to be enthusiastic about, but he would be a career to Phoebe. She did not think of it humbly like this, but with a big Capital—a Career. . . . Who can say she was not as romantic as any girl of twenty could be? Only her romance took

an unusual form. It was her head that was full of throbbings and pulses, not her heart.

Mrs. Oliphant could not properly end her Chronicles without some last word on the Dissenting church. In *Salem Chapel* she had confined herself to an attack on its system of lay government, showing through Vincent's rejection of the ministry the destructive effects of the domination of a church by its uneducated lay congregation. There is a faint echo of Arthur Vincent in the character of Horace Northcote, who appears at the beginning of *Phoebe, Junior* as a vigorous Dissenter. He launches his battle against the Establishment with his attack on Reginald May's sinecure. But the two clergymen of differing sects gradually discover that at the heart of the matter there are no differences between them. Meeting in the beautiful fifteenth-century chapel of the college they arrive at a mutual understanding:

> They meant everything that was fine and great, these two young men, standing upon the threshold of their life, knowing little more than that they were fiercely opposed to each other, and meant to reform the world, each in his own way; one by careful services and visitings of the poor, the other by the Liberation Society and overthrow of the State Church; both foolish, wrong and right, to the utmost bounds of human possibility. How different they felt themselves standing there, and yet how much at one they were, without knowing it.

At the end of the novel Northcote, like Vincent before him, has offended the members of Salem Chapel. They have had enough of brilliant young men who think themselves superior to their congregations. Tozer, who once defended Vincent, now rises to condemn Northcote: " 'If any more o' them young intellectuals turns up at Carlingford, I'll tell him right out, 'You ain't the man for my money.' I'll say to him as bold as brass, 'I've been young and now I'm old, and it's my conviction as clever young men ain't the sort for Salem.' " Northcote goes much further than Vincent. Not only does he give up the ministry ("for which he was not fitted," Mrs. Oliphant adds, with her mind still on the pastoral vocation) but Dissent as well—"coming to see that Disestablishment was not a panacea for national evils any more than other things."

Mrs. Oliphant's final judgment on Dissent, however, does not appear in this rather solemn decision of Northcote's. Rather it comes at the beginning of the novel in the richly satirical chapter on the Beechams, Phoebe's parents. Over the years Beecham has risen from the humble Dissenting chapel in Carlingford to a magnificent church in London:

> Mr. Beecham had unbounded fluency and an unctuous manner of treating his subjects. It was eloquence of a kind, though not of an elevated kind. Never to be at a loss for what you have to say is a prodigious advantage to all men in all positions, but doubly so to a popular minister. He had an unbounded wealth of phraseology. Sentences seemed to melt out of his mouth without any apparent effort, all set in a certain cadence. He had not, perhaps, much power of thought, but it was easy to make up for such a secondary want when the gift of expression is strong. Mr. Beecham rose, like an actor, from a long and successful career in the provinces, in what might be called the Surrey side of congregational eminence in London; and from thence attained his final apotheosis in a handsome chapel near Regent's Park, built of the whitest stone, and cushioned with the reddest damask, where a very large congregation sat in great comfort and listened to his sermons with a satisfaction no doubt increased by the fact that the cushions were as soft as their own easy-chairs, and that carpets and hot-water pipes kept everything snug underfoot.

The higher his economic fortunes, the higher his religious views. The Beechams never abandon their Dissenting principles. Crescent Chapel, his London church, is nominally as much a Dissenting church as Salem Chapel. But as they climb the social ladder they come more and more to tolerate, then admire, and finally to emulate the church of the Establishment:

> When Mr. and Mrs. Beecham commenced life, they had both the warmest feeling of opposition to the Church and everything churchy. All the circumstances of their lives had encouraged this feeling. The dislike of the little for the great, the instinctive opposition of a lower class toward the higher, intensified that natural essence of separation, that determination to be wiser than one's

neighbour, which in the common mind lies at the bottom of all dissent. In saying this we no more accuse Dissenters in religion than Dissenters in politics, art, or in criticism. The first dissenter in most cases is an original thinker, to whom his enforced departure from the ways of his father is misery and pain. . . . But that Non-conformity which has come to be the faith in which a large number of people are trained is a totally different business, and affects a very different kind of sentiments. Personal and independent conviction has no more to do with it than it has to do with the ardour of a Breton peasant trained in deepest zeal of Romanism, or the unbounded certainty of any other traditionary believer.

By 1876 when *Phoebe, Junior* was published, Mrs. Oliphant herself had come a long way from her humble origins in Scotland, the dingy Scotch church in Liverpool where she had worshipped as a young girl, and the sententious moralizing of her first heroine, Mistress Margaret Maitland. Religion was and remained a serious issue with her. Indeed, her faith was so firm that she could view it critically and even satirically without risk. *Phoebe, Junior* concludes the Carlingford series with a slightly mocking laugh at Dissent. It is not a "religious novel" in the sense that *The Rector, Salem Chapel,* and *The Perpetual Curate* are religious novels, having clergymen and their spiritual problems at their centers. Instead, it reduces sectarianism to social comedy. What interested Mrs. Oliphant, and her readers, in *Phoebe, Junior* is no matter of church doctrine but of human behavior. If Mrs. Oliphant sees Dissent with cynical eyes, it is only because she is looking at society in the same way. And Carlingford, in its modest way, has made its contribution to the Victorian human comedy.

Chapter III

The Seen And The Unseen

The Carlingford novels are rare, among Mrs. Oliphant's numerous works, for their relative objectivity. That is, they are the least personal in subject matter and characterization of all her fiction. Almost everywhere else she drew deeply from her own experience —in literal detail as well as in the subtler qualities of tone and spirit. Three themes certainly appear in her work—motherhood, widowhood, and the adjustment or reconciliation to the deaths of loved ones. Motherhood and widowhood especially dominate her novels of the 1860's and '70's. Her favorite subject of this period was the widow struggling to raise her family in a cold, unfriendly world. Here was the ideal subject for a novel, full of pathos, tenderness, homely truths, and homely emotions. Love stories had of course captured the literary market, but Mrs. Oliphant was impatient of them: "I have learned to take perhaps more of a man's view of mortal affairs,—to feel that the love between men and women, the marrying and giving in marriage, occupy in fact so small a portion of either existence or thought." Life had imposed a sterner reality upon her.

Within only a little more than a year after her husband's death Mrs. Oliphant had reconciled herself to her position as widowed mother and bread-winner for her family. Perhaps in the end no one was more surprised than she at her ready adjustment to her new life. There was even an element of guilt in it—an uneasy sense that the tranquility and happiness she now knew had been strangely lacking in her married life. She stopped wearing her widow's cap after a year or two because, she confessed, "I found

75

it too becoming! That did not seem to me at all suitable for the
spirit of my mourning: it certainly was, as my excellent London
dressmaker made it for me, a very pretty head-dress, and an expensive luxury withal." Like other sources of deep personal concern to her—her brother's alcoholism, her husband's failures—
she explored this problem of her widowhood in her fiction, treating
it with startling candor. Her widows are always beautiful in their
mourning; black sets off their complexions; the cap frames their
faces becomingly; their figures draped in crape are "willowy" and
"graceful." They have the joy of full possession of their children,
the admiration and pity of the world, and, not least, a freedom and
independence such as they never enjoyed in marriage. In a novel
called *Innocent* (1873) Mrs. Oliphant digresses with a paragraph
on widowhood:

> Life *à deux* (I don't know any English phrase which quite ex-
> presses this) is scarcely more different from the primitive and
> original single life, than is the life which, after having been *à
> deux,* becomes single, without the possibility of going back to the
> original standing ground. That curious mingling of a man's posi-
> tion and responsibilities cannot possibly fail to mould a type of
> character in many respects individual. A man who is widowed is
> not similarly affected, partly perhaps because in most cases he
> throws the responsibility from him, and either marries again or
> places some woman in the deputy position of governess or house-
> keeper to represent the feminine side of life, which he does not
> choose to take upon himself. Women, however, abandon their
> post much less frequently, and sometimes, I suspect, get quite
> reconciled to the double burden, and do not object too much, and
> often enough they fail; but so does everybody in everything, and
> widows' sons have not shown badly in general life.

She was happiest in the society of other women and her own
children. Albertinelli's *Visitation,* the painting to which she often
alluded, epitomizes that bond of intimacy and affection—woman
confiding in and leaning upon woman, sharing the precious secret
of approaching motherhood. Friendships with women figured large
in her life—Isabella Blackwood, Mrs. Tulloch, Emma FitzMaurice,
Geddie Macpherson, Lady Charlotte Eliot, Lady Cloncurry and
her daughter the Honorable Emily Lawless. In life, as in literature, Mrs. Oliphant tended to idealize and sentimentalize these

friendships. Describing her first meeting with Mrs. Tulloch, for example, she recalls how they sat together exchanging "matronly confidences": "These things were more to us than the movements of the spheres. We were two women together, with nobody to note whether we were silly or wise; and we communed in our fashion, with the best result of all communings, that we were friends from that day."[1]

In her fiction too she portrays this kind of relationship in almost idyllic terms. The heroine of *Madonna Mary* (1867), widowed in India, returns to England with her children and settles down in a country cottage with a spinster aunt:

> There followed after this a time of such tranquility as had never yet entered in Mrs. Ochterlony's life. Mary had known joy and she had known sorrow, as people do to whom life comes with full, giving and taking; but it had always been life, busy and personal, which left her little leisure for anything beyond the quickly recurring duties of the hour and day. . . . They [Mary and her aunt] were not unhappy, nor was their existence sad,—for the three boys were world enough to satisfy the two women and keep them occupied and cheerful.

The idyll, however, is not entirely woman-dominated. The flattering widow's weeds, the softly muted sorrow, the quietly courageous independence, all have an unmistakably romantic appeal. The degree to which Mrs. Oliphant identifies herself with her widowed heroines is striking. The heroine of *Madonna Mary* receives her title from an adoring younger man, "perhaps with some faint foolish thought of Petrarch and his Madonna Laura . . . and Mary herself did not object to be addressed by that sweetest of titles." Neither did Mrs. Oliphant object to the same title when it was bestowed on her by a younger and obviously admiring young man, the clergyman Robert Herbert Story. Story first called upon her in Edinburgh in the grim winter of 1860 to offer help in her research into the life of Edward Irving, a commissioned biography. Years later he recalled that meeting:

> I had heard but little of her previously, and only knew that she was a successful authoress and a widow. My idea of such a personage did not prepare me for the vision I beheld when she

entered the little parlour in Fettes Row, where I awaited her. A slight figure, draped in black; a very calm and gentle manner; a low and pleasant voice, marked with that homely Scottish accent which she never lost or wished to lose; a pair of the most delicate and beautiful hands I had ever seen; and such eyes I had never looked into, large, intensely dark, and lambent, with a pure and steady flame. The upper part of her face, with these wonderful eyes, and crowned with what was then very dark brown hair, bore a singular resemblance to the Madonna di San Sisto. Indeed, "Madonna Mia" was a name she was not unused to hear.[2]

Still another heroine is the charming Mrs. Severn, called "Padrona" by her friends, in the novel *The Three Brothers* (1870). The penniless widow of an artist who, like Francis Oliphant, had failed in his career, she takes up painting to support her family and becomes a competent "hack" painter. She too is completely absorbed by and devoted to her children and finds an almost perverse delight in her widowhood:

> . . . and out of her sorrow [she] had grown softly happy again, without knowing how—happy in her work, and her freedom, and her independence, and her children. Alas, yes; in her independence and freedom. She liked that, though many a reader will think the worse of her for liking it. But it is not as a perfect creature she is here introduced, but as a woman with faults, like others. Everybody knew that she had been very fond of poor Severn, and had stood by him faithful and tender till his last breath; and that she was very desolate when he was gone, and cried out even against God and His providence a little in her anguish and solitude; but pondered and was silent, and pondered and was cheerful; and, at last, things being as they were, got to be glad that she was free and could work for herself. And she was comparatively young and had plenty to do, and there were her children. A woman cannot go on being heartbroken with such props as these. And it pleased her, we avow, since she could not help it, to have her own way.

Mrs. Severn has an admirer in Laurie Renton, a young artist. At one point the relationship takes an almost alarming turn. Renton falls in love with her and declares himself passionately. Mrs. Severn dismisses him kindly but firmly:

> "I am very fond of you. I will say I love you, if you like. Patience and hear me to an end. If you go away I will miss you

every hour; but if my child's finger were to ache I should forget your existence, Laurie. A single hair on their heads is more to me than all the world besides. Do you understand? My poor Harry is past, if you will. God forgive me for saying so—but today is so full, there's no room in it for any other. Laurie, I want my friend. I want nothing else—nothing else that any man can give.

We have no way of knowing whether Mrs. Oliphant's relationship with Story proceeded quite this far, or if it even moved in this direction. Nevertheless, it was and for years remained a warm friendship. Story married in 1863, became an eminent reformer in the Church of Scotland, and in 1886 was appointed chaplain-in-ordinary to Queen Victoria. But Mrs. Oliphant continued to play the Candida-role of bossy but kindly matron, to read and encourage his literary efforts, to help him find publishers, to introduce him to influential people. In his journal for May 1862 Story recalls visiting her, when she was living at Ealing. Here he met the publishers Blackett and Macmillan, Miss Isabella Blackwood, and George MacDonald. A few days later he writes: "Spent the evening with Mrs. Oliphant at 5 Cheyne Row—no one but ourselves and Mr. and Mrs. Carlyle. Tea, and endless talk from Tom, who was most affable and brilliant."[3] Meanwhile, Mrs. Oliphant was persistently but unsuccessfully besieging Blackwood with requests to publish a volume of Story's. In an undated letter, probably in 1862, she urged Macmillan to let him review MacDonald's *David Elginbrod* in *Macmillan's Magazine*: "Mr. Robert Story would do it very well I am sure if you would put it into his hands. And I wish you would shake that young man up and make him do magazine work. If you would only get him into harness, I am sure he would prove a valuable addition to your team."[4] She finally persuaded Macmillan to publish Story's biography of his father, *Memoir of the Life of the Rev. Robert Story*, in 1862, and Blackett to publish a volume of his verse, *Poems by a Parson*, in 1863. Story was not unappreciative of her efforts. "I begin to believe in human perfectibility," he wrote her on January 8, 1869, "when I see how good you are, Madonna. It is very kind of you not only to read what I have written, but to criticise it, and to criticise it knowing as you do my amiability under criticism."[5]

Children, friends, country holidays—all this suggests a healthy recovery from the terrible blows of 1859-60. But it was work mainly that proved her salvation, as it was to do again and again in later years under even more terrible blows. Characteristically, the work that engaged her mind so completely was not fiction, but the strenuous intellectual effort of the Montalembert translation and the even more challenging and absorbing task of writing a biography of the Scottish clergyman Edward Irving. Irving's brief but spectacular career had ended in 1834, when Mrs. Oliphant was only a child; but he was well remembered in Scotland and in England, and a group of his disciples continued active down through the middle of the century. Today he is probably best known as the tutor of the precocious little Jane Welsh, who grew up to marry his friend and rival Thomas Carlyle. In his own day, however, his celebrity as a religious leader was almost unrivalled. Handsome and commanding, a brilliant speaker, he captivated fashionable London with his eloquent sermons. His theories of a Second Advent created a brief but intense movement of religious revivalism until the conservative elders of his church had him removed from office for heresy.

Mrs. Oliphant's interest in Irving originated naturally enough in her own religious background. The Church of Scotland, the Free Kirk, the various Dissenting movements she encountered during her girlhood in Liverpool, her brother Willie's brief career in the clergy—all these influences found expression in her early novels. In undertaking the Irving biography she embarked on a more formidable task. She was no theologian. Neither was she, for all her religious sympathies, a profound thinker on religious subjects. To complicate matters, simultaneously with her work on the Scotch-Presbyterian Irving, she was translating Montalembert's French-Catholic *Lives of the Monks of the West*. Eventually she reconciled these two seemingly conflicting influences, distilling from them her own deeply personal and emotional faith. From the outset she handled her work with admirable balance, though not perhaps to the complete approval of either ardent Irvingites or of devout Catholics. The biography had been commissioned in 1858 through the efforts of Henry Drummond (1786–1860), one of the founders of the Irvingite Church. Drummond was pleased with her

article on Irving which had appeared in *Maga* in November 1858.
He invited Mrs. Oliphant and her husband to his home in Albany,
Surrey, and they went down there just before their departure for
Italy, spending three days rather impatiently listening to the old
gentleman's recollections of Irving. The book had to be postponed
during the trip to Italy. Not until the winter of 1860, now
desperate for remunerative work, did she return to the subject.
Her first step was to seek out and interview people who had known
Irving. She began with Robert Story, whose clergyman father had
been an intimate friend of Irving's and who had in his possession
at Rosneath, where he had succeeded his father, a number of Irving letters. In the *Autobiography* Mrs. Oliphant recalled her visit
to the manse at Rosneath in the bitterly cold winter of 1861—the
friendly family consisting of Story ("the handsome young minister,
quite young, though already beginning to grow grey—a very
piquant combination"), his mother and his sister, the huge packet
of almost illegible letters which disappointingly proved not to be
by Irving but by others writing him, the growing despair as she
realized how difficult the undertaking would be.

But the Rosneath connection led to happier things. She returned
in the summer of 1861 with her children, the country now beautiful and gentle and sweet. Here she met the Tulloch family—the
learned, melancholy John Tulloch, Principal of Glasgow University, his wife who became her devoted friend, and their brood of
children who became almost as close to Mrs. Oliphant as her own
children. Here she resumed her friendship with the Storys, as well
as with the Moirs and with Isabella Blackwood. She took a house,
"Willowburn," on the side of the loch: "I doubt if I had ever been
so gay. I was still young, and all was well with the children. My
heart had come up with a great bound from all the strain of previous trouble and hard labour and the valley of the shadow of
death."

The research on Irving continued to engross her, leading among
other things, to the Carlyles and a warm friendship with them. She
approached the great Thomas cautiously, applying first to Dr. John
Carlyle, who then referred her to his more eminent brother. She
took time out during the happy summer of 1861 to go to London
to seek him in Cheyne Row. "I bearded the lion in his den." The

first interview was disappointing. He was kind but vague, telling her only that "the wife" could tell her more. Two days later, to Mrs. Oliphant's surprise, "the wife" appeared at her lodgings in Bayswater, took her for a ride in her brougham, and poured out her memories of her childhood tutor. But for Mrs. Oliphant the principal delight was Mrs. Carlyle herself: "What warmed my heart to her was that she was in many things like my mother; not outwardly . . . but in her wonderful talk, the power of narration which I never heard equalled except in my mother, the flashes of keen wit and sarcasm, occasionally even a little sharpness, and always the modifying sense of humour under all." Their friendship remained close until Mrs. Carlyle's death in 1866. The "lion" himself softened remarkably, Mrs. Oliphant recalling him in subsequent meetings as a benign figure—"not much like the old ogre his false friends have made him out to be."

In the autumn of 1861 Mrs. Oliphant moved her small family to the suburbs of London, to a modest house in Ealing, a "doll's house" she called it, warning her prospective guest Isabella Blackwood to dispense with crinolines when she came to visit. It was a cheerful place with tiny rooms and a pretty garden. She chose Ealing to be near another of her publishers, Henry Blackett, who lived in the neighborhood. The association with Blackwood continued—now, thanks to the Carlingford novels, on a livelier and more mutually profitable basis. Blackett was to publish the Irving biography and since she was now hard at work on this book, she may have felt a closer bond to him at the moment. Otherwise there were no personal ties such as she had established with the Blackwoods. She in fact rather looked down upon Blackett and thought his gentle, pretty wife Ellen much more clever than he, though admitting that neither was literary nor particularly cultivated. They had a lively family of young sons the ages of Mrs. Oliphant's boys. Moreover, and probably most important, Ealing had an ideal location, close to central London, healthful for the children, and living was inexpensive there.

Economy figured in this move, but it was an economy against which Mrs. Oliphant chafed constantly. Her personal extravagance, to which she admits freely in the *Autobiography,* her taste for good living, added considerably to the financial burdens which she

carried. At Ealing she played at thrift. At times, when she con-
templated the education of her sons, it was rather serious play.
Thus when Isabella Blackwood wrote to express her disappointment that she had not remained in Edinburgh, Mrs. Oliphant
replied:

> Where could I have got a cheap house in Edinburgh? If the ad-
> miring and enlightened public will present me with the *other* cor-
> ner house in Charlotte Square and a few hundred pounds to
> accomplish this removal, I should not mind flitting again tomor-
> row. But I doubt whether the public is likely to show so much
> discrimination. It is all very well for you rich people to talk, but
> supposing my stories were to run out, or my brain to get just a
> little duller than it is, what would become of my chicks? Not to
> say that I am ambitious and dream of Harrow and Oxford for my
> bright boy. If Tiddy is spared and turns out according to his
> promise, he will be somebody, or I deceive myself. There is a
> little outbreak of maternal vanity for you! So you see I am wading
> in rather deep water. All the social disadvantages in the world are
> bearable when one can get a house for fifty pounds a year.[6]

In spite of financial worries, the period from 1861 to 1864 was
one of relatively little personal anxiety. Mrs. Oliphant's income
was never sufficient for her needs, but she was working produc-
tively and confidently. The Carlingford series was shaping itself
into an astonishing success, with Blackwood writing her congratu-
latory letters and the reviewers enthusiastic. The Irving biography,
published in 1862, won the highest critical praise—perhaps the
most gratifying being Carlyle's tribute, reported by his wife, that
she was "worth whole cartloads of Mulocks, and Brontës, and
Things of that sort. . . . Nothing has so taken him by the heart for
years as this biography." There is an almost triumphant note in
her letters to Blackwood: "I cannot tell you how much gratified
and affected I am by what you kindly say of my writing. I take it
as one of the most valuable compensations for a lot more laborious
and heavily burdened than that of most of my neighbours, that
Providence has given me friends who judge my endeavors so
kindly." And in another: "Your note of this morning put me in
great spirits: I am more pleased than I can tell you that you
approve of Irving." And another: "I am perfectly charmed to hear
that you continue to like 'Salem' . . . I am delighted with your

approbation. I mean to make what one of the poor London painters despised by the academy calls an 'it if I can with this story."[7]

By 1863 Mrs. Oliphant had reached a kind of zenith of literary success. She was busily at work on her next Carlingford novel which was running serially in *Maga*. She was also under contract to Macmillan for "A Son of the Soil." In the spring of that year her old friend Geddie Macpherson returned to England from Rome to convalesce from a serious illness. She stayed with Mrs. Oliphant at Ealing and there met the Tullochs. John Tulloch was already showing symptoms of the melancholia which darkened his later years. In an effort to relieve the condition he took a trip to Greece, accompanied by his eldest son. Mrs. Tulloch and the other children planned to travel to Rome and meet him there on his return journey. Meanwhile Geddie Macpherson sought to persuade Mrs. Oliphant to spend the winter with her in Rome. Only the renewed confidence and energy which had come to Mrs. Oliphant recently could have influenced her to embark on such an ambitious undertaking. It was she who organized the party of women and children —Mrs. Tulloch and her two daughters, Mrs. Macpherson, the loyal servant Jane, a French governess, and her own little family. She planned the finances of her share of the trip with great care. Alexander Macmillan was to pay for it with the serial publication of "A Son of the Soil," the details of which she worked out during the summer of 1863 which she spent in Scotland near the Blackwoods at St. Andrews. In November the party set out. The expedition was quite a contrast to the dismal journey she had made four years earlier with a dying husband, almost no money, and no sympathetic female companionship. Now they were a gay group— "all with the sense of holiday, a little outburst of freedom, no man interfering, keeping us to rule or formality." They arrived in Rome in beautiful, springlike weather. There were friends to greet them —jovial Robert Macpherson and Willie, "my poor brother William," feebly but cheerfully helping Macpherson and "pouring out his stores of knowledge upon all visitors."

The travellers took a house on the Pincian hill, in Capo le Case street. The weather turned cold, but their spirits were not dampened: "We are having dreadfully cold weather, almost as cold as England, but the English community seems bent upon dancing itself into warmth, for one hears of nothing but balls," she wrote to Macmillan on January 20, 1864.[8] Exactly one week later her daughter Maggie, aged ten, died of gastric fever. The little girl, a healthy, happy, beautiful child, had been her greatest joy—her "ewe-lamb," her "woman-child." Her death was a blow such as Mrs. Oliphant had never sustained before. She buried her in Rome —"Oh this terrible, fatal, miserable Rome!"—and faced the dark hours of her grief alone. Her husband was dead. Her boys were too small to understand the loss; her friends and her brothers could offer sympathy but could not share the pain. In the blackest moment of her despair she wrote in her journal: "I am alone. I am a woman. I have nobody to stand between me and the roughest edge of grief. All the terrible details have to come to me. I have to bear the loss, the pang unshared. . . . O Lord, Thou wouldst not have done it but for good reason! Stand by the forlorn creature who fainteth under thy hand, but whom Thou sufferest not to die."

Of all the losses she had suffered and was to suffer, Mrs. Oliphant admitted thirty years later that Maggie's death was the one that grieved her most. Perhaps it was because she had died so young, before she had a chance to grow up and disappoint her mother, as her brothers were to do; or perhaps it was because she was a "woman-child" in a closer and more intimate relationship than the boys could have been with their mother. At earlier moments of crisis in Mrs. Oliphant's life writing had provided some distraction and relief. She tried now once more to resolve her grief in work. On March 2 she wrote to Blackwood from Rome:

I thank you for your kind sympathy. I had begun again to think that life was sweet—but it does not seem God's will that that should be anything but a shortlived delusion with me. I have been very happy this year or two. Now that is past, but I am still living, God help me, and like to live. I wish I could have some mechanical work to do like that translation [Montalembert's *Monks of the West*] you once charitably gave me the last time. Fiction is hard work just now.[9]

Though fiction was "hard work," she had commitments to several publishers which forced her to grind on. Under the pressures of work she once again gradually recovered from her grief. But the memory of Maggie haunted her and ultimately opened a new course of inspiration from which issued the most moving work she ever achieved. The group, known collectively as the Stories of the Seen and the Unseen, was inaugurated with a nouvelle called *A Beleaguered City* (1880), which undeniably belongs among the minor classics of Victorian literature and which was followed by a series of lesser tales of pathos and haunting power. In all the stories her scene is removed from precise locale to the uncircumscribed regions of the spirit, and her interest in religion becomes transfigured into a quest of the soul after its origins.

There is every evidence that Mrs. Oliphant's Stories of the Seen and the Unseen engrossed her creative mind more deeply and thoroughly than did her more realistic fiction. Whereas the best of the Carlingford novels and her other domestic novels are penetrated with keen wit and shrewd intelligence, *A Beleaguered City* and its successors reveal new qualities of imagination. They reflect at once her most serious mood and her most delicate sensitivity. One gathers too that these stories were close to her heart. It is easy to recognize in their basic themes—the attempts at reunion of dead people with their beloved who have survived them, the adventures of the soul after death—an expression of her own grief, as well as her curiosity about the life beyond the grave. This mystical strain emerged relatively late in her fiction, but as early as January 1865, in a poem called "Day and Night" contributed to *Maga,* she sought escape from her anguish in death:

> So might I wake e'er I was half aware
> Among the angels in the faithful heavens,
> And ope my eyes upon the Master's face,
> And, following the dear guidance of his smile,
> Find in my arms again what I had lost:
> Such are the gentle chances of the night.

Here death is regarded as a surcease and a release. In this psalm of despair Mrs. Oliphant anticipates the idea which was to pervade her supernatural stories—that death clears away the mists from the soul and brings it into immediate contact with the Creator.

Probably because she was emotionally involved with them at the same time that they challenged her imagination, the Stories of the Seen and the Unseen represent Mrs. Oliphant at her best also purely as a writer. Stylistically they are lucid and compact, in welcome contrast to the flatness and flaccidity which mar too many of her longer, more plotted novels. They stimulated her last period of creativity before the decline that set in with her later years. Another reason for their superiority is that she was able to bring to them her deepest interests, literary and intellectual. Early in the poem "Day and Night" occur these lines:

> I have withdrawn
> The veil from Love's fair face, and Joy has flashed
> Upon my soul the sunshine of his eyes,
> And grief has wrapped me in his bitter cloak;
> And, pausing in the midway of my life,
> Like him who once scaled heaven and fathomed hell,
> The path obscure and wild has made me fear.

This obvious allusion anticipates the pervasive influence of Dante over her stories of the supernatural. (She quotes the opening lines of the *Inferno* in Italian in a footnote to the poem.) In *A Beleaguered City* the mystic Paul Lecamus writes to Mayor Martin Dupin, describing the strange sensation he feels while wandering through the frightening darkness that suddenly envelops their city: "In the unseen world described by a poet whom M. le Maire has probably heard of, the man who traverses Purgatory (to speak of no other place) is seen by all, and is a wonder to all he meets— his shadow, his breath separate him from those around him." The story itself abounds in echoes from the *Inferno*. The title character of another of the tales, "Old Lady Mary," finding herself suddenly transported to an unfamiliar region, queries a stranger, "It cannot be the—Inferno, that is clear at least . . . perhaps Purgatory?" One of the shorter tales, "Earthbound," is based upon a passage from the *Purgatorio*. *A Little Pilgrim in the Unseen* begins with an epigraph from the *Purgatorio*: "Puro e disposto a salire alle stelle."

Mrs. Oliphant had steeped herself in the *Divina Commedia*

before she wrote these stories, in connection with the series of essays she did for Macmillan entitled *The Makers of Florence* (1876), as well as for the monograph she contributed in the following year to Blackwood's Foreign Classics for English Readers. In her essay on Dante she declared:

> We will not attempt to follow the crowd of learned Italians who live and breathe and have their being in Dante through the many convolutions of history, which sometimes bid fair to strangle, like the Laocöon, the poet himself and his great poem in their multiplied and intricate folds. Indeed we think the time has come when, in as far as the *Divina Commedia* is concerned, a reverse treatment would be advantageous, and those parts of the poem which belong to humanity, and are everywhere comprehensible, might be separated from those which are woven into the tangled web of Tuscan history.[10]

In her stories of the supernatural, as in her essays and biographical sketches, Mrs. Oliphant was intent on rescuing Dante from the scholars and bringing him home to the general reader.

Early in her career, in her novels and in her biography of Irving, Mrs. Oliphant had revealed a sympathy for the visionary mystic, the prophet without honor in his country—just such a figure as is represented in the tragic Paul Lecamus of *A Beleaguered City*. Her study of Montalembert brought her into contact with the French monastic revival, the continental counterpart of the Oxford Movement. The interest she developed in the ideas of Montalembert and his fellow crusaders Lamennais and Lacordaire account in particular for the French setting of *A Beleaguered City* as well as for the socio-religious milieu of that impressive story. Moreover, one of her closest friends, Principal Tulloch, was the leading Scotch churchman of the age and an eloquent apologist for theism against skepticism and rationalism. In the light of this background one can account for an important theme that underlies all the Stories of the Seen and the Unseen—the affirmation of the existence of an immanent and transcendental Creator and of the immortality of the soul in the face of the growing number of agnostics, scientists, aesthetes, hedonists, and materialists who were undermining traditional faith.

In her 1862 *Maga* article on "Sensation Novels," Mrs. Oliphant had protested against the *outré* in fiction. It is significant that in her own supernatural tales her spirits are beneficent ones, not demons, the emotion she arouses being awe rather than terror for the world beyond. For the same reason, the Stories of the Seen and the Unseen generally avoid lurid incident of any sort, achieving their effects rather through delicacy of feeling and sympathy with man's longings for transcendental experience. Her reviews in *Maga* of spiritualistic novels like *The Gates Ajar* by Elizabeth Stuart Phelps and *Hitherto* by Mrs. Adeline Whitney give us some idea of the popular stories that Mrs. Oliphant was to imitate and excel in her own writing. Another influence came from one of her favorite novelists, Edward Bulwer-Lytton. Writing an obituary article on him for *Maga* (March 1873), she classified his versatile output into stories of life and manners, historical romances, crime novels, and tales of magic and mystery. The latter—as represented particularly by the theosophical novels *Zanoni* and *A Strange Story*—she reserved for the last, remarking in words that make clear her own affinity for them that "the mysterious unseen world which surrounds us, of which we know so little by our reason, and so much by our fancy, about which every one believes much which his mind rejects, and feels much which his senses are unconscious of, must ever have a charm, not only for the fanciful and visionary, but for all to whom fact and certainty do not sum up the possibilities of existence."

Through all these observations we can feel Mrs. Oliphant groping her way towards her own tales of "magic and mystery." The sudden intimation of immortality, the evanescent inner light that is extinguished as suddenly as it is ignited—these are the spiritual phenomena that lie at the center of her religious consciousness. Like Dickens and Wilkie Collins, she tried to awaken readers to the romance of real life, but through spiritualizing rather than sensationalizing the mundane world.[11] Behind her supernatural fiction, as with that of many forgotten writers then in vogue, lay the need articulated by theologians and ministers and felt by sensitive laymen for a general revival and revitalization of the religious emotions. Also hovering in the background is the contemporary interest in the phenomena of parapsychology, or what we speak of today as extra-sensory perception. The baffling experiences of such characters as Martin Dupin in *A Beleaguered City,* Colonel Mortimer in "The Open Door," Edmund Coventry in "Earthbound," while leading them to a new religious insight, bring out the inability of the human reason to account for the nature of ultimate reality. Mrs. Oliphant refers to the supernatural simply as the Unseen, with the implication that our failure to achieve mystic insight is due to an obfuscation of our faculties, a spiritual blindness that results from living too much in the realm of the Seen. Significantly, the vision denied to the more intellectual and sophisticated characters of these stories is imparted to children like Connie in "Old Lady Mary," to the pure in heart like Madame Dupin in *A Beleaguered City,* or to innocents like the elderly heroine of *A Little Pilgrim in the Unseen,* "a gentle soul which never knew doubt." These are, as with Wordsworth, the "first philosophers." For the old, the learned, or the worldly to gain so much as a glimpse into the Unseen is an arduous process of removing mists and lifting veils.

Mystery and wonder suddenly obtruding themselves in the midst of the bustle of ordinary life, the depths of spiritual life concealed beneath the placid surface of familiar things, but momentarily emerging to jolt us out of our dull complacency—such is the keynote sounded by *A Beleaguered City,* the first and most ambitious of the Stories of the Seen and the Unseen. The story begins on a late afternoon in June 1875. Martin Dupin, Mayor of Semur, a prosperous farm town in the Haute-Bourgogne, is returning home from an inspection of the vineyards in the country when he witnesses a shocking incident. As Monsieur le Curé leads a procession along the Grande Rue carrying the rites of the church to a dying man, an atheist of the village tries to block his path and shouts sacrilegious words. Dupin, like all the others present, is shocked at the outrage, though it is rather his social sense than his religious feeling which is wounded. One of the more religious townspeople is moved to exclaim: " 'It is enough to make the dead rise out of their graves!' " Shortly afterwards a strange pall settles over Semur. Various explanations are offered for this phenomenon. The superstitious of the town suspect witchcraft, the rationalists attribute it to an eclipse or a horde of insects, while the pious immediately

conclude that all of the people of Semur are being punished for
the blasphemy of the few. Mayor Dupin wavers between the religious and scientific viewpoints as he struggles to take control of
the situation.

Meanwhile, mysterious sights and sounds pervade the atmosphere. Boats sail down the river propelled apparently by nothing
but air; various citizens claim to have seen their dead beloved; the
bells of the cathedral are heard to toll, though nobody is known
to be inside; the cathedral suddenly becomes ablaze with light.
Soon all the inhabitants feel themselves being pushed out of the
gates of the town, and they encamp before the walls of Semur,
refugees from an unknown, unseen, vaguely felt enemy. In time
the stranded populace are confronted by the town pariah, the dis-
credited visionary Paul Lecamus, who claims to have had contact
with the unearthly visitants and to have recognized among them
some of the dead of Semur. He assures his fellow citizens that the
spirits have come to save them, not to destroy them. Persuaded
by Lecamus, Mayor Dupin and Monsieur le Curé form an embassy
of good will to the visitors. They grope their way through the quiet,
seemingly empty town to the cathedral where the priest performs
the Mass. Suddenly the darkness is dispelled, and Semur is bathed
once more in radiant sunlight. The citizens re-enter, raising hosan-
nas, and the town is swept by a religious revival. Then all settles
back into normal routine, while Mayor Dupin ponders the significance of these "remarkable events."

The cumulative power of *A Beleaguered City* derives in part
from the contrast between the surface simplicity of the narrative
and its larger implications. The subtitle—"A Narrative of Certain
Recent Events in the City of Semur in the Department of the
Haute Bourgogne"—suggests a document to be filed in a government archives; indeed one of the Mayor's alleged motives for telling his story is to set the record straight. While aware that "the
faculty of imagination has always been one of my characteristics,"
Dupin hastens to assure his readers that, "Had it been possible for
me to believe that I had been misled by this faculty, I should have
carefully refrained from putting upon record any account of my
individual impressions." His narrative, in accordance with this
preamble, is remarkable for its lucidity and objectivity (resem-

bling in this respect Defoe's *The Apparition of Mrs. Veal*). The mode of narration of *A Beleaguered City*—the most intricate Mrs. Oliphant ever attempted—contributes further to its texture and stature. It is the only one of her stories told by multiple narrators, a method of presentation justified again by Martin Dupin's fidelity to facts. As "one who is the official mouthpiece and representative of the commune, and whose duty it is to render to government and to the human race a true narrative of the very wonderful facts to which every citizen in Semur can bear witness . . . it has become my duty so to arrange and edit the different accounts of the mystery, as to present one coherent and trustworthy account to the world." This device has been likened by some critics to the assemblage of the testimony of the various witnesses in Wilkie Collins' *The Moonstone,* but Mrs. Oliphant was probably influenced here more by Browning's *The Ring and the Book,* which she very much admired. At any rate, the several eyewitnesses of the "extra-ordinary events" of Semur contribute not so much different information as diverse viewpoints towards the confusing circumstances, giving Mrs. Oliphant opportunity for varied and dramatic characterization.

Dupin carries the burden of the narration. With his combination of pride, humility, officiousness, and sensitivity he emerges as one of Mrs. Oliphant's most complex portraits. Most moving is the growth of a religious consciousness in this *honnête homme* intended to represent the *haute bourgeoisie* mind of modern France —rationalistic, materialistic, state-centered and man-centered. But dimension is added to the story by the superposition of other religious attitudes. Mrs. Oliphant's sublimest style is reserved for the account by the mystic Paul Lecamus, befriended by the Mayor, though shunned by the others as "a dreamer of dreams." The language in which he describes his reunion with his dead beloved is at once Dantean and apocalyptic: "Her presence wrapped me round and round. . . . She was more near to me, more near, than when I held her in my arms. How long it was so, I cannot tell; it was long as love, yet short as the drawing of a breath. . . . We said to each other everything without words—heart overflowing into heart. It was beyond knowledge or speech."

At the opposite extreme is Monsieur de Bois-Sombre, a *déclassé* aristocrat and retired *mousquetaire,* humane, but snobbish and obtuse, who looks upon these same untoward events as connected somehow with the unleashed forces of republicanism. As a worshipper of reason and "the logic of circumstance," he sees Lecamus as "a hare-brained enthusiast." One gathers that so far as Monsieur is concerned, Church and State alike exist mainly to control the canaille. The two women who contribute accounts, Mayor Dupin's wife and mother, represent two antithetical types of piety. Madame Dupin is the serene, cheerful Christian, quite removed from the turbulent spiritual world of Lecamus. She is the simple, charitable, saintly soul who grasps religion mainly by intuition. Madame Veuve Dupin, on the other hand, is the stern evangelical, ever walking in "the light of reason" and recalling others to their sense of duty. It is significant that it is not she but Madame Dupin who sees the heavenly emissaries.

The various figures of *A Beleaguered City* seem to be intended as archetypes of religious and intellectual positions rather than as individualized personalities. Minor figures in the story are given generic names, such as the timorous *adjoint* M. Barbou, the miser Gros-Gain, and the ironically named M. Clairon, the ineffectual scientist from the Musée who is as baffled as the rest when challenged to explain the "miracle" of Semur. Even a place-name like Bois-Sombre (Dante's "selva oscura") has symbolic overtones. It is possible, in fact, to read the story throughout as a parable of the human faculties, with Jacques the atheist and the other peasants representing the irrational part of the soul, Dupin representing reason and courage, Madame Dupin natural piety, and Lecamus spiritual wisdom. The sparseness of setting, the lack of extensive physical topography in Mrs. Oliphant's fictitious Semur, as well as the confinement of sensuous impressions to light and darkness, music and silence, all make for a concentration of effect characteristic of a fable.[12]

Apart from its literary quality, *A Beleaguered City* is endowed with remarkable depth of feeling. The ultimate effect of the miracle of Semur is to strengthen the Dupins in their marital devotion. Before the story opens, they have suffered the death of a young daughter, Marie. (Thus the author projects her grief over her own Maggie.) In the course of the visitation of the spirits, Madame

Dupin is consoled by her communion with the spirit of Marie. Martin Dupin, lacking his wife's spiritual faculty, never gets to see Marie, but at one point, while he is groping about the house in the darkness, he suddenly discovers an olive branch hanging over her veiled portrait. His final narrative ends when he and Madame Dupin pay obeisance at the grave of Lecamus, the one citizen of Semur who apparently grasped the full significance of the return of the dead. Dupin is deeply moved when he notices that carved on the cross of Lecamus' tomb is an olive branch—a replica of the one he had seen suspended over the portrait of the dead Marie. Gazing at his wife, he muses: "Who but she could have done it, who had helped him to join the army of the beloved?" His wife seems to have read his mind. Her explanation brings the story to its muted end: " 'This was our brother,' she said, 'he will tell my Marie what use I made of her olive leaves.' "

Despite this touching close, the tone of *A Beleaguered City* is not predominantly sentimental. It offers no easy consolation in the manner of so much of the more conventional religious fiction of the period. Mrs. Oliphant makes it clear, for one thing, that it is not open to all to see the angels. Not only is Monsieur le Maire denied the privilege, but Monsieur le Curé as well. She also is aware that the way to mystic revelation is a thorny one, and that such vision brings its pains as well as its pleasures. Although Paul Lecamus, for example, achieves ecstasy, the experience proves so shattering that he dies as a result of it. Also, the inhabitants of Semur are not permanently converted by the visitation to a Christian way of life. When Monsieur le Maire and Monsieur le Curé walk courageously hand in hand through the gates into the benighted city to confront the spirits, Mrs. Oliphant seems to be offering the hope that Church and State may come to support each other, instead of working at cross purposes. But such is not to be. Once the threat is removed, Dupin finds himself again scoffing at superstition, as he sees Monsieur le Curé too ready to accept insincere devotion for true religion. The wave of religion that momentarily swept Semur proves to be but an epidemic of hysterical evangelism and a reign of false prophets. Nevertheless, she leaves us with some hope at the end of her story, through the image of the domestic and temporal orders, personified by the

Dupins, bowing before the spiritual order—in awe of Last Things.

The tautness of structure and beauty of style of *A Beleaguered City,* shaped by a controlling idea, make this story something unique in Mrs. Oliphant's writings. It was produced out of a rich fund of experience, from her life as well as from her reading. And, as happened rarely with her, her emotions, her mind, and her imagination were equally and simultaneously engaged in the creation of a work of fiction.[13] That it was a labor of love for her is apparent from the unusual amount of time and effort she expended upon it.[14] One regrets she could not allow herself this luxury more often, for the account of the strange events in Semur lends support to those critics who contend that Mrs. Oliphant might have been a major writer had economic pressures not forced her to write too much and too quickly. On the whole, posterity has rewarded her for her pains. *A Beleaguered City* has been the most frequently reissued of her books and one of the few to see print in recent years.[15]

Two years after the appearance in book form of *A Beleaguered City,* Mrs. Oliphant published a shorter and simpler tale, "The Open Door," in the January 1882 issue of *Maga.* Quite possibly because it is the most "Gothic" of her supernatural stories, it has been the one most frequently anthologized, and it has therefore maintained something of a reputation among connoisseurs of horror stories. But "The Open Door" is not a mere ghost story. The effect it leaves on the reader is more of pathos than of horror. It is related in theme to *A Beleaguered City,* as an attempt by a spirit to communicate with the living. Like its predecessor it is told by a character who stands midway in attitude between credulity and skepticism towards the inexplicable events described. The narrator, Colonel Mortimer, is a retired gentleman recently returned from India with his family. They settle in an old country house near Edinburgh to permit the young son, Roland, who is in frail health, to go to school while remaining under his parents' surveillance. On the grounds are some old ruins of unknown origin, including the remains of a door. Shortly after the family arrives, young Roland begins to show alarming symptoms. It develops that he has heard a wailing sound in the vicinity of the ruins which leaves him physically weak and emotionally shattered.

Upon investigating the grounds, Colonel Mortimer also hears this eerie noise, which sounds to him like a plea of a homesick youth crying to be let back into the house. Fearing for the possibly fatal effect of this disturbance upon his sensitive little boy, he is determined to get at the source and rid the neighborhood of it. After various unsuccessful attempts to find the mysterious wanderer or to account for his presence, he summons the minister, Dr. Moncrieff, who has lived in the vicinity for many years. Upon hearing the voice, the minister recognizes it immediately as that of a young man, presumed dead, who had lived on these premises but who had run away from home years before. He gathers that this spirit is trying to make amends belatedly for desertion of his family, and he speaks gently to him, trying to persuade him of the futility of knocking on the door of his former house of which nothing remains and telling him that his mother has long since gone "home" to a distant place where he is now free to seek her out. Apparently placated, the spirit is heard no more and young Roland is restored to health.

Embedded in this strange tale are personal preoccupations never far removed from Mrs. Oliphant's heart—the grief of parents, the erring son. She writes here of a sensitive boy in delicate health, reflecting her constant concern about the health of her own children. Her giving the name Willie to the vagrant, "weak, foolish, easily imposed upon and 'led away,' " who returns as a spirit, indicates how she could wear her heart on her sleeve at times. However, just as she so beautifully transmuted her grief over Maggie's death in *A Beleaguered City,* in "The Open Door" she is able to elevate her private sorrows into something close to poetry. The reader is left by this plaintive tale with a haunting sense of that loneliness, alienation, and remorse that fall to the general human lot.

"The Open Door" is generally associated with the later story "Old Lady Mary" because the two were republished together in the volume called *Two Stories of the Seen and the Unseen* (1885). Two years separated the original serial publication of the tales, and, for all evidence to the contrary, they may well have been conceived independently of each other.[16] Nevertheless, the stories serve as pendants to one another, "The Open Door" being concerned with the efforts of one who is living to alleviate the suffering of a dead person, "Old Lady Mary" being concerned with the attempts of a dead person to bring succor to a loved one who has survived her. On the whole, "Old Lady Mary" is superior, more deeply moving, warmer and mellower in its pathos, and finer in characterization—qualities, one gathers, that have not commended it to compilers of collections of ghost stories. Its theme is the recurrent one in Mrs. Oliphant's supernatural fiction of the struggle of spiritual beings to 'get through' to earthly ones, but this time the spirit is made palpable; in fact, it is the central character of the story. In this respect "Old Lady Mary" is transitional between those supernatural stories already considered that take place on earth, and the dream-vision type, represented by the "Little Pilgrim" series, which depict the voyages of spirits in the after-world.

"She was very old and therefore it was very hard for her to make up her mind to die," begins this tale in a gently foreboding tone. Lady Mary is caught in the situation of Everyman, overtaken by Death summarily and without previous preparation. Her predicament is all the more unfortunate because she is carried off so suddenly that she is unable to make known to her executor the provisions she has made for her young god-daughter and companion who is dependent upon her. However, she is allowed the unusual dispensation of returning to the land of the living in order to rectify this oversight, and her frustrating attempts to make restitution to her god-daughter are the burden of the story.

Lady Mary has much reason to cling to life. She has reached that silver age when all strong emotions have subsided, when pain and sorrow are absorbed into muted memory, and when one is content to sit back as a calm witness of the passing scene. "To passion, to joy, to anguish, an end must come," the author comments, "but mere gentle living, determined by a framework of gentle rules and habits—why should that ever be ended?" In one of the loveliest passages in all her writing, Mrs. Oliphant gives us a composite of Lady Mary's pleasant regimen. Lady Mary has had her share of cares and vexation, youthful vanities and sorrows, but now:

She had a pretty house full of things which formed a graceful *entourage* suitable, as she felt, for such a woman as she was, and in which she took pleasure for their own beauty—soft chairs and couches, a fireplace and lights which were the perfection of tempered warmth and illumination. She had a carriage, very comfortable and easy, in which, when the weather was suitable, she went out; and a pretty garden and lawns, in which, when she preferred staying at home, she could have her little walk or sit out under the trees. She had books in plenty, and all the newspapers, and everything that was needful to keep her within the reflection of the busy life which she no longer cared to encounter in her own person. The post rarely brought her painful letters; for all those impassioned interests which bring pain had died out, and the sorrows of others, when they were communicated to her, gave her a luxurious sense of sympathy yet exemption. . . . She came down-stairs at a certain hour, which she kept to as if it had been of the utmost importance, although it was of no importance at all; she took just so much good wine, so many cups of tea. Her repasts were as regular as clockwork—never too late, never too early. Her whole life went on velvet, rolling smoothly along, without jar or interruption, blameless, pleasant, kind. People talked of her old age as a model of old age, with no bitterness or sourness in it. And, indeed, why should she have been sour or bitter? It suited her far better to be kind. She was in reality kind to everybody, liking to see pleasant faces about her. The poor had no reason to complain of her; her servants were very comfortable; and the one person in her house who was nearer to her own level, who was her companion and most important minister, was very comfortable too.

But the calm balance of Lady Mary's gentle sybaritism is destined to be upset. With all her virtues she has a streak of stubbornness and perversity in her nature which is responsible for her being unprepared for death, although she is over eighty. She refuses to yield to the continued importunings of her lawyer to allow him to draw up her will for her signature. Instead, as a little joke on him, she writes her own will one night, signs it in the presence of two illiterate servants, and hides it in a cabinet. Her intention is to surprise the lawyer by producing this will the next time he broaches the subject. But one winter day she catches a chill while out on a carriage ride and dies suddenly, apparently intestate since she has not confided her prank to anybody.

Lady Mary awakens in a vast, unfamiliar place which she cannot identify, although she recognizes among the strangers here the face of a friend who, she is certain, had died. " 'I suppose,' " she inquires of this friend, " 'that we are not in—what we have been accustomed to call heaven?' " " 'That is a word,' " he replies, " 'which expresses rather a condition than a place.' " Lady Mary infers that she is not yet ready for this "condition." In this penitential hall, akin to Dante's Purgatorio, she is stung with remorse for her sins of omission as she realizes that her young companion, whom she knows as little Mary, as well as her servants, are left destitute. She gains permission to return to earth briefly to right her wrong to these people, although warned that the path back is a "dark and dreadful way," and that the journey is likely to be a fruitless one.

We are spared Lady Mary's perilous voyage, picking her up as she arrives one winter day, a lonely spiritual derelict, in her home village. Although she is overjoyed to be back, we soon feel with her a sharp sense of isolation as she recognizes former friends with whom she cannot now establish communication because they are completely unaware of her presence. "It is hard to be left out in the cold when others go into their cheerful houses," Mrs. Oliphant comments, "but to be left thus outside of life, to speak and not to be heard, to stand, unseen, astounded, unable to secure any attention! She had thought they would be frightened, but it was not they who were frightened. A great panic seized the woman who was no more of this world." Lady Mary's return to earth proves to be a journey through the Valley of Humiliation. She must overhear herself upbraided by her former servants for her thoughtlessness without being able to plead her extenuating circumstances. She re-enters her former house to find it now occupied by *nouveaux riches*. Young Mary has been taken in by neighbors until she can find suitable employment. She finds young Mary but is unable to convey any message even to her. However, she does have the deep satisfaction of discovering that her god-daughter, the one she has most wronged, remains faithful to her memory, never once speaking out against· her. Ironically, the only character in the story who can see Lady Mary is little Connie, daughter of the new tenants of her house, whom young Mary is hired to tutor. But the child's vision is dismissed as hallucination by the village doctor. In a scene of almost unbearable anguish, Lady Mary tries in vain to reveal herself to her erstwhile ward, but is finally forced to give up in despair:

> "I have failed. What am I that I should do what they all said was impossible? It was my pride, because I have had my own way all my life. But now I have no way and no place on earth, and what I have to tell them will never, never be known. Oh my little Mary a servant in her own house! And a word would make it right! but never, never can she hear that word. I am wrong to say never; she will know when she is in heaven. She will not live to be old and foolish, like me. She will go up there early, and then she will know. But I, what will become of me?—for I am nothing here, and I cannot go back to my own place."
>
> A little moaning wind rose up suddenly in the dark night, and carried a faint wail, like the voice of some one lost, to the windows of the sleeping house. It woke the children, and Mary, who opened her eyes quickly in the dark, wondering if perhaps the vision might come to her. But the vision had come when she could not see it, and now returned no more.

In time, presumably, justice is done. Some months afterwards, in the course of the removal of Lady Mary's furniture from her old house, the cabinet is opened by some boys: "And there the paper was found in the most natural way, without any trouble or mystery at all." It was far from Mrs. Oliphant's intention to write just another story of secreted wills and their unexpected discovery. Such was the staple of all too much murky sensational fiction at which she had scoffed. God's mysteries are made of subtler stuff, and so the story takes a different turn at its conclusion. Lady Mary, it develops, not her ward, is the principal gainer from her earthly mission. Upon her return "home," one of her companions in the after-life asks her if she has accomplished her goal:

> She had come to herself by this time, and the dark lines were melting from her face. "I am forgiven," she said, with a low cry of happiness. "She whom I wronged loves me and blessed me; we saw each other face to face. I know nothing more."
>
> "There is no more," said all together. "For everything is included in pardon and love."

One is tempted to read into the description of Lady Mary's round of life before she is taken off an idyll of the kind of old age Mrs.

Oliphant herself longed to enjoy; just as the story that follows might be taken as a dramatization of her perpetual fears of leaving her own dependents in a state of poverty. Old Lady Mary in fact had a real-life prototype—a Scotch *grande dame,* "that dear and bright old lady" Mrs. Duncan Stewart, whose London salon in Sloane Street, was often filled with luminaries of the day. Mrs. Oliphant recalls her in a charming sketch in the *Autobiography.* By coincidence, Mrs. Stewart's death occurred shortly after the publication of "Old Lady Mary" in *Maga.* "Even in the shock of loss," writes Mrs. Oliphant, "it was impossible not be consoled by the thought of that vivid curiosity and interest and enjoyment with which she would find a new sphere before her, with everything to be found out."[17] Subsequently, when the story was reprinted in *Two Stories of the Seen and the Unseen,* it bore the dedication: "To An Old Lady Ever Young, Harriet Stewart Now Gone Where Youth and Age Are No Distinction."

Another Story of the Seen and the Unseen in which a phantom is made palpable is the enigmatic Hawthornesque tale "Earth-bound," first published in *Fraser's Magazine* (January 1880). Like many ghost-spirit stories, it has a Christmas connection, beginning at a Christmas party in a country house. However, this is not a gay time for the hosts, the Beresfords, who are in mourning for the death of their young son. The narrative centers on one guest, Edmund Coventry, who is engaged to the Beresfords' daughter Maud. While strolling about the grounds alone, Edmund sees a strange young woman moving lightly along the lime tree walk. From a distance she resembles Maud, but her dress is old fashioned, suggesting a figure posed for a formal portrait. She disappears as suddenly as she had appeared, and Edmund makes futile inquiries about her throughout the neighborhood. Eventually he meets her again on the walk and this time engages her in conversation. He learns that her name is also Maud, her age a perpetual nineteen. She refers vaguely to having been condemned to remain indefinitely on earth because she had loved it so much. She disappears again, and Edmund confides this conversation to his host, Sir Robert Beresford. A skeptic, Sir Robert has a rational explanation. He shows Edmund an album of portraits of ancestors, among them one done by a pupil of Sir Joshua Reynolds a century earlier which looks exactly like the figure Edmund saw. Sir Robert assumes that Edmund had seen the portrait before and that it had impressed itself on his mind as a vision. Left alone with the portrait as night falls, Edmund kneels before it. Suddenly the subject materializes again. He pleads with her to promise that they will meet again in death if not in life. This she refuses to do, affirming that the future is not at her disposal, but she takes a fond farewell of him. Shortly after, Edmund is found in a coma. In time he recovers and marries Maud Beresford. The other Maud never returns. "Perhaps the time of her willing punishment is over, and she is earthbound no more," the author conjectures.

It is possible to interpret Edmund Coventry's shattering experience, as does Sir Robert, as hallucination. Just what his vision is supposed to signify is not altogether clear, but Mrs. Oliphant has left a clue. The influence of Dante, implicit in most of the Stories of the Seen and the Unseen, is explicit in this one. Maud's cryptic words to Edmund are glossed by these lines from Dante:

> Prima vuol ben; ma non lascia il talento
> Che divina giustizia contra voglia,
> Come fù al peccar, pone al tormento. . . .
>
> (*Purgatorio,* XXI, 64–66)

> It wills indeed before, but is not free
> From that desire, God's justice against will
> Sets, as toward sin once, now to its penalty. . . .
>
> (Binyon translation)

These are the words addressed to Dante and Virgil by the poet Statius, now on his way to everlasting bliss after having lain for five hundred years in penance, to account for the readiness of penitent sinners in Purgatory to accept what seems unendurable suffering. The desire which formerly inclined them towards sin, Statius explains, is turned in this state of penance towards its expiation. Apparently it is with this in mind that Mrs. Oliphant refers to Maud's "willing punishment." Presumably Edmund, represented earlier as a somewhat callow though sensitive young

man, rather "earthbound" too in his love of nature and of the
things of this world, goes to his wedding a sadder and a wiser
man.[18]

Concurrently with these stories in which dead people return to
the world of the living, Mrs. Oliphant wrote a group of fantasies
centered on the dead and taking place in the after-world. The
central figure of these tales is a gentle, saintly lady whom Mrs.
Oliphant called "the Little Pilgrim." After first appearing in
various magazines, they were collected in two volumes, *A Little
Pilgrim in the Unseen* (1882) and *The Land of Darkness, along
with Some Further Chapters in the Experience of the Little Pilgrim* (1888). With an exception to be noted, the Little Pilgrim
series is inferior work. In her best writing in this genre, we have
observed, Mrs. Oliphant achieves a fine balance of tough-minded-
ness with tender feeling, sophistication with pathos, and affirmation
of faith with a sense of man's spiritual limitations. By contrast, the
adventures of the Little Pilgrim soon cloy with an over-sweetness
smacking too much of consolation literature. While the various
realms through which the Little Pilgrim travels have their obvious
parallels in the Inferno, Purgatorio, and Paradiso, Mrs. Oliphant's
attempts to give topography to the world beyond the grave merely
betray the deficiencies of her imagination. These superterrestrial
travels evoke not so much the poems of Dante as the hymns of
Adelaide Procter and the stained glass of the Gothic Revival.

A Little Pilgrim in the Unseen, like "Old Lady Mary," had its
inception as a tribute to a friend. This was a neighbor called Aunt
Nelly by Mrs. Oliphant's sons (she herself refers to the lady as
"Little Nelly" in her *Autobiography,* but does not identify her),
known for her self-effacing charity to family and friends. "She
was far from being wise or clever," Mrs. Oliphant wrote, "generally reputed rather a silly little woman; but with a heart of gold,
and a straightforward, simple, right judgment, which was always
to me like the clear shining of a tiny light." She later describes
Aunt Nelly's "dying in her sleep without so much as the movement
of a finger," just such an easy passing away as is experienced by
her fictional counterpart. When the story was published in book

form, Mrs. Oliphant spoke of it in the dedication as "little more than a wistful attempt to follow a gentle soul which never knew doubt into the New World, and to catch a glimpse of something of its glory through her simple and child-like eyes."[19]

The adventures of this innocent in the New World demonstrate that the pure in heart will see God and remind us that nothing evil can happen to a good person. Our sympathies are enlisted for the fate of proud Old Lady Mary as she is progressively humbled, but the Little Pilgrim is already among the saved when she arrives in the upper regions; therefore little distance remains, spiritually, for her to travel. As a result, her journey through the after-world turns out to be an extended and monotonous anthem in praise of the Almighty, as she brings solace to various sinners and sufferers, is accompanied into Heaven by the Lady Ama, and becomes herself a welcoming angel to the newly arrived souls released from earthly bondage.

This apotheosis of Aunt Nelly was obviously intended to confirm the pious in their faith and to bring comfort to the aggrieved, but it becomes evident in places that it served Mrs. Oliphant as a personal catharsis also. In one episode early in her adventures, the Little Pilgrim meets an apparition in the form of a child and holds a conversation with her:

> "Are you a child?" said the Little Pilgrim, "or are you an angel? Sometimes you are like a child; but then your face shines and you are like—You must have some name for it here; there is nothing among the words I know." And then she paused a little still looking at her, and cried, "Oh, if she [the Little Pilgrim's friend on earth] could but see you, little Margaret! That would do her most good of all."
>
> Then the maiden shook her lovely head: "What does her most good is the will of the Father," she said.

Just as she places her dead daughter among the angels, Mrs. Oliphant finds a place for her unfortunate late husband within Heaven's many mansions. In the second part, called "The Little Pilgrim Goes Up Higher," the Little Pilgrim, having been brought into the presence of the Father, wanders about the Holy City and there meets a painter. He is apologetic about his limitations, telling her that he gains his satisfaction from drawing figures for a greater master who fills in the faces and endows them with life. One's own work always falls short of one's ambitiońs, the artist explains, "whereas in your master's work you have full content, because his idea goes beyond yours, and as he makes every touch, you can feel 'that is right—that is complete—that is just as it ought to be.' " If this is intended as Francis Oliphant's reconciliation to his failure on earth, perhaps here too Mrs. Oliphant offers her own apologia for the literary artist whose reach exceeds his grasp.

A Little Pilgrim was among the most popular of Mrs. Oliphant's books. Macmillan printed over 20,000 copies—a considerable figure for that time. It was frequently reprinted in America. Obviously feeling that this record warranted a return engagement, Mrs. Oliphant wrote to Macmillan's editor George Lillie Craik three years after its original publication to ask if he was willing to bring out a second series. This is the first we hear of the sequel volume, published in 1888—something of a hodgepodge made up of three magazine pieces, "The Land of Darkness," "The Little Pilgrim in the Seen and the Unseen," and "On the Dark Mountains."[20] After what has been said, a modern reader may feel that he has had a sufficiency of Aunt Nelly, alias the Little Pilgrim. However, as with many a greater writer, sin challenged Mrs. Oliphant's imagination more than virtue could. As a result, "The Land of Darkness," which begins this volume, stands out in stark contrast to the inanity of the rest of it. A macabre fantasy, the nightmare that offsets the dream vision to follow, it is a chilling picture of human degeneration and evil that anticipates some contemporary dystopias. "I found myself standing on my feet, with the tingling sensation of having come down rapidly upon the ground from a height," begins the unidentified narrator. "There was a similar feeling in my head, as of the whirling and sickening sensation of passing downward through the air, like the description Dante gives of his descent upon Geryon. . . ." Mrs. Oliphant clearly intends this as her version of the Inferno, but the woes of this Land of Darkness stem from modern spiritual ills. We accompany the narrator through a busy, populous city which proves to be a kind of Beleaguered City without hope of redemption. In this diabolical metropolis, each man is sufficient unto himself. Traffic moves along at a dizzy pace without regulation. People greet each other and part company with curses instead of "hello" and "goodbye." To see a sick wretch lying in the street is to make one take satisfaction in his own health rather than pity on the sufferer.

At times this Land of Darkness, intoxicated with science and technology, seems like a forerunner of Aldous Huxley's Brave New World. At other times it is a Kafkaesque world of unmotivated brutality and imprisonment. The narrator, seeking escape, comes to the startling discovery that he is really trying to run away from himself. Hell, we soon realize, is humanity purged of morality and affection, knowledge pursued to no end or purpose, art and beauty debased by materialism, perpetual desire and dissatisfaction. After a number of harrowing adventures, this sufferer eventually succeeds in wresting himself free from the city—or state of mind—of aimless hedonism and endless torment.

The connection of "The Land of Darkness" with the Little Pilgrim series is tenuous. A brief epilogue explains that it does not belong to the adventures of the Little Pilgrim as such, but "is drawn from the Archives in the Heavenly City, where all the records of the human race are laid up," and is included to give the reader a full understanding of her experience. What follows, as we expect, is the presentation af the blissful state of the saved in contrast to the despair of the damned. The Little Pilgrim briefly returns to earth, her wish being granted to become an emissary to the grief-stricken who are left behind. She learns that God forgets nobody, not even sinners, so that the Way is always open. In the concluding portion of her adventures, called "On the Dark Mountain," she becomes a guide to those stumbling on the stony peak that leads heavenwards, helping those who have managed to struggle out of the Land of Darkness to make their painful journey into the Light. In what is perhaps intended as a symbolic self-effacement, Mrs. Oliphant indicates that one of the travellers supported by the Little Pilgrim has come from the City of Art, where men have wrought everything in beauty only to find that the aesthetic life leads to vanity, greed, and discontent.

Considered out of their time, Mrs. Oliphant's stories of the supernatural are striking fables of the unsatisfied yearnings of the spirit and of the frustrations of communication between human beings. In their own age they were part of the religious ambience that included the Dante Revival, the Oxford Movement, and Ritualism, making their modest contribution to the protest against an emergent scientism. The Stories of the Seen and the Unseen assert the power of the mysterious and the supra-rational in the face of those who sought to or claimed to be able to bring all phenomena within the realm of the knowable. The central characters of her supernatural stories struggle with various degrees of success to free themselves from imprisonment in the world of the senses. Their difficulties lie typically in trying to reach others through "non-conductors"—mists, darkness, thick foliage, stone walls—suggesting that Mrs. Oliphant was well aware of the new discoveries in physics concerning light waves and sound waves and optical and aural illusions. But telepathic rather than telegraphic communication was what preoccupied her—the *cor ad cor loquitur* which penetrates the most impermeable of media. In this respect, *A Beleaguered City,* "Old Lady Mary," and the other tales of this group reflect the spiritualism that swept over England during the 1880's and 1890's. The breakdown of traditional faith, along with dissatisfaction with "rational" explanations of phenomena undeniably contributed to the theosophical societies, "miracle clubs," Swedenborg and Madame Blavatsky circles that burgeoned during this period. It was an age when, as a literary historian has recently remarked, "those who felt that Christianity was almost bankrupt turned eagerly to the study of Eastern philosophies and to the exploration of occult forces of all kinds."[21] In this period of disruption and ferment, Mrs. Oliphant, rather than turning to new religions, clung to the old one.

In December 1880 Mrs. Oliphant had occasion to comment on the passing of the greatest of her sister novelists and, as it happened, a skeptic. "It seems to me while I write that probably you will be in London for George Eliot's funeral," she wrote to William Blackwood. "How sad it is! . . . There is something very solemn in the thought of a great spirit like hers entered the spiritual world which she did not believe in. If we are right in our faith, what a blessed surprise to her!" Without being dogmatic Mrs. Oliphant was firm in her own faith. Unlike many of her contemporaries, she turned not to ethical systems or to faddish spiritualism, but to a reaffirmation of that faith in its simplest, most elemental terms. As she was to write shortly before her death: "I can only claim to be one of the people whose nature it is to believe rather than to doubt, and to whom, where all is mysterious, the way which I have been taught to believe is God's way of accounting for the universe seems more realistic and less difficult (where all is difficult) than any other way." Thus she expresses the essence of her faith, that which sustains her in grief:

> There is one thing and only one, in which I have taken refuge in such bitter extremity,—always I remind myself, that in the universe with which we are acquainted there are but two continually face to face with each other—God and man, or rather, the Godhead and the man, the Saviour and the saved, the Father and the child. I think that every incident in life is secretly, and in a manner which no other spirit knows of, discussed between them, and —above all the smaller matters, most eminently and supremely the great question of death.

When beset with doubt she, like Newman, leans for sustenance on "the two and two only absolute and luminously self-evident beings, myself and my Creator" of which she can have certitude. And like Newman in "The Dream of Gerontius" she lays stress on spontaneous communion with God and individual salvation: "We stand alone among the spheres: we have our way: it is our birthright: we grope, but know not how to take hold of the hand stretched out to us; perhaps we deny it or thrust it away. But the moment of choice is not once as in the old fables, but continually repeated. It is before us till our last breath—"[22] Mrs. Oliphant was clearly in accord with her friend Principal Tulloch, who marked out as the tendency of the age "a general breaking up of the old close traditional systems transmitted from the earlier time." Tulloch saw Christianity moving towards "the idea of God as the loving father of all men—the religious life as having its root in immediate contact with the Divine, rather than in adherence to any definite forms whether of Church belief or Church order . . . the desire after a more concrete and living faith merging into one the abstractions of theological nomenclature."[23] Mrs. Oliphant's personal faith, cutting through ritual and dogma and arriving at the immediate apprehension of the Divine, receives its ultimate expression in her Stories of the Seen and the Unseen.

Chapter IV

Boiling The Pot

Writing—especially her stories of the afterlife—ultimately brought consolation to Mrs. Oliphant for the sudden death of her daughter in Rome. Relief did not come easily nor swiftly. At first she tried to lose her memories in restless, rapid travel. A pathetic odyssey began in Geddie Macpherson's little house in Frascati, where she spent the week immediately following Maggie's death, recalling not only that loss but the two months she had spent there in the summer of 1859 with her dying husband. For a brief period in March she was in Albano, then back to Rome, which she left finally that spring, never to see again. "I dared not while I had still the boys to think of. Twice fatal to me, I did not venture to face it a third time." But she could not yet face the thought of returning to England: "I have no wish to go home. To do so, diminished and impoverished as I am, is more than I can bear. One's courage may be good for once and not answer a second time. The effect of the second blow, so sudden and unforeseen, makes it look as if this was the rule and order of my life."[1] Early in April she went with her sons and the Tullochs to Capri, then a quiet, untouristed island. There she found a measure of peace. "I always long for the sea when I am in great trouble, and I think it will be good for my little boys," she wrote Macmillan before leaving Rome.[2] They spent about six weeks on Capri, during which she regained a good deal of her self-possession, though her grief was by no means mitigated. "I am better than I was," she wrote Isabella Blackwood on May 15, "if not more resigned as people say, at least more accustomed to the impossible life to which God

109

has seen fit, He alone knows for what mysterious reason, to ordain me."[3]

At the end of May Mrs. Oliphant left Italy—"this dearest, saddest, murderous Italy." She traveled in Switzerland during the summer with her sons and the two little Tulloch girls. In July they were in Lucerne and Vevey, in August in Lausanne and Montreux. They spent the autumn and winter in Paris in a bright apartment overlooking the Champs Elysées. Here she established an expensive household—a French governess for the little boys, the faithful nurse Jane, and "a servant and a half." But financial problems were relatively unimportant. Paris was lively and beautiful: "It was at the height of the gaiety and prosperity of the Empire, and I used to say that the sight of all the gay stream of life from the windows, all the fine people coming and going, the brightness and the movement, were a kind of salvation to me in that dark and clouded time."

Mrs. Oliphant had come a long way from her isolated and provincial girlhood. In Paris she found a charming cosmopolitan society—not the shabby-genteel, second-rate social circle in which she had moved during the first years of her marriage, but worldly, sophisticated people. She was never a lion-hunter. Her preference, in fact, was not exclusively literary society but a more diversified one. Paris offered the widest variety. Her most distinguished friend was the Count de Montalembert—urbane, educated, and deeply religious. "He had that curious mixture," she wrote, "of the—shall I say?—supernaturalist and man of the world (not mystic, he was no mystic, but yet miraculous, if there is any meaning in that) which has always had so great an attraction for me." He had the courtesy and bearing of the *ancien régime:* the son of an émigré, he was not too distantly removed from the elegance of the eighteenth-century French court. His fervent Roman Catholicism fascinated her even while she viewed it with her characteristic skepticism as "mere fables of a fond and excited fancy."[4] The ladies of the Montalembert family, his wife and young daughters, held less interest for her. Madame de Montalembert was a *grande dame,* "ready and capable to do anything in the world of which there might be need, to defend a castle or light a fire, or nurse the sick, but helplessly unable to 'do' her own hair."

Mrs. Oliphant also had a taste of a more bohemian society in which she delighted—Giovanni Ruffini, an Italian refugee; the colorful old Father Prout, the "reprobate" priest who had been a contributor to *Fraser's Magazine* in earlier and more prosperous days; the American actress Charlotte Cushman, "who touched my heart with her evident deep knowledge of trouble and sorrow." There were also visits from old friends from home—Robert Story, Principal Tulloch, and that witty, over-dressed spinster Miss Blackwood. But it was the new society which exerted the healing influence. Her association with Montalembert opened her mind still wider to the mystical appeals of Catholicism. At his suggestion she began to attend services at Notre Dame. In 1867 she heard Père Félix preach his Lenten sermons—"a most impressive and wonderful sight, such as it would be difficult to find any parallel to in this country, with all its boasted gravity."[5]

At quite the other extreme she acquired a sophisticated tolerance of the "irregular" relationships so frowned upon in her own country. In Paris, for example, she found "a delightful innocence and naturalness" in the fact that Ruffini openly lived and traveled with his widowed English landlady. "They made their *villeggiatura,* those two together, sometimes in a couple of chalets on a Swiss mountain, as if there had not been such a thing as an evil tongue in the world, which interested me exceedingly." With equal delight she entertained Father Prout and his elderly friend ("a very dauntless, plain-spoken old person in an old shiny black satin and lace, and looking as if everything was put on as well as the satin—hair, teeth, and everything else"): "It was wicked of me, I fear, but it amused me to think that these old people had perhaps indulged in a *grande passion* and had defied the world for each other. I thought no worse of them, somehow, which I am aware is a most immoral sentiment. But perhaps there had never been anything in the least wrong."

The beginning of the new year 1865 saw Mrs. Oliphant much improved in spirits though by no means recovered from her grief. In a letter of January 3 to Macmillan she writes: "Happy and merry don't seem to be words I can use at a season which by reason of its universal rejoicing throws a deeper shadow than usual upon those who have done with joy."[6] Her main consolation was her sons: "Oh, my little boys! and the happiness of watching over them and all their ways and sayings, though I was sad enough then, thinking there was no sadder mother, longing for my Maggie wherever I went." Cyril, now eight, was beginning his formal education with an English tutor, an Oxford man somewhat fallen in the world, and Cecco, six, was learning French with the governess. They were handsome, bright, lively children—Cyril full of jokes, Cecco retaining his baby charm. Still reluctant to return to England, she took her small family to Normandy and Brittany in the spring. It was a pleasant, leisurely time, marred only by the financial problems forever plaguing her. After brief stays in Avranches and St. Malo, she rented a house in July at St. Adresse, near Le Havre, which belonged to Queen Christina of Spain. On the 29th she sent an urgent appeal to Blackwood for a £100 advance: "I have got into a little complication stupidly by want of attention, and should be much obliged if you would have the goodness to do this *at once*." A few days later, discovering that she had not blundered after all, she rather cavalierly informed him: "I hope, however, you have done or will do what I asked all the same. When I come home I am going to ask you to give me some two or three hundred pounds on credit of Miss M[arjoribanks]—or rather, of her ultimate price."[7]

Her work on *Miss Marjoribanks* was proceeding well and she was also occupied with critical articles for *Maga*. *Good Words* had offered her £1,000 for a new piece of fiction *(Madonna Mary)*. Successful in her writing, contented for the moment in the comparative good health of her sons, Mrs. Oliphant played vaguely with the idea of settling permanently in France. But she was influenced by more sober considerations, especially the matter of schooling for the boys. The only decision to make was the choice between Eton and Harrow, her preference being Eton. It did occur to her that it was both extravagant and impractical to educate her boys as though they were rich men's sons. Consulting Blackwood on the question, she wrote: "I have written to Mr. [W. Lucas] Collins asking him what is after all the fundamental question, whether boys of no particular pretensions and who have their own way to make would be in their right place at this most aristocratic of schools. I have a selfish interest in this question for it would be much pleasanter to live near Windsor than at Harrow."[8] Her only concession to economy, and this was more probably a concession to mother love, was that the boys should live with her at home rather than at school. This dictated the choice of Eton and the decision to live in Windsor, almost in the shadow of the great castle.

After a leisurely and expensive journey by carriage along the French coast from St. Malo to Boulogne, the Oliphant party crossed the channel and returned to England late in September. They stayed in rooms in the Bayswater Road while she looked for a house in Windsor. She was delighted by the town—the river, the castle, "the air of cheerful life about"—and soon rented a sunny house with a pleasant garden at 6 Clarence Crescent, to which they moved in November 1865. Mrs. Oliphant's associations with Eton lasted for more than thirty years and continued, in a grimly permanent way, with her burial alongside her two sons in the Eton parish cemetery. In spite of the bitter disappointments and losses which she suffered during all those years, she never lost her idealized and almost idyllic conception of the school and its surroundings. Its traditional gentility and social eminence no doubt were at the root of its attraction for her, but to this must be added the fact that it was, for her boys at least, a thoroughly happy place. Of the rigors of English public school life one reads nothing in her fiction, nor in the accounts her son Cecco left of the Eton days.[9] The boys were bright and had no difficulties with their studies. At this early stage she had relatively few anxieties about their future. They fitted well into the social life of Eton and Windsor. By 1865 Mrs. Oliphant's prestige as a novelist and critic was considerable and assured her admission into the best society. Everything—her work, her choice of living arrangements and friends—reflected only one thing: total dedication to the happiness of her sons: "I see no reason to decline the American's offer, magnificent as it is," she wrote to Blackwood at this time, touching apparently on the reprint rights to one of the Carlingford novels. "It will buy Tiddy a pony, which he will think highly satisfactory—and which is certainly better than nothing."[10]

Life was organized around the boys. Even the work providing them with these luxuries was subordinated to their happiness. She did her writing late at night or in the early morning hours. Mrs. Coghill recalled that once the local police officer, making his rounds on a summer night and seeing lights burning so late, suspected burglary in her house. When he discovered it was Mrs. Oliphant working late, he chatted with her and frequently returned thereafter for friendly midnight visits.[11] During the day she was always free for her sons and their friends—from the early breakfast and Bible-reading sessions after which they left on their one-mile walk to school, through pleasant afternoon and evening parties and theatricals. A. C. Benson, a schoolmate of the boys at Eton, described them years later in his memoirs: Cyril, "a small, lightly-built, curly-haired boy, handsome, attractive-looking, stepping rather jauntily and with an air of entirely unembarrassed amusement—indeed, a charming-looking creature, with an expression which seemed at once sensitive, impressionable, and whimsical"; and Cecco, "a very quiet boy, with a highly animated and I thought roguish expression, with bright black beady eyes, very friendly and amiable, but decidedly silent." Mrs. Oliphant herself he recalled as "a quiet-looking, grey-haired lady," graceful and dignified, almost beautiful except for her mouth, "which had something roughly shaped and abrupt about it, the upper lip projecting sharply over the lower. About the whole face there was a look of reserve, even of endurance, more of repression than of suppression, as if a naturally expansive and genial nature had been thwarted and baffled." Benson remembered too the cheerful, comfortably insulated life she had created for her family: "She stood between them and life, warded off every sort of trouble and discomfort, and arranged everything for their pleasure and enjoyment . . . and she herself seemed to have nothing to do except to arrange matters for the young people and to share their delightful and delighted companionship."[12] A similar picture remained in the memory of another schoolmate, Howard Overing Sturgis, who recalled visiting her as a schoolboy and "finding always a gracious lady, apparently occupied with nothing more serious than some piece of delicate needlework, always ready to pour out tea and listen patiently to my selfish confidences. Only once she mildly asked me not to come till after four o'clock as that was post time and she was 'rather busy'—and I remember I was somewhat hurt!"[13]

Their friends, besides the Eton boys, were mainly from the Eton faculty—the Hawtreys, relatives of old Provost Hawtrey, a large family of elderly brothers and sisters; Francis or Frank Tarver, a French master at Eton who, through the good offices of Mrs. Oliphant, met and married Sarah, eldest daughter of Principal Tulloch; and of course the Tullochs and Blackwoods and the other old friends. There were also Windsor neighbors, officers from the Castle and genteel ladies whose names Mrs. Oliphant neglected to record in the *Autobiography,* perhaps the most significant of them the modest, simple little woman who lived next door, "Aunt Nelly," who was the inspiration for the Little Pilgrim series.

It was a good life, so gay that when she looked back at it in the *Autobiography* she marvelled that "I should have risen again into absolute gaiety thus, twice over." There were short trips to London for art exhibitions and theatre, and little theatricals at home in which both the children and the adults participated— simple children's plays like *Barbe Bleue* and even more ambitious bits of Shakespeare and Molière. Mrs. Oliphant herself overcame her reticence on one occasion to play Mrs. Hardcastle in *She Stoops to Conquer.* Her writing was proceeding well, despite the fact that the fiction was not selling as well as she and her publishers would have liked. But she was working on a large body of serious non-fiction for *Maga* which stimulated her mind more thoroughly than her fiction did—book reviews, a series of "Historical Sketches of the Reign of George II" (which appeared in *Maga* from April 1868 through August 1869 and was published in book form by Blackwood in 1869); and, for Macmillan, a biography of Saint Francis of Assisi (1868). With a good income and faith in her power to continue working, she was living extravagantly. She dressed so well indeed that on a visit to the Blackwood offices in 1866 she went unrecognized: "I don't know whether I told you how much humbled I was on calling at George Street when I was in Edinburgh. Neither Mr. Simpson nor anyone knew me," she wrote Blackwood. On the manuscript of this letter someone, probably the faithful Mr. Simpson himself, scribbled: "No wonder! the style of Ladies dress now defies recognition. That of Mrs. Oliphant on the occasion referred to impressed me so that I expected I was to address a Duchess."[14]

Finally there was the minor triumph of royal recognition. In 1868 Mrs. Oliphant was awarded a Civil List pension. The circumstances of the award are amusing and revealing. In her published writings Mrs. Oliphant always showed a proper awe and respect for Queen Victoria. In later years when she came to know the Queen personally, she wrote a proper and conventional little biography of her and, on the occasion of the Queen's Diamond Jubilee, a patriotic poem.[15] The unpublished Blackwood letters, however, reveal a far more sophisticated and cynical attitude. She was not alone among her generation in regarding the Queen's mourning over Prince Albert's death as excessive. Having suffered what she regarded as even more tragic losses, Mrs. Oliphant had little sympathy to spare her sovereign. She wrote to Blackwood on August 8, 1867:

> I think all the same that if any of us ordinary people were to treat our friends and visitors and society in general in the same way, we should simply put ourselves out of the path of society— and lose both visitors and friends. I doubt whether *nous autres* poor women who have had to fight with the world all alone without much sympathy from anybody, can quite enter into the "unprecedented" character of the Queen's sufferings. A woman is surely a poor creature if with a large, happy affectionate family of children around her she can't take heart to do her duty whether she likes it or not. *We* have to do it, with very little solace, and I don't see that there is anybody particularly sorry for us.

At this time, apparently, Blackwood asked her to review *The Early Years of His Royal Highness the Prince Consort* by C. Grey, issued under the supervision and approval of the Queen and published by Smith, Elder. He evidently suggested that a favorable review might be of some personal benefit to her. Mrs. Oliphant's reaction speaks for itself:

> What have I done, oh great editor, that I am to be Maga's permanent Jenkins or Jeaves? I thought I had done my duty that way. I am neither moved by an enthusiasm of loyalty nor do I put much confidence in the problematical benefits to be desired. I don't think her Majesty *could* do anything except in the way of personal notice, which would no doubt be flattering but unsatisfactory. Praise is sweet, but I don't think there is any pudding

to bestow. However, *since you wish it,* I will try to make something of the Royal lucubrations if they are sent to me, and if it
is possible. I suppose it will be very harmless, well-conditioned
sort of pratter. I will try it on condition that I am not to be asked
to tackle the holy Albert again in his later volumes. It is a dreadful thing to begin writing. She may be going in for novels yet if
she is to get a review in Blackwood every time she takes pen
in hand.

In another note to Blackwood written about the same time she observes: "I will do the S. [sic] Albert paper if you wish it, but I am
sick of the name of him and so I suppose is everyone else. I don't
think you at all appreciate in Scotland the exasperated feeling
with which people here regard the Queen's doings."

Nevertheless, obliging hack that she was, Mrs. Oliphant wrote
an enthusiastic review ("A Royal Idyll," *Maga,* September 1867).
She sent it off to her publisher with a sigh of relief: "I hope you
will like it. I have done my best with what is not a very comfortable subject—for one must eulogize and one can't tell lies,
though loyalty may go the length of a fib occasionally. One thing
the book proves that at least her Majesty is an innocent-minded
woman—it is wonderfully youthful and unsophisticated. Poor
prince! What a bore his life must have been to him."[16] As she had
predicted, the Queen, once bitten by the writing bug, fell prey to
the disease. Blackwood was still holding out the promise of
pudding as well as praise, and with this in mind he sent her,
in January 1868, *Leaves from the Journal of our Life in the
Highlands.* "The Queen's book has arrived," Mrs. Oliphant wrote.
"It looks mighty like a little girl's diary of travel and is innocent
to the last degree. Would that it was consistent with loyalty to
make fun of it! It would be ten times easier than any other mode
of treatment. However, in case there should be anything in the
mysterious hopes you hold out to me, I will try what I can do."[17]

The review, "The Queen of the Highlands," published in the
February 1868 number, was kind, though one can detect a note
of sarcasm. Mrs. Oliphant begins, for example, with a rather am-
biguous statement. It is now sixty years, she observes, since Sir
Walter Scott "threw open" the Highlands: "And had Sir Walter
lived till now, here is a book about the Highlands that would have

brought tears to his loyal and kindly eyes." She stresses the book's simplicity and homeliness and ventures one humble point of domestic criticism in a footnote. When the Queen mentions that she ate hodge-podge, "mutton broth with vegetables which I did not much relish," Mrs. Oliphant offers a gentle correction: "not hodge-podge, or *hotch-potch,* but simple broth; the other being a lordly soup, made of youthful lambs and the earliest dainty vegetables,—something like soup *à la Julienne,* but much better, of course."

Thus Mrs. Oliphant earned her reward. The Blackwood correspondence includes an official paper from 10 Downing Street, dated 20 June 1868: "The Queen has, on Mr. Disraeli's recommendation, granted a pension of the Civil List of £100 a year to Mrs. Oliphant." Her reaction was one of pleasure, not unmixed with cynicism and practical considerations. On receipt of the official certificate she wrote to Blackwood:

> Curiosity however mingles with my rapture. Are pensions of this kind generally paid in the lump once a year? It is very good of the Queen if she has anything to do with it—which you will say is a doubt of the profanest kind. But I don't suppose she has taken the trouble to make any special stipulation in my favour.
>
> And please don't take a mean advantage of me and make me review her books that are coming! I feel the tremendous vantage ground this gives you.[18]

With the award went presentation at court. In later years Mrs. Oliphant had several private visits with the Queen, but the 1868 meeting was only an official ceremony. "I have no doubt," she wrote Blackwood, "you would hear every detail of my royal visit from Isabella to whom I thought it right to communicate all the circumstances! Her Majesty has not yet looked in to five o'clock tea—but that of course is a thing that may happen any day."[19]

Frequently in Mrs. Oliphant's letters there is an expression of an almost superstitious dread that the moments of happiness in her life are mere delusion and are fated to be momentary. The few short years of happiness following her adjustment to her husband's death ended abruptly with Maggie's death. The gradual recovery and return to normal life at Windsor were interrupted, though less catastrophically this time, by the financial ruin of her brother Frank Wilson in 1868. Frank's downfall came later than her brother Willie's, but it was in some ways more unfortunate since he had a wife and four children to support, a burden which he transferred with rather surprising willingness to his sister. In earlier days Frank had always been the steady and reliable brother in the Wilson household. He had been devoted to his younger sister. Along with their mother he had been the first admiring audience for her fiction. His attachment to his sister and the family was so strong that when she married and her parents moved to London to be near her, Frank, "discontented and wounded . . . married too, hastily, but very successfully in a way as it turned out." He married his cousin Jeanie Wilson, younger daughter of George Wilson, and they remained in Birkenhead. They had one son, Frank, and three daughters—Nelly, Madge, and Janet Mary (Denny). Mrs. Oliphant lived for a while with him and his family after her husband's death. It was not a satisfactory arrangement, although she acknowledged that the failure was in no way his.

During the 1860's Mrs. Oliphant saw little of the Wilson family. They were living a "very humdrum but happyish life" and were poor correspondents. She knew only that Frank was in poor health, suffering from a nervous condition which caused his hands to tremble but did not interfere with his work. Then quite suddenly, early in 1868, she learned that he was in serious financial trouble. He did not seek her help, but she went to Liverpool at once, only to discover that he had left home. As had happened in other Wilson family crises, the women took over. With his wife's feeble but willing assistance she tried to straighten out his tangled affairs. He was absolutely ruined financially:

> He was a man without an expensive taste, the most innocent, the most domestic of men, but what he had had always slipped through his fingers, as I well knew. Poor dear Frank! how well I remember the use he made of one of my mother's Scotch proverbs to justify some new small expense following a bigger one which he would allow to be imprudent. "Well," he would say, half-coaxing, half-apologetic, "what's the use of eating the coo and worrying [choking] on her tail?" Alas! he had choked

on the tail this time without remedy, and the only thing to be
done was to wind up the affairs as well as possible, and to further
the little family, whom he could not live without, after him,
which was what we did accordingly, with a prompt action which
was some relief to our heavy hearts.

No businesswoman herself, Mrs. Oliphant nevertheless settled his
affairs. Years later, after her death, the author of an unsigned
obituary article on her in the *Quarterly Review* wrote: "Men at
Liverpool remember to this day the apparition of Mrs. Oliphant
at the financial crisis in her brother's affairs, when the adverse
balance was re-adjusted by her frank acceptance of the whole responsibility, present and future."[20]

From that point Frank Wilson never recovered, either financially or morally. He found a job with a railway construction
company in Hungary and went off to that remote country with
his wife and two younger daughters, leaving Frank, now fourteen,
and Nelly in his sister's care. With a now expanded family she
again settled down to tranquil life in Windsor. There were added
responsibilities, another boy to educate, but she found some
patronizing comfort in this: "I am not sure that I had not a sort
of secret satisfaction in getting Frank, my nephew, into my hands,
thinking, with that complacency with which we always look at our
own doings, that I could now train him for something better than
they had thought of." The crisis seemed over, but relief was only
temporary. "One seems to be always dragged back by the heels
when one hoped to have got the better of the world," she wrote
wearily to Blackwood in the spring of 1870.[21] In the midst of a
gay supper party on the river that she had been giving for her
sons and their friends, a telegram arrived from Frank in Hungary:
"Jeanie is dead, and I am in despair."

She kept the news from his young son that evening so as not
to spoil the party. Within a few weeks Frank came home with his
two little girls and established himself and them as permanent dependents upon his sister. She had tried earlier to find work for
him, appealing to both Blackwood and Macmillan for simple editorial tasks, indexing, or perhaps work in a library. The horror of
Frank's situation now was how closely it paralleled that of his
younger brother Willie. Not an alcoholic, he nevertheless showed

the same symptoms of moral inertia. Just as, years before, Willie had slipped into indolence, staying home, smoking cigars, reading French novels, and copying his sister's manuscripts, so Frank contentedly "settled down to a kind of quiet life, read his newspaper, took his walk, sat in his easy-chair in the dining room or in his own room for the rest of the day, was pleased with Frank's progress and with Nelly's love for reading, and with his little girls, and so got through his life, I think not unhappily." Whether Mrs. Oliphant's willingness and ability to assume his responsibilities contributed to his passive acceptance of his fate we cannot say. She did so in good spirit on the whole, but there were moments of irritation. The old intimate brother-sister relationship, the respect which she had once had for him, were gone—"he drifted one way and I another." For a while he talked of going off and living by himself as their father had done in his last years, but even this act of independence was too much for him. He lingered on another five years. At the time of his death in July 1875 he was not quite sixty, "but worn out and his life withered away to the barest skeleton of living." Even in his dying he inconvenienced his sister who was obliged to delay work on a manuscript for Macmillan while she nursed him.[22]

There was still another addition to Mrs. Oliphant's household at this time, her second cousin Annie L. Walker, later Mrs. Coghill. A distant relative, she had written to Mrs. Oliphant in 1865 while she was living in Paris, to introduce herself. Miss Walker had some literary ambitions which Mrs. Oliphant did not take very seriously. However she did encourage her to turn from poetry to novel writing, and in the period from 1877 to 1894 Miss Walker published five novels, as well as a collection of plays for children and an anthology of English and Canadian verse. She proved useful to Mrs. Oliphant in various literary and secretarial jobs. In 1884 she made an autumnal marriage to a wealthy man, Harry Coghill, of Coghurst Hall, a union which Mrs. Oliphant viewed with cynical amusement. Commenting in a letter to William Blackwood on reports of the remarriage of John Blackwood's widow, she wrote: "It is the most extraordinary of elderly successes—greater even than my cousin Miss Walker with her 10,000 a year."[23]

All these domestic responsibilities forced Mrs. Oliphant to undertake even more writing. Often in her letters of this period she speaks of being "up to my eyes in work" or "dazed" with work. She was at a decisive moment in her career. With her output of the 1860's she had established herself as a serious writer, potentially a good or even (from the critical point of view of some of her contemporaries) a great one. Certainly the Carlingford series and the Irving biography showed a promise that, if it was ever to be realized, must be fulfilled now when she was experienced and mature. Good serious writing demanded time and careful labor but the needs of her family demanded rapid, ever-increasing and unending production:

> I remember making a kind of pretence to myself that I had to think it over, to make a great decision, to give up what hopes I might have had of doing now my very best, and to set myself steadily to make as much money as I could, and do the best I could for the three boys . . . I never did or could, of course, hesitate for a moment as to what had to be done. It had to be done and that was enough, and there is no doubt that it was much more congenial to me to drive on and keep everything going, with a certain scorn of the increased work, and metaphorical toss of my head, as if it mattered! than it ever would have been to labour with an artist's fervour and concentration to produce a masterpiece. One can't be two things or serve two masters.

The price that Mrs. Oliphant paid for her choice was hackmanship. She never had taken her writing very seriously. It came easily to her, and after a while she grew to look upon her talent with a faint contempt. She had an almost sublime indifference to good style: "I am afraid I can't take the books *au grand sérieux.* Occasionally they pleased me, very often they did not . . . I have always had my sing-song, guided by no sort of law, but by my ear, which was in its way fastidious to the cadence and measure that pleased me; but it is bewildering to me in my perfectly artless art, if I may use the word at all, to hear of the elaborate ways of forming and enhancing style, and all the studies made for that end."

She worked methodically and mechanically—perhaps not with the well-oiled efficiency of Trollope, for she seems to have set herself no daily quota of wordage, but with a kind of quiet industry that could produce in a single year novels ranging from sheer triviality to real merit. Her method of composition was casual. She kept no notebooks, made no elaborate drafts. She simply wrote a story, often with no notion at the beginning of how it would develop or end. Once she confided to William Blackwood: "I always find with my work that it shapes itself, and I am never quite sure in beginning a story what character it may take."[24] And she described her composition of *The Curate in Charge* in this fashion to Alexander Macmillan:

> There is an old, amiable, feckless "Curate in Charge." There are two pretty daughters, and there is a young Rector, spick and span from Oxford, viewy and tender-hearted, who has to oust my old man. Exactly what these people are going to do I cannot tell, as the story is not finished and my personages have an unaccountable liking for their own way and never conduct themselves exactly as I intend them to. But in somewhere about a fortnight, I think, if the tide keeps flowing, you shall have the story.[25]

Small wonder then that her novels are full of inconsistencies and errors, that her characters' names sometimes change within the space of a few chapters, that her plots, when complicated, become so confused and involved that she neglects to iron out all the issues. With such working habits it is not surprising too that, except for Carlingford and a few Scotch scenes, she rarely recreates a milieu or a society; that, except in a few stories of the supernatural, she rarely rises above plodding literalness of language. She had no time for the exercise of imagination or even for careful thought. Her major concern in novel writing, she cheerfully admitted, was boiling the pot:

> God help us all! what is the good done by any such work as mine, or even better than mine? 'If any man build upon this foundation . . . wood, hay, stubble; . . . if the work shall be burned he shall suffer loss: but he himself shall be saved; yet so as by fire.' An infinitude of pains and labour, and all to disappear like the stubble and the hay. Yet who knows? The little faculty may grow a bigger one in the more genial land to come, where one will have no need to think of the boiling of the daily pot. In the meantime it was good to have kept the pot boiling and maintained the cheerful household fire so long, though it is smouldering out in darkness now.

The bulk of her work from 1870 to her death consisted of pot-boilers. Yet in that mass of fiction are a few novels and short stories of distinction and many that, for a variety of reasons, are interesting and worthy of attention. She tried her hand at every popular genre of fiction, but her talents shine, generally, in only two types—social comedy and the anti-romance. At its best her social comedy captures and impales with deadly accuracy and effect some segment of a recognizable society. Carlingford, and particularly its community of Dissenters, is so caught for us, fluttering with brief but unmistakable vitality. Nowhere else does she quite so successfully mark or hit her target. Not a systematic critic of society, for the most part she accepted the world around her without question or serious complaint. Her satirical shafts are directed not at institutions, customs, classes, but at individuals, personal idiosyncracies, and fallibilities. Miss Marjoribanks, for example, is ridiculed for her bossiness and complacency, rather than for what she reflects of the complacent provincial society in which she lives. Only rarely, as with the tradesman Tozer in *Salem Chapel* or the prosperous Dissenting clergyman Mr. Beecham in *Phoebe, Junior,* does Mrs. Oliphant rise above the merely personal and project recognizable social types. But on the more modest level of individual portraiture she does occasionally write delightful satire. Snobs, boors and bores get their share of drubbing, but it is in the less noxious types that she excels—well-meaning but ineffectual husbands and fathers, loyal but faintly disillusioned wives, idealistic and naive young heroes and heroines. She is at her best when she maintains the balance between satire and sympathy —the bookish Mr. Proctor of *The Rector,* the middle-aged newly-wed Morgans, and rock-ribbed Aunt Leonora in *The Perpetual Curate.* Her potboilers offer a few similarly felicitous examples.

The Curate in Charge (1876), a slight but appealing novel which, as Mrs. Oliphant's note to Macmillan quoted above indicates, was spun out of air, introduces a sweet old man whose rather literal acceptance of the Christian duties of meekness and humility has kept him for many years in a low-paying post of curate in charge for a rector who has gone off to seek health and diversion in Italy. When the rector suddenly dies, the curate is out of a job. His problem is complicated by two grown unmarried

daughters and two baby sons, the latter acquired when in a
moment of Christian charity he marries his daughters' plain-
looking governess because he lacks the heart to discharge her.
The hero of the novel is the well-to-do, aesthetic young rector who
comes fresh from Oxford to replace him. Here again Mrs. Oliphant has a character whom she can gently satirize without destroying her reader's sympathy for him. The old curate dies peacefully and the young rector falls in love with one of his daughters
whom, after the predictable obstacles are overcome, he marries.
The romance, however, is significantly underplayed. Thus, by skirting sentimentality on the one hand and cynicism on the other,
Mrs. Oliphant achieves a delicate balance which gives *The Curate
in Charge* a sparkle and freshness unexpected in a potboiler of
this nature.

She achieves this balance again, though somewhat more precariously, in a novel generally uncharacteristic of her fiction, *The
Duke's Daughter* (first published as "Lady Jane" in *Good Words*
in 1882, then in book form in 1890 by Blackwood with the present title to avoid confusion with her *Lady Car,* a novel published
in 1889). The aristocracy rarely figures in Mrs. Oliphant's fiction.
Wealthy characters are plentiful, but they are usually not higher
in the social scale than the squirearchy. *The Duke's Daughter* is
therefore an interesting oddity. Except for raising the rank of her
leading characters and underscoring their snobbishness, however,
she is writing simply another domestic love story with a plot cen-
tering on a proud father's opposition to his daughter's marriage to
a man of a lower social class. The charm of the novel is its sustained tone—that of a fable, a kind of latter-day Sir Walter Scott
romance, told with tongue-in-cheek irony. Although it is a contemporary novel with a London scene, Mrs. Oliphant's proud
Duke of Billingsgate, Pendragon Plantagenet Altamont Fitz-Merlin
(who "believed devoutly that he and his family tree and the straw-
berry leaves that grew on the top of it, overshadowed the world")
and his aristocratic daughter Lady Jane ("she accepted undoubt-
ingly the creed of her race, and never questioned the fact that she
was something entirely removed from the crowd, elevated above
the ordinary level of humanity") might have stepped out of a
fairy tale.

Jane is the unawakened princess, getting on in years at twenty-eight, unmarried simply because no one worthy of her has offered himself. She falls in love quite perversely with a commoner—a man of excellent birth and income, but, alas, no title. The Duchess, Jane's mother, is a realistic woman interested only in seeing her daughter happily settled for life. Knowing that her husband will be unalterably opposed to the marriage, she advises the young man to forget his passion: " 'If you had spoken to me I should have said, Try and get over it, Mr. Winton; don't disturb her, poor girl, by telling her. Try if a little trip to America, or tiger-shooting, or to be a *Times* correspondent, or some other of those exciting things which you young men do nowadays, will not cure you.' " But when she realizes that he will not be dissuaded, she does her best to promote the match, even inviting him to their home to meet the Duke. The latter has no objection to his coming —" 'There must always, I suppose, be a few nobodies to fill up the corners,' " he observes tolerantly. But when the young man asks for his daughter's hand, the Duke is horrified, forbids the marriage, and, on later discovering his daughter's plan to elope, locks her up and keeps her a prisoner. Here again Mrs. Oliphant maintains a balance, skirting the pitfalls of melodrama and of farce. The Duke is stubborn but very human. He feels guilty about his harsh treatment of his daughter and painfully disturbed by the gossip which his tyrannical behavior has caused. Ultimately coming around, he gives his blessing to the marriage.

There is something of the same air of fable, lightly dusted with homely realism in this case, in the short story "Queen Eleanor and Fair Rosamond," first published in *Cornhill* in 1886 and later collected in the posthumous volume *A Widow's Tale and Other Stories* (1898). The historical framework of adulterous king, jealous queen, and devoted mistress is reduced by Mrs. Oliphant to a modern bourgeois marriage crisis. For Henry II and his queen she offers a prosperous, middle-aged Liverpool businessman and his contented wife. The famous bower becomes a cozy suburban London villa, "fanciful with a Cockney sentiment," where the erring husband sets up a bigamous household with his young Rose. The wronged wife has none of the passionate jealousy of her historical counterpart. Happily and securely married, she is not even alarmed at first by her husband's long absences on "business" in London:

> Marriage is a tie which is curiously elastic when youth is over and the reign of the sober everyday has come in. There is no such union, and yet there is no union that sits so lightly. People who are each other's only confidants and cannot live without each other, yet feel a half-relief and sense of emancipation when accidentally and temporarily they are free of each other. A woman says to her daughter, 'We will do so-and-so when your father is away,' meaning no abatement of loyalty or love, but yet an unconscious, unaccustomed, not unenjoyable freedom. And the man no doubt feels it perhaps more warmly on his side.

When she discovers her husband's infidelity she reacts with shock but without any loss of her sound feminine common sense. She telegraphs a trusted family friend, " 'Come to me directly if you can. I have great need of your advice and help. Tell no one,' was what she said. She liked, like all women, to get the full good of the permitted space." The domestic crisis is settled with a minimum of emotion. The wife returns to her Liverpool home; the scandal is hushed up and gradually forgotten. The only victim (we learn almost nothing of poor Rose) is the husband, whose single misstep cuts him off from his business and his family and reduces him to shabby cockneyism. Years later he visits his family, a pathetic little man: "To see him elderly, stout, and . . . oh so commonplace! and fallen from his natural level, shuffling his feet, reddening, smiling that confused and foolish smile, conciliating his children, gave his wife almost the keenest pangs she had yet suffered. She could not bear to see him so lowered from his natural place. Tragedy is terrible, but when it drops into tragi-comedy, tragi-farce at the end, that is the most terrible of all."

From this sophisticated outlook, it is not a far move to the anti-romance, a form for which Mrs. Oliphant had a rather special fondness and talent. We have already met in Carlingford the two best of her anti-sentimental heroines—the domineering Miss Marjoribanks and the level-headed Phoebe, Junior. In creating these characters Mrs. Oliphant was not perhaps engaged in any deliberate program of satirizing the sentimental love story, although she frequently indicated her weariness with its conventions. She tells her readers in an aside, for example, that she debated the ending of *The Curate in Charge,* preferring actually to leave her hard-working heroine struggling in poverty to marrying her off to the hero. A "happy" ending, she observes, "is simply a contemptible expedient. But, alas! it is one which there can be no doubt is much preferred by most people to the more legitimate conclusion." Furthermore, she points out, improbable marriages occur every day in real life—"a disgrace to any romanticist or dramatist, if they were not absolute matters of fact and true."

The heroine who emerges from Mrs. Oliphant's novels after 1870 has plenty of Phoebe, Junior's common sense, but she is often harder, more scheming and less charming.[26] She is never, however, morally corrupt or vicious. Mrs. Oliphant despised what she called "the cold-blooded school of novel writing" and deplored the tendency of the sensation novelists to portray as heroines women of weak morality, like Lady Isabel Vane in *East Lynne,* or of positive depravity, like Lady Audley.[27] Hers, at their worst— like the unsympathetic governess who is the heroine of *Janet* (1891), or the fortune-hunting Laura Lance of *The Sorceress* (1893), or the thoughtless and over-indulged Stella of *Old Mr. Tredgold* (1896)—are selfish, shallow, and unethical; but they do not deliberately, or even usually accidentally, inflict serious injury upon others. The outcome of their stories is invariably happy in the respect that they get what they want even if their goals are not admirable. Phoebe, Junior married her millionnaire and rejected a more idealistic and romantic suitor without any suggestion by the author that her heroine will regret her choice. Indeed, where in one novel, *For Love and Life* (1874), Mrs. Oliphant has a young widow refuse a handsome and wealthy suitor because she loves a poor ne'er-do-well, she concludes almost bitterly: "Ah me! if Margaret had made that 'good match,' though it was not all for love, would it not have been better for everybody concerned?"

Phoebe had warmth and sensitivity, but most of the heroines of the anti-romantic novels are "hard-boiled," tougher in mind and character. Generally this is the result of the circumstances of their lives. Less generously endowed than Phoebe, who had money and a loving family, these girls, though pretty, are often poor, unedu-cated, and vulgar. They seek the status and security of a "good" marriage. At the same time they are not always mere fortune hunters. *Mrs. Arthur* (1877), for example, presents a kind of transitional heroine who marries a young man of a higher social class for love but loses him temporarily because of her vulgarity and her stubborn unwillingness to improve herself. She softens, however, in time for a reconciliation and happy ending. But many of Mrs. Oliphant's heroines of this type do not undergo such total transformation. Sometimes they are sobered and mature in the course of the novel, but they remain essentially unchanged. In a particularly bleak and unpleasant novel, *Within the Precincts* (1879), Lottie Despard, seeking to escape from a poor, dreary household, falls in love with a younger son of an aristocratic family. Jilted by him, and further afflicted by the loss of her beautiful singing voice, she ultimately marries a poor canon whom she does not love. The novel ends on a note of weary resignation: "She would do her best, she would be a good wife, that would be within her power. She would serve him humbly, that he might forgive her for not loving him."

Lottie is unlucky. She has spirit at the beginning of the novel but is beaten down by a series of blows. A stronger young woman and a luckier one is the lively Patty Hewitt, heroine of the realistic, almost Hardy-esque novel *The Cuckoo in the Nest* (1894). This is a village Phoebe, hardened by the circumstances of her life. The daughter of the owner of a country pub, she is energetic, capable, proud, uneducated: "She was never afraid to do whatever she had a mind to. She never stood swaying from one foot to another unable to make up her mind. She was all swiftness, firmness, alertness—ready for anything." Patty is adored by Gervase Piercey, the feeble-minded son of the rich local squire, but is herself in love with Roger Pearson, the village athlete. Nevertheless, when she has an opportunity to marry Gervase she seizes it and glories in her new position. Not until after her husband dies does she realize the loneliness of her life, shunned by her higher class neighbors and cut even by former friends of her own class. She feels no guilt, however, about her mercenary marriage; when she finally renounces her title and estate it is not out of remorse but as the result of the common-sense recognition of the fact that is not, after all, the kind of life she wants. She then marries Pearson, now a prosperous cricket champion, and settles down to happy domesticity in a " 'andsome 'ouse."

The Cuckoo in the Nest completely rejects sentimental clichés. The heroine of the subplot, a genteel, penniless widow, ultimately fares well too, thanks to Patty's renunciation of her estate, but sh· is bloodless beside the vigorous blooming Patty. And we *like* Patty, though we are shocked by her insensitivity. Another young woman who shares Patty's appeal, in spite of her hardness of character, is Constance Waring of *A House Divided Against Itself* (1886), the daughter of a couple who are separated. Her gentler sister Frances lives a sheltered life with their father in Bordighera. Constance, who has been brought up in London by their mother, Lady Markham, is completely the product of her environment, worldly and mercenary. The girls exchange visits with their parents. While Frances is disgusted by the shallow, superficial life of London society, Constance is bored by the simple provincial life of Bordighera and amuses herself by flirting with a sensitive young officer. She is cold and unfeeling, yet curiously likeable. In the end she makes an entirely practical, loveless marriage which the reader is made to feel is a happy and proper conclusion.

Such cynicism and weariness with the conventions of sentimental fiction was not merely a literary reaction on Mrs. Oliphant's part. It was the reflection of her life, her disappointments in her marriage, her family, her career. It therefore takes the form in her work not only of anti-romance but also in a kind of general disillusion, an anti-idealism which is infinitely more serious and more sobering. As early as 1863 in *A Son of the Soil* she was exploring the whole pattern of disillusion in a man's life—in which romantic love is only one small episode. Colin Campbell, the brilliant young son of simple Scottish peasants, wins a scholarship to Balliol, but idealistically seeks his career in the humble kirk of his fathers in Scotland, to "breathe a new breath into the country he loved." He soon discovers, like Arthur Vincent in *Salem Chapel,* that his congregation is ignorant, unappreciative, and unworthy of the light he brings them. Reconciling himself to this disappointment, he even more pathetically marries Alice Meredith whom he had once loved but now has outgrown spiritually. He acknowledges frankly to himself that "he could not cheat his own heart, or persuade himself that he wanted to marry her, or that it was less than the sacrifice of all his individual hopes to enter again upon the old relationship, and fulfill the youthful bond"; but he has made his promise and must honor it. Mrs. Oliphant cannot resist an anti-sentimental thrust:

> If this had been anything but a true history, it would have been now the time for Alice Meredith to overhear a chance conversation, or find a dropped letter, which would betray to her Colin's secret; but this is not an accident with which the present history can give interest to his closing chapter, because, in the first place, it did not happen, and, in the second, if a second should be thought necessary, because Colin never confided his secret either to writing or to any mortal ear—which is of all ways of securing a private matter the most certain.

After his marriage he retains his ideals but cannot share them with his wife; he settles down to a calm, reasonably happy life. "He was as happy as most people are . . . a man can live without that last climax of existence when everything else is going on so well in his life."

The fading ideal then is not only romantic love. It can be career, or those ideals which Mrs. Oliphant herself cherished so deeply—motherhood, children, family life. Long before she was forced to acknowledge her bitter disappointment in her own sons, she had candidly recognized the fact that motherhood is not always a glorious and exalted condition. The mother in *Harry Joscelyn* (1881) is tyrannized by a brutal husband. She seeks but fails to find consolation in her children:

> She had a large family—plunging into all the roughnesses of life, its nursery prose and bread-and-butter, without any interval of repose, without money enough or leisure enough to put any glow of prettiness upon the rude circumstances, the band of children— noisy boys who made an end of all her attempts at neatness, and gobbled their food and tore their clothes—and were dirty and disorderly as any cottage brood. She struggled on among them as best she could, always watching every new baby wistfully to see if perhaps something like herself, a child who would be her very own, and speak her language and understand her meaning, might be born to her. But alas! they were Joscelyns every one, big-limbed creatures with light blue eyes, and great red cheeks,

who stared at her cynically out of their very cradles, and seemed
to demand what she was making a fuss about when she sang
them to sleep.

An even more unhappy mother is Lady Caroline, who appears
in two novels, *The Ladies Lindores* (1883) and its sequel *Lady
Car* (1889). The first of these is a striking book, far above the
run of Mrs. Oliphant's later fiction. A study of the effects of sudden wealth upon a family, it is starkly powerful in places. Once
again the theme is disillusion. The Lindores family, after living
happily in genteel poverty for many years, suddenly becomes rich
when the father inherits a title and an estate. Almost immediately
his pleasant, easy-going character changes. Now proud and ambitious, he forces his eldest daughter Caroline into marriage with a
rich vulgar brute, Pat Torrance. A gentle, sensitive girl, she bows
to her father's will although she loves another man. Her children
give her no comfort in this wretched marriage:

> They were their father's children: they had his black hair, a
> peculiarity which sometimes is extremely piquant and attractive
> in childhood, giving an idea of unusual development; but, on the
> other hand, sometimes is—not. Little Tom and Edie were of those
> to whom it is not attractive, for they had heavy fat cheeks, and
> the same light, large, projecting eyes which were so marked a
> feature of their father's face. Poor Lady Car thought they fixed
> their eyes upon her with a cynical gaze when she tried to sing to
> them—to tell them baby-stories. She tried her best, but that was
> perhaps too fine for these children of a coarser race. . . . Poor
> Lady Car! They were a wonder and perplexity to her. She was
> half afraid of them though they were her own.

Lady Car wins her freedom at last when her husband is killed in
a quarrel with her brother. She rejoices in her widowhood and
exults in language hardly characteristic of a nineteenth-century
heroine:

> "Oh my innocent mother!" she cried. "Oh mother! you only
> know troubles as angels may have. Look at me! look at me! I am
> like a mad woman. I am keeping myself in, as you say, that I
> may not go mad—with joy! . . .
> "To think I shall never be subject to all *that* any more—that
> he can never come in here [her bedroom] again—that I am free,

that I can be alone . . . I have never had so many hours to myself for years. It is so sweet to sit still and know that no one will burst the door open and come in. Here I can be sacred to myself, and sit and think: and all quiet—all quiet about me!"

She even temporarily enjoys the reward of a conventional heroine, marrying her former suitor, a refined, scholarly man, and settling down to a happy ever-after. But in *Lady Car* the second marriage too is chilled with disillusion and unhappiness. Her second husband fails to achieve his scholarly ambitions to write a great book on political economy and contentedly compromises on a dilettante's existence, lazy and idle, living on his wife's fortune. Her children from the first husband grow up boorish and insensitive. Lady Car finally dies of disappointment: " 'I have had everything —and nothing. The heart of it has always been stolen from me, all the lights put out; but the dark is sweet too; it is only dim, dim, not discernible—don't call it dark.' "

Lady Car is Mrs. Oliphant's most extreme expression of romantic disillusion. It is certainly the most pathetic of these novels, unrelieved by her generally balanced view of life. She has moved from a brusque, satirical treatment of conventional, sentimental love and heroines into a more serious tone that tries to echo the whole "still, sad music of humanity." Yet we cannot chart her emotional development in these novels in any regular course. Throughout her career, even while she was creating hard-boiled, anti-romantic heroines and melancholy, disappointed mothers, she was spinning conventional love stories as well. One novel that curiously bridges the gap between them is *Kirsteen* (1891), produced in a period of such personal unhappiness that one marvels at its relative sparkle. Possibly this is because in *Kirsteen* Mrs. Oliphant returned to her favorite setting, the quaint, simple and colorful Scotland of the beginning of the century and drew a new breath of life. It is nowhere so good a novel as some of its earliest readers, J. M. Barrie and W. E. Henley in particular, thought it. Henley was so enthusiastic about it that he insisted that his friend Henry James read it. Though a sympathetic admirer of Mrs. Oliphant's work, much impressed by her "extraordinary fecundity," James recognized her limitations. He confessed himself baffled by *Kirsteen*—its charm, its vivid recreation of Scottish life and speech—but also its failure, when it had so much to offer, to rise to the level of art.[28] Largely this failure was the result of her relentless stretching of a thin plot to a full-length novel and the inevitable padding it demanded. The novel is, however, an interesting variation on the traditional love story, in that the heroine, a soft and sentimental young girl in love with a young soldier, defies her strict, overbearing father, runs away to London, and becomes an enterprising career girl, working in a mantua-maker's establishment. When she learns of her lover's death in India, she is broken hearted but not broken in spirit. She builds up a successful business, remains a spinster, and helps her married sisters in their domestic difficulties. What is extraordinary about Kirsteen's fate is that Mrs. Oliphant sees it as not particularly tragic or pathetic but suggests, in fact, that Kirsteen in her spinsterhood is better off than her spoiled, sheltered married sisters.

Kirsteen is a compromise novel with all the ingredients of romance the public demanded but also with a touch of homely cynicism that expressed Mrs. Oliphant herself. She could also deliver on demand the thoroughly conventional love story and she wrote a large number of them—sweet, pallid, innocuous stories which won favorable if unenthusiastic reviews, sold modestly, and were soon forgotten—by the author as well as by her public. They dot her career from 1870 with *John* to 1894 with *A House in Bloomsbury: Ombra* (1872), *Diana Trelawney: The Story of a Great Mistake* (1892, but written twenty years earlier), *A Rose in June* (1874), *Carità* (1877), *The Primrose Path* (1878), *The Greatest Heiress in England* (1879), *In Trust: A Story of a Lady and her Lover* (1882). Among this dreary spate one novel stands out for its simple appeal—*It Was a Lover and his Lass* (1883), which so delighted A. W. Kinglake that he wrote Mrs. Oliphant: "I 'pitied myself,' as they say in Cumberland, when I got to the end of the book, but I hear of the 'Ladies Lindores' in a way that promises me pleasure to come."[29] While we may not share Kinglake's enthusiasm, we must admit that this quiet little Scottish love story has a charm which even the most ruthless padding could not entirely dissipate. The formula is substantially the familiar one— a sheltered, sleeping beauty of a heroine who lives with two adoring spinster aunts in a lonely country house. The hero is a pleas-

ant, well-meaning young man who quite innocently disinherits her
—he has been adopted by her uncle and made his heir. He comes
to the village, his identity disguised, to put things right by marrying someone in the family. Before he meets the heroine, he offers
himself improbably but rather touchingly to one of the elderly
aunts. As soon as he meets the girl of course he falls in love with
her, but their marriage is opposed by the other aunt who has
ambitious plans for marrying her to a man with a title. The hero
goes away, the heroine pines, and the aunt relents. All this is told
as a kind of fairy tale—the creaking old country house, the lovely
tranquil countryside, the benevolent "good fairy" aunt, the awakening heroine, the hero fighting his benign dragons for her—and it
has a tenuous appeal even for the modern reader.

In addition to the romances Mrs. Oliphant kept the pot boiling
with a number of conventional family or domestic novels. Here the
heroines are mature, wise, considerably sobered by the hardships
of life. In this genre, as we have already observed, she often revealed herself—the widowed heroines of *Agnes* (1866), *Madonna
Mary* (1867), *The Three Brothers* (1870), and the deserted wife
in *At His Gates* (1872) all reflect aspects of her own marriage
and domestic struggles. The introduction of a personal note lends
these novels the only interest they possess for modern readers. At
worst, however, they are merely banal—*Cousin Mary* (1888),
A Poor Gentleman (1889), *The Railwayman and his Children*
(1891), *Two Strangers* (1894), *Lady William* (1894), *The Two
Marys* (1896).

These quiet, chatty novels made relatively few demands upon
Mrs. Oliphant. She could write them swiftly, without bothering
about setting, construction, characterization. But the demands of
the literary market for sensation novels, stories of intrigue and
violent action, were persistent. Reluctant as she was to work in
this genre, especially after the signal failure of the melodramatic
episodes of *Salem Chapel,* she nevertheless yielded to pressure.
While skirting the extremes of horror and of overt violence, she
followed the general formula here with murder, treachery, and
even a few "criminal" types. These novels are her poorest work—
murky, dull, improbable: *The Minister's Wife* (1869),[30] *Innocent*
(1873), *Young Musgrave* (1878), *The Second Son* (1888),[31]

Madam (1885), *Oliver's Bride* (1886), *The Son of his Father* (1887), *The Mystery of Mrs. Blencarrow* (1890), *The Heir Presumptive and the Heir Apparent* (1892), *Who Was Lost and Is Found* (1894), *Sir Robert's Fortune* (1895).

Not too far removed in spirit from melodramas like these are a large number of novels dealing with problems of estates and their inheritance. Melodramatic episodes are often introduced, but for the most part the problems are solved by compromise and the peaceful settlement of misunderstandings and quarrels. The theme of the "rightful heir," so popular in Victorian fiction, appears in some of Mrs. Oliphant's earliest novels and turns up throughout her career, beginning with a short novel serialized in *Maga,* September to November 1860, "The Romance of Agostini." One of her most dramatic in this genre was *Brownlows* (1868). Of a more routine nature were *Squire Arden* (1871) and its sequel, *For Love and Life* (1874), a short novel, "The Two Mrs. Scudamores" (*Maga,* December 1871 to January 1872), *May* (1873), *Whiteladies* (1875), *He that Will Not When He May* (1880), *The Prodigals and their Inheritance* (1894).

By far the best treatment of the "rightful heir" formula is Mrs. Oliphant's delightfully sentimental *The Story of Valentine and his Brother* (1875). Written during a period of relative tranquility, with her sons healthy and happy at Eton, it is a bright, cheerful, thoroughly engaging story of boyhood. The improbable plot is handled like a contemporary fairy tale. Twin brothers are separated in their infancy when their gypsy mother leaves one son with his wealthy grandparents and raises the other herself. Valentine, the baby who grows up in the sheltered loving care of Lord and Lady Eskdale, meets and is strongly attracted to the young, uneducated tramp Dick while he is a student at Eton. Heir to a title, Val is spoiled, but good-natured and charming. Dick, as the reader quickly surmises, is his missing brother, and since he is the older twin, the rightful heir. The complications of the plot—another claimant to the estate, the gypsy mother's pathetic attempts to conceal the relationship and later, when she is restored to wealth and comfort, her longing for a free life on the road, Dick's renunciation of the title—are insignificant. What matters here is the atmosphere—the bright, innocent world of childhood where everybody is kind, the scenery is always beautiful, and even the villain is warm-hearted. Mrs. Oliphant never wrote more happily or felicitously than she did here. With her sons and nephew flourishing at home she drew a sensitive and knowledgeable picture of an adolescent boy growing into manhood: "He began to be conscious of himself, that most confusing and bewildering of experiences. . . . Me—how much has been said about it, philosophies based upon it, the whole heaven and earth founded on this atom! but there is nothing that bewilders the young soul so much as to see it surging up through the fair sunny matter-of-fact universe, and through the world of dreams, disturbing and disarranging everything. This change befell Valentine early." And finally she closes with a touching sketch of the old grandparents, lonely but happy now that their children's problems have been solved:

> The avenue was very steep; it tried them both as they went up slowly leaning on each other. When they stopped to take breath, they both spoke, the same thought coming to their minds at the same moment. "The house will be dull without Val," Lady Eskdale said with a sigh. "When the bairns are gone, the house grows quiet," said her husband. Then they set forth again and climbed the last turn to their own door, holding each other with a kind of mutual pressure of their old arms. Both of them were beyond the measure of man's years on earth. "The bairns come and the bairns go—but, thank God, you and me are still together, Catherine," said the old Lord.

No one was better aware of the weaknesses of these commercially fabricated novels than Mrs. Oliphant herself. Never guilty of self-deception, she made no apologies: "I have written because it gave me pleasure, because it came natural to me, because it was like talking or breathing, besides the big fact that it was necessary for me to work for my children." Yet even she could not resist the temptation of speculating occasionally on the possibility that under more favorable circumstances she might have written better. Almost at the end of her life, now neither rich nor famous, and painfully alone, she wrote: "I might have done better work. I should in all probability have earned nearly as much for half the production had I done less; and I might have had the satisfaction of knowing that there was something laid up for them [her sons] and for my old age; while they might have learned habits of work which now seem beyond recall. Who can tell? I did with much labour what I thought the best, and there is only a *might have been* on the other side." All this remained, as she conceded, in the realm of pure speculation. Meanwhile, however unpalatable and un-nourishing the ingredients, she kept the pot boiling and the wheels turning—a "great *improvisatrice*," as Henry James called her, "a night-working spinner of long, loose, vivid yarns, numberless, pauseless, admirable, repeatedly, for their full, pleasant, reckless rustle over depths and difficulties."[32]

Chapter V

Author And Publisher

On June 19, 1877 Mrs. Oliphant celebrated the twenty-fifth anniversary of her association with the firm of Blackwood's by giving a party at Runnymede, on Magna Carta Island. It was a gala affair, attended by a large number of Blackwood contributors and friends—among them Sir Edward Hamley and his brother General William Hamley, Alexander Innes Shand, Colonel Lockhart, R. H. Hutton, Henry Reeve, Dinah Mulock Craik, and R. D. Blackmore. The guests of honor were Mr. and Mrs. John Blackwood. Lunch was served under a canopy on the lawn. Mrs. Oliphant, exquisitely dressed in grey silk, with a white lace bonnet, was escorted to her place by Mr. Blackwood, and Cyril Oliphant, then a twenty-year-old Oxford undergraduate, conducted Mrs. Blackwood. Cyril also served as toastmaster and made a graceful speech of tribute to the publisher. The principal speaker was of course Mr. Blackwood himself, who, in his remarks, joked about the historical significance of the spot on which they were gathered, saying that "he hoped the Barons of Blackwood would always rally round for his support." He concluded by observing that "Mrs. Oliphant's eyes were undimmed by her twenty-five years' writing."[1]

The association was to continue for still another twenty years. Thus for nearly half a century Mrs. Oliphant was a Blackwood's author. She had many other publishers and contributed to many other periodicals, but the Edinburgh firm remained her longest and her steadiest connection. In the course of her relations with the firm she wrote primarily to three people—Major William Blackwood II, who died in 1861; John Blackwood, who died in 1879;

and his nephew, Major William's son, William Blackwood III, who outlived her and died in 1912. There are also letters to other members of the firm—J. M. Langford, George Simpson, and Archie McColl Smith, a cousin of the Blackwoods. The letters are a mirror of Mrs. Oliphant's career. They reflect vividly those cycles of happiness and tragedy which marked her life—the eager deference of the young author, the growing confidence of the established author, the irritability and disappointment of an author whose reputation was declining, the mournful despair of a lonely, sometimes querulous, old woman. They reflect her personality—her wit, her candor, her pride (*amour-propre* as she so often referred to it), her desperate need for money—and, most of all, that extraordinary temper which could flare into sharp anger one day and soften into mellow good humor the next. In a sense too they are a mirror of the publisher—benevolent, generous, yet shrewd and canny in all business operations.

We have already seen the extent to which she revealed herself personally to the Blackwoods. Indeed, much of the material for her biography is to be found in these letters. A Blackwood's author from the age of twenty-four, she came to regard her relationship with them as almost a family one. She was an intimate friend of John Blackwood's sister Isabella, a frequent visitor to his home, a friend of his wife and daughters. When he died and the editorship was assumed by his nephew William, Mrs. Oliphant transferred her confidences to him, never forgetting her seniority, quick to advise and criticize him, yet always aware of the power of his position and the respect due him.

The main records we have of Mrs. Oliphant's earnings in a lifetime of literary work are in these letters. They are curiously unsatisfying, because she was a poor businesswoman. As far as can be learned, she kept no formal business records, only scraps of notes. Always in debt, working simultaneously on so many projects for so many publishers, she was herself probably uncertain at any given moment of her financial condition. Her writing was her collateral, and she paid off her debts, when she paid them, in stories and articles, rarely in cash. Yet like so many women who profess an ignorance of business, she nevertheless managed to keep her head above water at all times and always to collect what

was owing to her. For most of her career she had no literary agent
to handle her affairs, no zealous guardian as George Eliot had in
George Henry Lewes, for example, to look out for her interests.[2]
But she worked with a firm in which she had full confidence, and
she was the first to admit that she had been treated honestly and
generously by them most of the time.

There were periods when her tangled finances seemed almost
hopelessly snarled. In April 1889 when she took her ailing son
Cyril to Beaulieu and was badly in need of money, she was horrified to learn from Blackwood that her debt to the firm was even
higher than she had thought. She had received an advance on the
novel, "Lady Jane," and had assumed that when that novel was
published her obligation would be cleared. She now learned that
she was still in debt: "I am utterly bewildered by the amount you
send me. . . . I suppose you must be right—and in any case I have
not any of my papers with me to show if there is anything forgotten on my side. . . . My impression was that the balance of
£100 lent in September '88 was all that was between us. . . . I
can say nothing in face of the account you send me by which I am
absolutely dumbfounded. I cannot imagine it possible that there
is not some error."[3] A month later, when Mrs. Oliphant returned
to Windsor, she wrote Blackwood suggesting that by way of repay-
ment she either sell her current work in progress (a biography of
Laurence Oliphant) to another publisher—"paying you the pounds
in reduction of that debt"—or "take counsel yourself as to an
estimate more satisfactory" by offering "adequate payment for my
work." This latter tart suggestion was hardly one that he could
have received with pleasure. The nature of his reply is suggested
by Mrs. Oliphant's remark in a return letter, "I am very sorry that
you should be vexed by my letter." She did not drop the subject.
Several months later, writing to say that she would be visiting
Edinburgh, she had the triumphant last word:

> I think I have found out the error in the balance which stunned
> me so when it came upon me like a thunderclap last April. If
> you please, we will go over it together, and I will show you
> my memoranda which I have found. The mistake I think I can
> prove to you is a very simple one. Your clerks have omitted
> to place to my credit for one thing a cheque of Macmillan & Co.

for £200 which I paid to you in the early part of 1888. The fact
that it was not drawn by myself must have caused this error.[4]

Her principal complaint against her publishers was that she
could never make as much money as she would have liked with
her writing. She was never in a good bargaining position, always
desperate for money and forced to accept the first offer. She had
to sacrifice the copyrights of most of her novels for the immediate
gain, though she knew well the value of reprints and new editions.
In 1886 she wrote to Blackwood:

> Anthony Trollope's list of his own earnings gave me a great shock
> —for he had evidently got twice and sometimes three times as
> much as I ever did. And though I suppose at the beginning and
> height of his career he was far more popular than I ever was, I
> don't think this would be the case towards the end. The same
> thing has happened with Mrs. Craik for instance. I remember
> being told by Hurst and Blackett that they had given her £1,500
> merely I think for the reprint of a book called Hannah, a very
> objectionable book, the worst of all hers, I think, in two volumes.
> Now this was the utmost I ever got in my life for any book. These
> things may not be true, but they are said and people believe
> them.[5]

She was quicker, however, to blame the public than her publisher
for this injustice: "It is either my own fault that the public don't
set a higher price on my work or the fault of the public which does
not know honest work when it sees it. It is strange that it should
be so, but I am sure it is no fault of yours anyhow, and I suppose
if the public prefer Miss Norton and Miss Mulock to myself, not
to speak of less or more worthy competitors, it has a right to its
opinion."[6]

The fact is that although she always had a loyal following of
readers, and although her novels were widely circulated by Mudie,
there was no time except 1863–1865, when the Chronicles of Carlingford and especially *Salem Chapel* were being published, in
which Mrs. Oliphant was a best seller. From about 1868 on,
Blackwood's rejected more of her fiction that it accepted. Nothing
ever matched the popular success of *Salem Chapel*, and in the
years following its publication she had the disheartening experience
of seeing her work constantly drop in marketable value. It is thus

not surprising that she was obliged to take so many of her novels to other publishers. In 1873, for example, she asked Blackwood to publish her novel-in-progress "The Story of Valentine and His Brother." We do not know how much the firm offered for it at this time, but the amount was clearly below her expectations:

> I do not see that I can do anything else than accept your offer in respect to my new story, for I don't care to carry my goods about for sale, or to haggle over prices—but I don't, I confess, like to come down in my price, or to be put down, by so old a friend as yourself. This is to neutralize all the advantages (such as they are) of years, and to return to a much earlier period of one's development. Of course it goes without saying that a person so heavily handicapped in this case as I am must be prepared to accept a little mortification now and then, and I do so without more grumbling than is indispensable. I hope you will find the larger price within your power before 'Valentine' is finished.[7]

They agreed finally on the conditional sum of £800, but the final amount that she was to receive remained unfixed. A year later, the novel almost completed, she wrote to press for more: "Now with anyone but you I should of course have a distinct understanding about money before anything else was done. I don't quite know why we shouldn't say something definite on this subject—as it is, you are aware, one of the greatest possible importance to me. . . . A thousand pounds is my general estimate of what such a story is worth. Shall we go upon this as a basis, leaving it to be settled definitely when you have all the story whether you think it worth more or not?"[8] Mrs. Oliphant was in no position to make demands. The prestige of the Blackwood imprimatur was important to her. When she offered John Blackwood a novel in 1878 and he asked if she thought it would be a "marked success" she replied humbly:

> I don't suppose that at fifty, one is likely to begin a new career or do much more than one has already attained, so that I can't assert this or even expect it of myself. And of course I can have no desire to thrust myself upon you if you do not find my books answer. This is quite simple. Happily as yet this has not proved to be the case elsewhere. However, if the matter of price is the only one—and I suppose it would be exaggerated modesty on my part to pretend to think myself below the level of your ordinary

contributors—I should almost prefer now and then to take a
smaller sum in order not to break an old connection.[9]

Too often apparently the Blackwoods found that her books did
not "answer." They rejected some of her best work—*Phoebe,
Junior, The Curate in Charge, A Beleaguered City*—as well as
some very poor novels. But Mrs. Oliphant's persistence sometimes
influenced them to reverse a decision. In 1881 she began working
on *The Ladies Lindores* and wrote to William Blackwood on
March 3 to offer it for serial publication in *Maga*. After waiting
three weeks for a reply, she wrote: "I think on the whole I had
better not trouble you with my story. I have taken your silence as
evidence that you did not want it." But on May 4 she tried again:

> At the risk of being importunate and although I had settled
> upon another destination for the book I wrote to you about,
> I cannot refrain from mentioning it to you again . . . This one
> I feel more and more to be better suited to the Magazine than
> to any other medium of publication. I wish if you are coming to
> .town that you would let me read two or three numbers to you
> as I am aware my hand is getting more and more cramped. . . . I
> really don't want to offer it to you yet cannot help doing it—
> so there is quite a metaphysical mystery involved! which ought
> to promise a good result.

Her salesmanship paid off in this instance. Blackwood took the
novel for £800, with the understanding that if the sales reached
1,250 she should receive an additional £200, "making it up to
the usual thousand."[10]

She was less fortunate, however, with the novel *Joyce* in 1887.
William Blackwood accepted it for *Maga*, but as the numbers
appeared, he became increasingly critical of the story. It lacked
action and moved too slowly. "I am sorry that some of your
readers do not like Joyce," Mrs. Oliphant wrote him on October
11. "My own impression was that a little local society of this kind
which was so successful (more successful than anything else I
have ever done in this way) in The Perpetual Curate would enrich
the story. But rapid sensation, you are aware, is out of my power.
The tragic portion of the tale is now begun." On November 3,
sending two more numbers, she wrote: "You have made me so

exceedingly nervous about it that I lose myself in cutting and carv-
ing and attempting to improve, and your last suggestion about
winding up in ten or eleven numbers takes me quite by surprise."
No amount of revision could redeem *Joyce* for Blackwood, and he
refused to publish the novel in book form. (Macmillan published
it in 1888.) To this Mrs. Oliphant replied bitterly:

> Your letter is very discouraging and I will not deny that it is a
> great disappointment to me. Of course I cannot at the end of a
> long life change my plans—nay, the entire nature of my mind
> and work, however much I might wish to do so,—and if the
> public no longer cares for that I have nothing for it but to sub-
> mit. It seems a little hard, but I suppose it cannot be helped. And
> I don't want certainly to make any change or hawk it about on
> the chance of getting a little more. . . . It is so difficult to change
> one's way of living, and I have been so sanguine of things mend-
> ing that I find myself in a very difficult position now, and of
> course the failure of public appreciation, or at least of the
> libraries, is at my age and in my circumstances very serious.[11]

Mrs. Oliphant became accustomed to rebuffs of this kind from
Blackwood's. On October 8, 1888 she offered them for *Maga* her
novel *Kirsteen* which she had already arranged to have published
in book form by Macmillan. "I am not given to falling in love
with my books, you know," she wrote Blackwood, "but I suddenly
find myself amused by it and begin to grudge that it should not
have the advantage of the Magazine—which it seems to me would
be a mutual advantage." She asked £400 for it. Within three days
she had her reply—"I quite expected what your answer would be
about the novel, but it does not matter."[12] *Kirsteen,* incidentally,
received favorable notices and proved to be, financially if not
artistically, one of her more successful books.

Throughout her life, her earnings were precarious. More than
anything she longed for the security of a fixed income, and for
more than three decades she besieged her publishers for steady
regular work and income. As early as 1867 when she was negotiat-
ing the sale of *Brownlows,* she wrote John Blackwood: "I don't
know that our system of leaving a settlement to the last is a good
one, especially to a person of my desultory turn of mind—for it
leaves everything vague, and one has no certainty what one has

to depend upon—and in small concerns like mine, which is little to you, makes all the difference between comfort and embarrassment." In the same letter she urged him to make a definite offer for her proposed "Sketches of the Reign of George II": "I don't think I am generally a troublesome person to deal with—but perhaps you may find it difficult to realize the difference between working steadily on a settled plan and doing bits of works precariously without knowing what one may calculate upon."[13]

She sounds the note again in 1880, writing to William Blackwood that Macmillan is paying her £1,000 to write a book on the literature of the nineteenth century (*A Literary History of England in the End of the Eighteenth and Beginning of the Nineteenth Century,* published in three volumes in 1882)—"something like a year's income to me." She continues: "I am very anxious as the years go on to get regular work which I can arrange beforehand and which will bring in regular payment. Though I have always done very well, yet there is an element of precariousness in literary work which is at once against economy and against comfort, and I am very much bent on some occupation of a continuous character, editorship or otherwise."[14] And in 1894, after making an urgent appeal for an advance on future work, she wrote: "I wish very much I could make myself practically useful about manuscript reading or any other actual business work, such as a great establishment like yours must require. I wonder if you could advise me as to the possibility of getting something of the kind to do, as a sort of permanent thread of income, if you have not any opening of the kind yourself. . . . I cannot but think that my long experience might be of use, to relieve me from constant and I fear now and then overproduction."[15] Blackwood's never offered her an official position. She did, however, serve from time to time as a free lance editor and reader for the firm. As early as 1863 she was rewriting articles for *Maga,* and as late as 1896 she was reading and reporting on manuscripts, but this activity provided no regular income.

One enduring problem Mrs. Oliphant had with her publishers was the matter of conflict of publication. Her industry, this "equivocal virtue" as she called it, the flaw of her whole writing career, was not only "little satisfactory in art" but was also seriously damaging financially. On many occasions she was her own competitor. Her principal publishers—Blackwood, Macmillan, Hurst and Blackett—were cooperative in their own interests as well as hers, holding back on publication and rescheduling whenever necessary. But she published through so many outlets—newspapers, magazines, American editions, foreign editions like Tauchnitz, cheap reprints of all kinds—that conflicts were inevitable. Not surprisingly, reviewers, and probably the reading public, viewed the situation with suspicion and dismay. In 1856 Blackwood's ran into the problem for the first time with her novel *Zaidee* which they had published serially in *Maga* in 1854–55. They issued it in book form in 1856 as, almost simultaneously, Hurst and Blackett published *Lilliesleaf,* a sequel to *Margaret Maitland.* Mrs. Oliphant hastened to apologize to the Blackwoods:

> I am very sorry to hear of the want of success of Zaidee, partly of course on my own account, but still more on yours, for I am disturbed to think you should have lost by your liberality to me. It never occurred to me till after the publication that Lilliesleaf and Zaidee could affect each other. I generally, indeed I think always till this occasion, find my manuscript kept by the Great Marlboro St. people at least six months after it is in their hands. This time they brought it out at once—and I suppose my illness and preoccupation had diverted my thoughts from these matters. At least I did not apprehend any unfavourable result. Another time I shall know better.[16]

Mrs. Oliphant could never afford to "know better," and her publishers could only bear patiently with her. Out of loyalty to Blackwood she usually sought their permission before selling her material to less eminent outlets, and this permission was usually granted. The Blackwoods, she once wrote confidentially to Mrs. Tulloch, "are my great dependence" and she valued her connection with the firm too highly to jeopardize it by publishing without their consent. In 1861 she wrote them with some embarrassment: "I have got into a scrape with Mrs. [Samuel Carter] Hall, that most persevering of *littérateurs.* I gave her a morsel of a story on condition that it should be anonymous: and now she makes the most touching appeal to me as a personal favour for my name. I fear you will think a person whose name has to do penance in Mrs.

Hall's Magazine is most unworthy of the honour of appearing in Maga—but it is only for once and I cannot help it."[17]

In 1865 she cleared with Blackwood before accepting an offer from *Good Words*. Her publisher's only stipulation was that the work not be advertised as by "the author of the Chronicles of Carlingford" which they had published. To this Mrs. Oliphant readily agreed: "I would never for an instant dream of giving a story by the author of the Carlingford Series to any periodical whatever on any terms, unless indeed you were first to throw me overboard. I have decided to tell the 'Good Words' people that they may have a novel by Mrs. Oliphant or the author of 'Margaret Maitland' if they wish it. The other I should never have thought of under any circumstances." Many years later, in 1897, she again sought Blackwood's permission before accepting an offer to write an article on the Queen's Diamond Jubilee for *Good Words*. She was already engaged in doing one on the same subject for *Maga* (" 'Tis Sixty Years Since," May 1897). "I am in no way inclined towards the work, but I should like to have your opinion on the subject. If you wish me to write a signed article on the Queen's Reign, of course I should refuse Dr. Macleod at once: if, on the other hand, you like the 'Looker-on' form (which I do myself), I might consider what he proposes."[18] Blackwood evidently gave his permission. The *Maga* article appeared without a signature, and an article called "The Queen," signed "Mrs. Oliphant," appeared in *Good Words* at the same time.

She felt considerably more embarrassment about allowing her stories to be serialized in newspapers. In 1870 she had an offer from *The Star,* a Glasgow paper, for a story to be published in daily installments:

> I suppose it is a thing which never has been done on this side of the Channel and I am quite at a loss what answer to make. Of course money is always a temptation, and the world in general is not likely to be much the worse for anything (in the way of literary publication) that occurs in Glasgow. Will you kindly advise me whether you think it is a thing I could do without derogation. Money is much but there are other things that are of more value. Had it been in London I should probably never have given it a thought, but in Glasgow it is different.[19]

Mrs. Oliphant was right to have had some qualms about publishing in *The Star;* she did not receive payment and was obliged to take the matter to law. "I have never got my Glasgow business settled yet," she wrote to Blackwood in August 1871. "Sheriff Ball gave a decision in my favour (it being submitted to him for arbitration) which I think I must bring down to show you, as it is rather amusing—but I have not received a penny as yet."[20] Her dealings with another newspaper, *The Graphic,* were also unfortunate. In 1872 she wrote apologetically to Blackwood: "I have made a bargain with the Graphic newspaper to publish a story in their paper, an odd proceeding rather—but in no way derogatory I hope. Anthony Trollope, they tell me, is to do the same after mine is finished. This is why I am so busy at present as I thought it best to write a story especially for them. Their pay is satisfactory."[21] The story she sold them was *Innocent,* published in book form in 1873 by Sampson Low. But in 1880 she got into serious difficulties with *The Graphic* over a "Life of the Queen" which she had written exclusively for them. "I was horrified the other day," she wrote Blackwood, "to see it advertised in book form by Messrs Low. I immediately remonstrated, but was met by a copy of my receipt, in which I had, it appears, given the 'entire copyright' to the 'Graphic.' I suppose I had never read the receipt at all when I signed it, and certainly no idea of republication had ever been suggested." Mrs. Oliphant appealed to Blackwood and again sought legal advice, but in the end it proved costly for her. "I hoped the solicitor, who is a very moderate and sober person, and was greatly against proceeding to extremities, would have managed a compromise. This is still possible, but only by a sacrifice on my part—buying back the copyright, which I never had the slightest intention of selling." The matter was finally settled by buying the copyright from Sampson Low for £30—"a shabby proceeding to take money from me."[22]

Careful as Mrs. Oliphant was to avoid offending Blackwood's by appearing too often in rival publications, she nevertheless embarrassed and inconvenienced them on several occasions by conflicts of schedule. In 1871 Blackwood accepted a two-part story, "The Two Mrs. Scudamores," for *Maga.* This same story she had offered to *Scribner's Magazine* in America, but they had decided to publish instead her novel *At His Gates.* Therefore she thought she was in the clear with the story. To her surprise she then learned that *Scribner's* had liked "The Two Mrs. Scudamores" so much that they had decided to publish it as well, although the first installment of the novel would appear in the same issue which contained the last part of the story. "I don't suppose," she wrote Blackwood, "that anybody in Great Britain except myself gets Scribner's Monthly Magazine, but still you must judge whether under the circumstances Maga will condescend to share with the Yankee."[23] *Maga* did "share with the Yankee," publishing her story in December 1871 and January 1872.

In 1883 three publishers were involved in a conflict over scheduling her work. Hurst and Blackett published *It Was a Lover and His Lass;* Blackwood published the three-volume *The Ladies Lindores;* and Macmillan published three of her books: *Sheridan* (in the English Men of Letters Series), her introduction to an edition of *Cowper the Poet,* and a three-volume novel, *Hester.* In addition, Macmillan had another two-volume novel (probably *Sir Tom,* published in 1884) in the press. There were hasty conferences between Mrs. Oliphant and George Lillie Craik of Macmillan and an urgent letter to Blackwood: "He [Craik] says that if you are bringing out the 'Ladies' in the ordinary three-volume form, that he does not think the one would affect the other at all. If however you do think so I fancy I can induce him to postpone his publication." Mrs. Oliphant did manage to persuade Craik to postpone the novel—"which, I daresay, will embarrass me further on, but at present leaves the coast clear."[24]

With such a maze of publishing complications and such extraordinary prolificness on Mrs. Oliphant's part, it is not surprising that from time to time a literary work was forgotten or even lost in the shuffle. On one occasion the fault was Mrs. Oliphant's. In 1875 she wrote in embarrassment to Blackwood: "I am obliged to ask you a very disagreeable thing to do, to send me back the paper on Dante, which I sent to you a couple of months ago. I had half forgotten that I had promised it elsewhere, in my desire to send what I thought was well done to you—but it has been claimed, and I cannot delay sending it. Would you be so very good as to return it to me at once?"[25] Another time the fault was apparently Blackwood's. In October 1879 John Blackwood died.

Some time before his death Mrs. Oliphant had sent him the manuscript of a two-volume novel, *Diana Trelawney*. The book had been offered as security for an advance of £400. On Christmas eve 1879 she wrote to his nephew William: "When I spoke to him last on the subject he seemed to have forgotten all about it. I should of course be very glad to have it appear in the Magazine when you have a vacancy."[26] Nothing more was heard of *Diana Trelawney* until 1892 when at last it appeared serially in *Maga* and Blackwood's published it with, ironically, the subtitle: "The Story of a Great Mistake." The circumstances of *Diana's* mysterious fifteen-year disappearance were explained by Mrs. Oliphant in the very revealing preface to another novel, *The Heir Presumptive and the Heir Apparent,* published by Macmillan in 1892—a year which also saw publication of two other three-volume novels, *The Cuckoo in the Nest,* published by Hutchinson, and *The Marriage of Elinor,* published by Macmillan, as well as her two-volume *The Victorian Age of English Literature,* published by Rivington. Such an appalling output in a single year demanded explanation and, indeed, apology. Mrs. Oliphant offered these:

> The conditions of literary work, especially in fiction, have so much altered since the time when a book came solidly before the world in one issue, that I think it right to say a word in explanation of the rapidity with which one work of mine has recently, within a few months, followed another. The fact is, that a writer of fiction is now so much drawn into the easy way of serial publication that he, or she, not unfrequently loses command of the times and seasons once so carefully studied. We have not yet come to the *feuilleton* of French newspapers, but there are said to be indications that this is on its way; and in the meantime the mode of publication in magazines, and country newspapers under the enterprising syndicate of Messrs. Tillotson, which are sometimes delayed and sometimes hurried according to the need of the periodicals rather than the calculations of the writer, brings together sometimes a small crowd of books by the same hand which have all run their little course, and ended at about the same time. These bring with them new complications with respect to American copyright, which must be claimed at once or not at all, one after another, so that the writer of fiction when such a combination occurs has little choice, and must bring out his books much more quickly, one after another, than he has any desire to do. And some are necessarily delayed by the stream which hurries on the others. The present work was written some years ago, be-

fore the days of American copyright (such as it is). And it has
happened that another recent publication of mine, "Diana Trelawney," published by Messrs. Blackwood went astray and lost itself
for many years in the dark recesses of the editor's cabinet, where
it came to light suddenly after the seclusion of half a lifetime,
its author herself having almost forgotten its existence. What the
little manuscript might be doing all that time among other drifts
of literature, who can say? But it had to come before the public
when it reappeared. Thus it is that, without intention, and without any helter-skelter of composition, it sometimes happens that
one work hurries on the heels of another, without any power on
the part of the writer to stay them in their career.

It is difficult, if not impossible, to separate Mrs. Oliphant's
business relations from her personal ones with Blackwood's. Because of her friendship with the family, her business letters are
personal letters too. They offer not only biographical information
but invaluable insights into her personality and temperament. The
public impression of Mrs. Oliphant was of a woman of utmost
reserve and reticence. She shunned publicity, deplored the practice of giving interviews to the press, and under the severest pressures maintained an outward pose of dignified self-possession. But
in her novels, as we have already noted, she aired her most intimate family problems. Very likely she assumed that the reading
public, ignorant of the details of her private life, would not recognize these parallels, and that her family and friends were well
enough aware of these secrets already. There is no reticence in the
Blackwood letters. Her pride, which was so easily and so often
wounded, her self-pity, her anger, her bitterness, her generosity,
and her warm affection are all freely displayed. The forty-five
years' association with the firm was marked on the whole by good
will on both sides. Nevertheless, there were moments of irritation
and often more serious clashes between author and publisher. In
the long run these were amply balanced—by Mrs. Oliphant's
loyalty to the firm, her willingness to work prodigiously hard for
them, and her basic respect for the Blackwoods personally. The
final reckoning is perhaps summed up in William Blackwood's
dedication of *Annals of a Publishing House:* "To the memory of
an old and valued friend, Mrs. Oliphant." However, the course of
a lifetime of association was not always smooth.

Even early in the relationship, in the 1850's, there had been some friction when Mrs. Oliphant and her husband tried to persuade the Blackwoods to allow him to illustrate *Katie Stewart*.[27] And there is a curious postscript in one of her letters to John Blackwood in 1856, "Don't be so very hard upon my unfortunate big boy," which suggests that Francis Oliphant's demands on the firm were irritating at the least.[28] There were misunderstandings over finances wounding feelings on both sides. In 1857 she wrote John Blackwood:

> I have been a good deal surprised by your letter which I have just received and don't quite understand it. You have been giving me, I think, for some time past, twenty pounds a sheet for my miscellaneous papers. This of course is your own estimate of what my services are worth to yourself—and if you find reason to change that I trust you will do me the justice to inform me of it. I asked you to give me a further advance when I should have placed in your hands the short paper I was thinking of on the House of Commons—expecting when I wrote that you would make use of the American paper for this month's number. I am surprised to find that my late articles have been so far short of the ordinary length. Still the American paper and the one I sent you yesterday will increase the thirty-seven pages you mention up to about sixty—(that is of course if you are inclined to use them), which after a close calculation will leave me just eight pages in your debt. This is not a very heavy arrear. If however you do not care for having these articles or have any reason to change your opinion of their value, that is a totally different matter—and one on which I can say nothing. I know what my work is to myself, but I do not pretend to judge what is its value to the Magazine.

Mrs. Oliphant's tone apparently offended the publisher. In her next letter she wrote: "I cannot conceive how it is possible that anyone could interpret my letter into complaint of my remuneration or of you [sic] taking advantage of me." She also antagonized, or feared that she had antagonized, his brother, Major William, and wrote apologetically to him:

> I am sorry to thinking [sic]—seeing the address of the paper which was returned to me yesterday to be in your handwriting—that you share in your brother's unaccountable change of senti-

ment and actions towards me. I have received so much personal kindness from yourself that I am grieved you should partake in Mr. John's offence, whatever the ground of *that* may be—and I trust you will understand me when I say that one ungracious act, however unlooked for, cannot efface from my recollection the many kind ones which are past. Temporary disappointment and vexation may express themselves at the moment, but that does not affect my appreciation of the former liberality and courteous treatment which I have received both from yourself and your brother, and still less can it diminish the remembrance I shall always retain of your own and Mrs. Blackwood's late kindness to myself and my children. With kind regards to your family.

Major Blackwood may have been the peace-maker in this dispute. In any event, it was settled about a month later and Mrs. Oliphant wrote again to John Blackwood:

> I have no doubt I expressed a momentary offence to the full as warmly as I felt it, and I did think your calculation unfriendly at the time. However, to set the matter right—as you recur in your last note to the advance I asked for—though I had not intended to mention it again—I do not mind returning to where we were before this misunderstanding, to repeat that I should be much obliged by your making me an advance of sixty or seventy pounds on account of miscellaneous articles. If you find it suitable to do so now it will be an advantage to me.
> And I am sure you cannot seriously suppose that I have ever imagined myself inadequately paid. So far from this, my recollection of my letters to you makes me sure that I have always been prompt and eager in acknowledgment of your general liberality and kindness.[29]

At times of crisis Blackwood's never failed her. They subsidized her trip to Italy with her dying husband in 1859, paying for articles they did not even use. When Francis Oliphant died they promptly sent her money to cover expenses until her return to England. In every subsequent family emergency Mrs. Oliphant turned to them for help. Once, some years later, the younger William Blackwood offered her money outright as a gift, not a loan, but this she refused: "You must not think me nasty. I am most grateful for your kind consideration, but let me re-indorse your kind present and forgive me for doing so. This is *impossible.* I ask advances and all that sort of thing as you know—but I have never gone further. Pardon me, and don't take any notice."[30]

Such a relationship obviously inspired frankness and confidence. Mrs. Oliphant did not hesitate to confide her financial dealings with other publishers to Blackwood:

> My story in Longmans ["The Lady's Walk"] ends next month. . . . By the way you asked about their pay. They consulted me as to what I got ordinarily, naming in particular the 'Little Pilgrim' and saying that they had intended to offer me £30 for the two numbers of the present little tale. I told them what Messrs. Macmillan had given me, adding that both you and Messrs. Smith-Elder were exceptionally liberal so that I did not quote you. They have sent me £30 accordingly for the first installment of the Lady's Walk which, as it is very short, is exceptionally liberal too. I hope they will be able to go on with these cheap selling prices and dear paying ones, but it seems a bold experiment—however, Good Words pays highly too. There seems likely to be great competition in the way of stories, so that we poor raconteurs should make hay while the sun shines.[31]

There was often a note of friendly, relaxed gaiety and teasing between them. In 1863, while *The Perpetual Curate* was running serially in *Maga,* John Blackwood held back a chapter because he had some questions about the plot. "I accept my drubbing with humility," she wrote, "oh virtuously-indignant editor—but all the same you are wrong. You were once saucy enough to say that a woman never did confess herself in the wrong, and I don't mean to depart from the habitudes of my kind. I have not changed my plot, but only advanced a step more rapidly than I had intended. . . . After having this explanation I trust you will tender an 'umble apology and confess yourself (as I suppose men always do) to be for once wrong."[32] In 1867 Mrs. Oliphant wrote from Paris, where she had been assigned to cover the Exhibition for *Maga:*

> I can't do it. I have been labouring on it at every spare moment for some time back, and only getting deeper and deeper into the mud. I am very sorry if it will disappoint you, but the fact is, I detest Exhibitions. Even the pictures are not striking, and, how, I appeal to your feelings, can one write about cotton or flannel, or manures, as 'Galignani' does today? I don't have headaches in a general way, but I have had half a dozen literary ones over

this wretched place. . . . I confess I envy you men your power of swearing at such prodigious humbug. . . . It would be a kind of satisfaction to my mind in my present state of feeling to go down to the Champs de Mars and break a lot of windows, but I fear that is a gratification impossible to anything but a boy.[33]

Finally, there is the cryptic note to John Blackwood in 1868 that can only make one further regret the one-sidedness of the correspondence: "I have been working hard at the proof and I hope have improved it, though as for your kissing——! I am much shocked by the suggestion and have closed the door upon it as you will perceive."[34]

With William Blackwood, John's nephew, who succeeded him in the editorship, Mrs. Oliphant sometimes took a more high-handed tone. By the time he assumed office in 1879 she was a senior contributor with more than a quarter of a century of experience with the firm. He was only about eight years younger than she, but many years younger, she must have felt, in terms of editorial and publishing experience. She never hesitated to express herself, sometimes very sharply. For example, in the July 1880 issue of *Maga* there was an article by Mrs. Oliphant, "School and College," a discussion of Eton and Oxford. When the article appeared, she discovered that he had cut out a passage in which she had argued against introducing tramways to Oxford. She immediately wrote an angry letter:

> May I say one word as an old contributor to a young editor? I think that a great part of your excellent uncle's unique position among editors was his very sparing use of this editorial privilege. I never like to do anything for the Edinburgh Review because Mr. Reeve interferes with the proof. . . . I don't think I am touchy, and I rejoice to see that the Magazine is keeping up admirably—but my long experience is worth something and I feel sure you will lose more than you can possibly gain by breaking the sequence of an article at the last moment where there is no appeal against your decision.[35]

When she did not like an issue or an editorial policy, she spoke candidly. In 1884 she wrote: "I wish you would pause a little before continuing the series of those matter of fact tragedies and libels upon life which you have been having lately—Alexander

Nesbit, etc. In the first place they are quite untrue. In the second, that sort of railing at humanity wants a very light touch and your contributor has a heavy one. Pessimism is always odious I think, but when it takes a matter of fact form like these it loses what little claim it has to be listened to."[36] In March 1885 she wrote at length reviewing every major article in that issue with such remarks as this: "Where have you disinterred that old rhymster Charles Mackay? Beware of him. I don't think he was ever worth paper and print at his best." A few months later, complaining of the low price Blackwood's had offered her—and she had accepted —for the serialization of *Joyce,* she observed sharply: "I doubt (impartially) whether your rule is wise. I fear you will find that the fiction you get cheaply is not worth very much. I think the 'Waters of Hercules' is a failure for your purposes—and 'Fortune's Wheel' is an old fashioned order of work which wants a most robust faculty of fun or strong adventure to carry it off. I hope it may turn out to have these qualities. I think if I were in your place I should go in for one number stories as strong and striking as possible. This is easier said than done, it is true."[37] And in March 1891: "I think the last number is a little feeble altogether, and one wants some stronger interest. And I do think it is a dreadful pity to encumber yourself with a number of unknown names."[38]

The thrusts were sometimes more personal. As the years went on and Mrs. Oliphant received less money for her work and as her family sorrows cumulated and were intensified, her tone became increasingly bitter. In 1887 Walter Besant, who had long been fighting for the rights of authors and had four years earlier established his Society of Authors, issued another attack on publishers for not compensating their authors more generously. Instead of springing to Blackwood's defense, as evidently he had expected, she needled him:

> Why should you be proud any more than the rest of us? Beside, you know, you are a little disposed to snub those poor creatures called authors, and when one of them gets elated and asserts himself too loudly, no doubt he has had his humiliations in his time. It is a great pity that nothing can be done without provocations of hot words, for the practical matter would seem to be but a

small one after all. Literature evidently in the majority of cases does not pay as well as it used to do. I confess myself that when I saw Anthony Trollope's table of his earnings in his memoirs, it gave me anything but an agreeable sensation, for his worst book was better paid than my best. In the same way when new beginners hear of the large sum got by their predecessors they are bewildered and wonder how it is. Mr. [James] Payn, you know, speaks in the same large way of what he gets. I can't for my part understand why he should get two or three times as much as I do —but I suppose simply it is because the public likes him better. Other people, however, with less experience than I have wonder and think that somehow it must be their publisher's fault. And as a matter of fact while writers barely manage to live, almost all publishing firms thrive exceedingly. There are of course many good reasons for this, but still you can scarcely wonder that the original producer chafes at it.[39]

Even in the days of John Blackwood's editorship, as we have seen, there had been occasional flashes of temperament. One dispute beginning in 1874 smouldered for almost a decade. Blackwood's had been publishing a series of small volumes called "Ancient Classics for English Readers," and Mrs. Oliphant had proposed to the firm a similar series on continental literature. In August 1874 W. Lucas Collins, who edited the Classics series, visited her to ask if she would contribute a volume to a new series on continental authors. Mrs. Oliphant wrote indignantly to John Blackwood:

I forget whether it is two or three years since being at St. Andrews for the summer . . . I originated the idea of this Continental Series, an idea which you received most cordially predicting that we should both 'make money by it,' a prospect very agreeable to me. Afterwards you cooled, very probably because you thought me wanting in the qualifications of an editor, an objection perfectly reasonable, and in which I could have found nothing to complain of, however much I might have regretted it. We had, however, several conversations on the subject, and I gave you, I think—or at least prepared—a list of subjects. After all these preliminaries I am sure you will allow that I had some reason to feel wounded when Mr. Collins asked me today whether there was any subject I would care to take up in the new series, requesting me to turn it over in my mind as if it had been quite a new idea. Do not you think that it would have been more

civil, not to say more friendly, had you yourself explained to me
—by letter or otherwise, a very easy thing to do—that you considered Mr. Collins best adapted for carrying out such a scheme?
. . . In the present circumstance I cannot but feel deeply hurt,
and I think with very good reason. I have no desire to make any
fuss on the subject, but I think it best to let you know what my
feelings are.[40]

Mrs. Oliphant evidently prevailed. There were no further argu-
ments on the subject, and she was named editor of the series, "Foreign Classics for English Readers." In 1876 she, not Collins, was
offering assignments: "Would it not be graceful at least to ask Mr.
Collins, who did the other series as well, to contribute to this?
Everyone has a pet author whom he would like to produce."[41]
But Foreign Classics, though for a time providing Mrs. Oliphant
with the small but steady income she so desired, did not have
smooth sailing. She clashed with William Blackwood over the
order of publishing of the volumes, writing in 1877:

> I am entirely taken by surprise by the unexpected accusation that
> *I* settled with the Principal [Tulloch] and that *I* made arbitrary
> arrangements and insisted on Pascal being published third. I have
> done nothing of the sort. I have written to him [John Blackwood]
> to say that I am ready to give up the place of editor altogether if
> he likes—and I confess I should be disposed to do so at once
> without any condition in the matter but that the withdrawal of
> my name would look like a quarrel and give the adversary occa-
> sion to blaspheme.[42]

There were further troubles involving the recruiting of authors
and the publicity for the series. Some authors were old Blackwood
regulars and friends—General Hamley did *Voltaire,* W. Lucas
Collins *Montaigne* and *La Fontaine,* his son Clifton Collins did
Saint-Simon, Mrs. Oliphant herself did *Dante, Molière* (with the
assistance of Francis Tarver), and *Cervantes.* Others were her
personal choices—Principal Tulloch for *Pascal,* Anne Thackeray
for *Madame de Sévigné,*[43] and Cyril Oliphant for *De Musset.* The
younger authors received £60 each. The more established contributors, the "swells" as Mrs. Oliphant called them, got £100.
Mrs. Oliphant, a "swell," received that sum for each of her volumes, plus £25 for editing each volume.[44]

The most serious vexations Mrs. Oliphant and her publisher had were with two contributors—Walter Besant, who did *Rabelais,* and Henry Trollope, Anthony's son, who did a single-volume *Racine and Corneille.* Of Besant, Mrs. Oliphant complained that he ignored her editorial comments, included references to too many extraneous matters, and did not concentrate sufficiently on Rabelais the man. She consoled herself and Blackwood, however, with the thought that Besant's book would be well received by the press.[45] She refused to find any consolation in Trollope or his work. In 1877 she wrote John Blackwood:

> I have just seen and had a long talk with, and, rather against my will, entrusted a volume on Racine and Corneille to Mr. Henry Trollope. He has an extremely *queer* look, and is anything but prepossessing and heaven forbid that he should have Molière! So far as I could make out he knows about the history of the French stage but nothing else. What a very odd creature to follow upon two generations of literature! I hope he may do the work decently, but the sight of him called from me a pious ejaculation. I thank heavens our boys are not like that![46]

There is no doubt that Mrs. Oliphant harbored a strong prejudice against the young man. When he finally submitted his manuscript, after sixteen months, in the summer of 1879, she rejected it, objecting among other things to his insufficient admiration of his subject and his failure to provide poetical translations. His father intervened with William Blackwood:

> I hope that Mrs. Oliphant and Harry will hit off their difficulty. I cannot but think that she has in some respect over-acted her part as editor, having assumed an imperiousness which would have been very foreign to Collins or to your uncle. . . . She then requires poetical translations of extracts, not at all knowing how often the attempts have failed always. She kindly offers to do it herself;—but look at the attempts in the Molière! Relieved from the superintendence of such an older critic as your uncle, she is I think a little without a guide.[47]

Henry also appealed over her head directly to Blackwood, unwilling, he wrote, "to abide by Mrs. Oliphant's condemnation without remonstrance," and he offered to submit the manuscript to a third party for a judgment. "If she wanted undiluted praise she should have said so; and I should have declined the task."[48] Blackwood defended his editor, and Mrs. Oliphant wrote to him approvingly:

> Your letter to Mr. Trollope is excellent and most judicious. I did not reject his book but said that he must either make or permit me to make great modifications before I could send it to the printer. He sent me a somewhat insolent letter, to which I have replied saying that he had misunderstood me, pointing out that in a work of this kind it is absolutely necessary to have quotations (of which he has given none) and offering to alter it myself so as to adapt it to the others without interfering either with his credit or remuneration as the author. What could mortal say more? I am sorry for his disappointment but the production is deplorable. I shall have to rewrite it altogether if he accepts my proposal.

Mrs. Oliphant revised the manuscript freely: "I have been at work on Mr. Trollope's Racine all day. I daresay the critics will be merciful to his father's son which is the best we can hope for."[49]

In the last decade of her life Mrs. Oliphant clashed more frequently and more bitterly with William Blackwood. One source of conflict was over her much esteemed friend Principal Tulloch. After his death in February 1886, Mrs. Oliphant wrote an obituary for the March issue of *Maga* and a longer memorial article for April. Almost at once Blackwood commissioned her to write a full biography. She approached the assignment with some reluctance, knowing that it would not be financially rewarding. She asked Blackwood to pay her £250 for the initial publication of which she planned to contribute £100 to a fund established in the Principal's memory. The final price agreed on was £200, and Mrs. Oliphant reduced her contribution to £50: "Your estimate of the cost and profit of the proposed life of the Principal is not very encouraging. It is not a thing which I should look upon in the mere point of view of profit—but still, as there seem many doubts about it, this is a matter which has to be taken into consideration, and I can scarcely afford to give my time and labour without compensation."[50] She began work in September 1886, receiving a number of the Principal's letters from Mrs. Tulloch. From these she drew much of her material. She did not expect to finish the book until the following spring: "I don't think this will be at all too late," she wrote her publisher; "indeed I shall have to bear the impertinence of the critics, no doubt, as to hurrying into print evidently before the grave is green. However, I have borne so much at their hands that I shall no doubt be able to bear that too."[51] The manuscript was not actually ready until June 1888: "It has taken me a much longer time and more labour than I had calculated upon. Indeed I have spent more of both upon it than I did on the life of Montalembert for which your uncle gave me £500, but I fear that was not a remunerative transaction on his side." When the book was finally published, sales were even poorer than anticipated. Deeply disappointed, Mrs. Oliphant wrote her publisher: "The question was whether it is very good at all spending so much labour and time in writing for so small a recompense. . . . I do not really think it is worth my while to go on to a second edition at all. The public had better just do without what it neither pays me to write nor you to publish. I don't feel at all generous towards the reader, nor see any reason why we should go on supplying editions."[52] Blackwood nevertheless went on, late in 1889, to publish a second edition, much to Mrs. Oliphant's indignation:

> I do not think you had any right to publish the edition in the face of my refusal, whether it was reasonable or not. It is a point of law, and not a matter of opinion. If it is as you say—I wonder what rights remain to the author at all? except to make him or herself disagreeable, which is the resource of the impotent. . . . And I cannot see how the proposal to suppress a book which pays neither you nor me should be unfair. What is it unfair? I am poor, but fifty pounds is not worth the sacrifice of one's *amour-propre,* and to you who are not poor the twenty-five pounds which you estimate as your share is certainly not worth the fuss which we have mutually made. . . . I have always said that you treat authors, who after all are the origin of all books, and without them publishing could not be very much—*de haut en bas*—too much, I think, and I have not hesitated to say this before. Your uncle entertained a good-natured contempt for us.[53]

It is unfortunate that the Principal's biography, a work which should have been a labor of love, produced such bitterness between author and publisher. When Blackwood suggested a third edition in 1891, she turned upon him furiously:

I must express my opinion that your conduct has been of the most arbitrary and imperious character. I had come to see that to suppress the second edition might be a little absurd, but that did not give you the slightest right to dispose of the book at your pleasure, and in face of my distinct prohibition. Such a right so far as I am aware was never claimed by any publisher before. It is difficult not to believe that your knowledge of my want of money to vindicate my rights has much to do with your most high-handed action. Certainly had I been richer and more independent I should not have acquiesced in it for a moment. . . . I don't care in the least, I must tell you, whether it sells or not— and am most deeply wounded and offended by the whole matter. As for the claims of the family to be considered, they are nil. The family may owe me something. Certainly I owe nothing to them. . . . I should be much obliged if you would kindly refrain from any further mention of the Principal's life. I am too much disgusted and humiliated to wish to hear of the book again. Of course when I say that I do not mean to abrogate my rights in respect to a third edition, of which I will not relinquish the full and absolute control.[54]

All this is very different from the confident, trusting tone characterizing most of the letters. One must remember, however, that at the time Mrs. Oliphant was making these accusations she was deeply disturbed by family problems, especially the health of her sons. She flared into anger quickly, but she calmed down quickly too. In the *Autobiography* she described her mother as having been "quick in temper," possessing "in perfection that dangerous facility of sarcasm and stinging speech which Sir Walter attributes to Queen Mary." With the years, as the letters demonstrate, she grew to resemble her mother even more strongly in this particular. She respected and admired William Blackwood, but she could not control her temper. She criticized, she carped, she nagged. Even the printer who ignored her directions for setting quoted matter in smaller type felt her wrath: "If the printer thinks he knows so much better than the author, he had better write the book in future. Nothing could be more unsatisfactory than the manipulation of the copy altogether, and the impertinence of it really should be punished by making the meddlar pay for the extra expense to which he must put you."[55]

When in 1891 Blackwood suggested that the new edition of the

Laurence Oliphant biography be issued in two volumes, the second to contain the letters, she snapped: "I think you are mistaken in making out books to a length scarcely justified by usual precedent. For instance your printing my little story 'Sons and Daughters' in a volume, and calling it a novel. My calculation is that three of such stories would fitly make up such a volume, and nothing has been published with my will as an individual publication of such a size (excepting of course the paper-covered shilling publication)." She raised a similar complaint about the firm's ethics in a letter to Archie Smith regarding an announced sixth edition of *Laurence Oliphant:* "I am greatly grieved that your cousin should have been induced to put forth these sham editions. I thought it was quite contrary to the usage of the Blackwood house to do such a thing, and I feel very much ashamed, as if I were a party to such a proceeding. Please be so good as to beg your cousin from me to stop short now and not add any more to these fictitious editions."[56]

The most serious quarrel that Mrs. Oliphant had with her publisher was over the series called "The Old Saloon." This was an omnibus type of article: reviews of books, plays, art exhibitions, the London season, published in *Maga* from 1887 to 1892. Originally it had been conceived as a monthly feature, but after the first year it appeared every two or three months. Mrs. Oliphant first proposed the idea to Blackwood in 1884: "By the way, a notion has been coming and going in my mind of a monthly article on 'Things in General.' Should you be at all disposed for anything of this kind? Short of politics, I should be inclined to take in everything that was going on—theatre, pictures, books, even a taste of gossip when legitimate. What do you think? It might be made very interesting, though whether I can do it or not remains to be seen." Nothing was done about her proposal, and she repeated it in 1886: "I should be glad to undertake this for you, very provisionally, for three or six months, as an experiment. I have a very strong feeling that it would answer." Blackwood was more encouraging now. Mrs. Oliphant began thinking over titles for it. Her first suggestion was "The Saloon at 45," referring to the firm's Edinburgh offices at 45 George Street; the name finally selected was "The Old Saloon."[57]

The articles were unsigned—partly because of the general policy of anonymity and partly because the feature was intended, by Blackwood at least, to be the work of a variety of contributors. Nevertheless, by the time six numbers had appeared—June 1887 —Mrs. Oliphant observed to him: "Much against my will these Old Saloon articles have got associated with my name in the public mind. I was most anxious it should not be so, but it is." Blackwood was evidently displeased by this development. In July he expressed his annoyance to her and received this stinging reply:

> I am extremely surprised by the letter I have just received from you. No man in the world has the right to accuse me of falsehood or bad faith—and I have repeatedly said that it was to my extreme regret that I had found the Old Saloon papers had been associated by various people with my name. In these circumstances your words, "It is annoying your having proclaimed yourself as the writer of the Old Saloon papers," is simply giving me the lie, and doing so in the most offensive way.

Blackwood withdrew his charge and soothed her feelings. A few days later she wrote a friendly and somewhat apologetic note: "Of course no offense can possibly exist after what you have said. I felt it sharply at the moment, being oppressed and irritable with a wretched cold and worried in many ways."[58] But the source of the irritation was still present. Mrs. Oliphant looked upon "The Old Saloon" as her property. She had agreed to share responsibilities in it—primarily with Alexander Allardyce, an editor with the firm—but she was jealous of her rights. In 1889 she complained to Blackwood:

> I scarcely think that the *ragout* of several different kinds of material is successful generally or carries out the intention of the Old Saloon which when first begun I meant to have a little of the character of a running commentary on literary affairs as well as a succession of reviews. In carrying out this idea I have always tried to make my papers light, and they do not always go in well with steady serious review articles such as those of last month and this month. . . . Altogether I think the Old Saloon loses its meaning when it becomes so completely a mixture by different hands. It wants individuality and unity, and the more important contributions would come better by themselves.[59]

The articles continued but appeared less frequently until 1892 when the quarrel over "The Old Saloon" reached an angry climax. For some time Blackwood had been chafing about what he considered Mrs. Oliphant's high-handed treatment of some of the books she reviewed and her habit of puffing favorite authors, especially her personal friends. In 1892, just before the explosion, he complained to her about her inclusion in the article of a highly favorable review of *Grania,* a novel by Emily Lawless, daughter of her old friend Lady Cloncurry. She replied: "I am sorry you think I say what I do about Miss Lawless' book because she is my friend. I have passed over several books of hers without notice because I did not care for them, but this I think very highly of, and I think you are the only person I have heard or seen to express disappointment in it—but that is of course a matter of taste, in respect to which there is nothing to be said." Blackwood had anticipated trouble. When he received this reply, he noted with relief at the head of the letter: "This is milder than I expected from what I had written, and I do not mind her kick at me about Miss Lawless as she had no write [sic] to include the book without telling me." But Mrs. Oliphant did not take her editor's hint. On October 28 she gave him proof positive of his charge of puffing. Writing of plans for the next "Old Saloon," she commented: "Of course for my little friend George Nugent Bankes, as well as for my other friends whom you mention, Dr. Boyd and Mrs. Ritchie, I should be delighted to say everything that is good. Geraldine Jewsbury was a great friend of mine too. I am afraid she might lead me back to the great Carlyle controversy in which, you know, my views are very distinct and strong."[60] This provoked Blackwood to an open declaration of war. His letter, fortunately, is preserved:

> So far from taking my view of the matter, you have of late confined 'The Old Saloon' to the notice of a very few of the biggest heads of game at whom you wished to poke your fun—very good fun it always is—so that readers turn towards it simply to find out what 'The Old Saloon' has got to say about Kipling or Louis Stevenson, Blackmore, Hardy, Rider Haggard or A. Lang. If you do notice a minor book, it is generally to serve some of your own friends, as you very frankly admit in your letter of the 28th. This is in no sense what I ever intended the 'Old Saloon' for, or wish

it to be. My desire is to have the 'Saloon' as much a comprehensive and representative review of the current literature of the time as its limits will admit of, and that young writers should, in accordance with the traditional practice of the Magazine, be noticed and encouraged on their first appearance, as well as pretenders of older standing exposed. . . . I do not say anything about the systematic neglect of my own books in the 'Saloon'—for I would never have it used as a means of puffing them—but it does seem to me that now-a-days I never publish a book fortunate enough to deserve your favourable notice.[61]

Mrs. Oliphant's defense was so lengthy that it required two letters. On November 9 she wrote:

I was so much surprised both by the matter and the tone of your letter received the other day that I did not reply to it at once, not wishing to do so with any angry feeling. In respect to the first, the object of the communication, I should have with great pleasure given up the Old Saloon at any time had you expressed a wish that I should do so without explanation. Indeed I have very nearly done so for a long time. There have been I think only two Old Saloon papers during the course of the year, so that the publishers and the public must be highly sensitive indeed if they have been affected as you say by such rare appearances. And in respect to the tone of your letter you must permit me to say that though I have done much work for the Magazine and received pay for it, yet we do not stand exactly in the relation of Master and servant, and that it has never been one of the rights of an editor to rate a contributor as he might do a shopman. The Saloon in George Street is unquestionably yours—but the Old Saloon as a seat of criticism was not invented or thought of by you, but by me. You did not make and cannot own it, nor is it any necessary part of Maga, any more than Ambrose's Tavern was. As for using it to serve my friends, I presume you mean the review of 'Grania,' which is anything but a minor book and which indeed, since large mention was made in the review of the author's previous work 'Hurrish,' which you published, I do not see could have been omitted with any regard to what was fit and becoming. It is not, however, necessary that I should defend myself. As we have disagreed so often as to literary merit, we must even make up our minds to disagree again. I will be more magnanimous than you and lay claim to no right in the series of papers which I originated. The one for next month is partly done so I will finish it as far as I can and send it. Otherwise I hereby return to you the key, so far as it is mine, of my Old Saloon and retire from the

field. There should perhaps in justice to me be some slight indication that it has changed hands, for if it continues people may continue to lay on my shoulders the responsibility for views which are
not mine. As for the general attribution to me of these papers, I
certainly have not originated it. I suppose it was made inevitable
by the fact that some people know and recognize my style.

On November 17 she concluded her argument:

> You must be quite aware that I never have used the Old Saloon
> as a vehicle for as you say puffing my friends. My letter of 28
> October of which you make such Jesuitical use was merely an
> answer to yours, in which you proposed a certain list of books
> to me, none of which was any suggestion of mine. I said what
> I did by way of hearty assent to your proposal. As a matter of
> fact I have never done anything of the kind. . . .
> Why the assistance of other contributors (which was originally,
> if I am not mistaken, my own proposal) should have dropped off
> I cannot tell. It has certainly not been my doing.[62]

Sharp as this exchange was, it did not permanently damage relations between Blackwood and Mrs. Oliphant. In the last years
of her life a happier association was restored. "The Old Saloon"
was dropped, but in August 1894 Mrs. Oliphant began a new
series, "The Looker-on," which was substantially the same type
of article though exclusively hers. She wrote about two of these a
year; the last one appearing in October 1896.[63] Mrs. Oliphant's
last major contribution to Blackwood's was her history of the
firm, *Annals of a Publishing House: William Blackwood and his
Sons, their Magazine and Friends,* published in 1897, two months
after her death. She wrote the first two volumes, carrying the history through the death of Major William Blackwood in 1861. The
third volume was written by Mrs. (Mary) Gerald Porter, John
Blackwood's daughter. Mrs. Oliphant had undertaken the assignment gladly—partly because it offered a measure of financial
security (she received £500 for the first year of her work),[64]
but largely because work of this nature provided the intellectual
challenge and stimulus which she particularly needed at this time.
Her younger son, Cecco, died at the beginning of October 1894.
A little more than a week after his death she wrote to Blackwood:
"If I live—which I most heartily pray God I may not, but one

knows how vain are one's desires in the face of His decrees—it will be a great relief from other work to undertake your family history: in any case, I will keep the materials safely and in their proper order. I have never been able to thank you for the kind thought that made you suggest this work to me as a kind of prop and support in the midst of my many expenses and cares."[65] The task of sifting, arranging, and reading the cases of company papers which Blackwood had sent was not always so absorbing as she had anticipated. She wrote to Mrs. Coghill in March 1895: "I spend half of my day reading old letters, which I thought would be a good sane piece of half-mechanical work; but I find it very fatiguing, and the letters not so interesting as I hoped."[66] Nevertheless, the work occupied her time profitably. In reviewing the old records she also reviewed her life. "I began my married life," she wrote Blackwood in November 1894, "by my first story in 'Maga' —the proofs of which ('Katie Stewart') I received on my wedding day: I should like to wind up the long laborious records (which seems to me now to have been so vain, so vain, my life all coming to nothing) with this."[67]

Mrs. Oliphant approached the work as very much her own personal right and possession. Blackwood gave her a free hand. It therefore came as a shock in January 1895 to learn that John Blackwood's widow and his daughter, Mary Porter, unaware of the proposed "Annals," were planning to publish a biography of him. Mrs. Blackwood wrote Mrs. Oliphant asking for any letters of her husband's that she might use in the book. Mrs. Oliphant immediately wrote in alarm to William Blackwood:

> What am I to do? Should I tell her that you are contemplating a work of a larger scope into which these letters would naturally come? . . . Such a publication would be very inconvenient to our design, would it not? . . . Don't you think it would perhaps be well to announce the fact of your intention in the Athenaeum? There can be no necessity for concealing it—and indeed if Mrs. Blackwood perseveres in her intention it would perhaps be a good thing to push on at once so as to get our first volume published as soon as possible.

Eventually the trouble that Mrs. Oliphant feared was averted by compromise. Mrs. Blackwood and her daughter agreed to abandon their project with the understanding that Mrs. Porter would write a biography of her father to be incorporated into the "Annals." Mrs. Oliphant had no intention of relinquishing her full authority over the book. She wrote Blackwood: "But if you like I will write to Mary and tell her that I would gladly put in anything she might wish to write, with her name, into my volume. This would be quite right and appropriate, I should think. It is not likely, I should think, that she would write very much, for unaccustomed persons soon get tired of literary composition. I don't know of course whether she is supposed to have any gift that way." She warned Mrs. Porter flatly to keep her contribution within limits:

> I shall be much pleased to have such cooperation from you as is reasonable and feasible in respect to the life of your father which ought to form one considerable volume of my projected work, but you must let me point out what seems to me would be reasonable and feasible. You will at once perceive that for you and me to write such a life in the same lines, you illustrating yours from such letters as you have collected and I doing the same on my side, would be rather an irrational plan in itself and one unlikely to produce a good book.[68]

Throughout these negotiations Mrs. Oliphant kept in close touch with William Blackwood. Though there were minor disagreements on finances and on other writing she was submitting, the work on the firm's history proceeded smoothly. She even had kind words to offer on *Maga,* writing to him on August 25, 1896: "I have several times intended to speak of the very great vigour and fresh start which the Magazine seems to me to have taken during the last year. It has been more full of interesting articles and altogether stronger than for a long time before."[69] The sometimes stormy relationship between Mrs. Oliphant and her publisher ended in peace and harmony. She died before she could finish the *Annals* but not before she had written a major part of it and revised the first volume. On her deathbed she proofread the title page and made the final corrections. In her last letter to William Blackwood she apologized: "I can't tell you how sorry I am not to be able to revise the second volume."[70]

Mrs. Oliphant's relations with her other publishers cannot be as thoroughly documented. Most of the records and letters have been lost. What remains, however, is enough to suggest that they followed a similar though less intimate and revealing pattern. This holds especially true for the Macmillan correspondence. Here again Mrs. Oliphant's association with the firm covered many decades—from 1859 when Macmillan published *Agnes Hopetoun's Schools and Holidays* to the posthumous publication in 1898 of *That Little Cutty; and Two Other Stories* and *A Widow's Tale and Other Stories*. With Macmillan, as with Blackwood, there existed a close personal association. She corresponded chiefly with Alexander Macmillan, whose son George was a schoolmate of Cyril's at Eton, and with George Lillie Craik, who married her old friend Dinah Mulock. With both men she was completely candid about her family and financial problems. Appeals for advances, for advice, for jobs for her brother Frank, her cousin Annie Walker, even for Principal Tulloch's son, for recommendations for Cyril's application for admission to the Inner Temple, for publication and reviews of the work of her friends R. H. Story, George MacDonald—all appear frequently in these letters. And also, as with Blackwood's, there were problems of publication conflict and, particularly in the later years, outbursts of irritation and anger.

The earliest letters are to Alexander Macmillan and deal with her novel *A Son of the Soil,* published serially in *Macmillan's Magazine* and in book form in 1866. She applied for money to finance her trip to Italy in 1863—a decade later he subsidized another Italian journey for *The Makers of Florence.* Her relations with him were cordial. The sharpest note was sounded, not surprisingly, over money, and this was relatively mild. On February 8, 1866 she wrote:

> It has just occurred to me to ask you about the Son of the Soil, whether you are going on the idea that our bargain for it is complete or indeed whether there was any bargain made. Since its beginning I have got dreadfully confused in my memory about business matters, and I really do not recollect what you said about it or what I said about it or if anything distinct was said. I know you gave me £250 over and above the payments on account of the Magazine. But I don't suppose you will think this sufficient for the reprint. I have always been accustomed to go on the perhaps erroneous idea that publishers know best what they could

afford to give,—but when I have gotten people in my track who do otherwise, I begin to think that I ought to act more energetically, for my little boys' sake.

The bulk of the Macmillan correspondence is addressed to George Lillie Craik. His marriage to Dinah Mulock in 1865 brought him even closer to Mrs. Oliphant who had known her since the early 1850's. Mrs. Oliphant's feelings toward Miss Mulock were somewhat ambivalent. They were not warm and intimate friends. For her fiction Mrs. Oliphant had nothing but contempt, and she felt a lively resentment at the fact that Miss Mulock's earnings were always so much higher than her own. In the *Autobiography* she recalled with irony her introduction of Miss Mulock to Henry Blackett—a meeting which resulted in the publication by his firm, Hurst and Blackett, of her phenomenally successful *John Halifax, Gentleman:*

> I had introduced Mr. Blackett by his desire to Miss Muloch [sic] in London,—he, apparently with some business gift or instinct imperceptible to me, having made out that there were elements of special success in her. Probably, however, this instinct was no more than an appreciation in himself of the sentimentalism in which she was so strong. He had at once made an arrangement with her of which 'John Halifax' was the result, the most popular of all her books, and one which raised her at once to a high position, I will not say in literature, but among the novel-writers of one species. She made a spring thus quite over my head with the helping hand of my particular friend, leaving me a little rueful,— I did not at all understand the means nor think very highly of the work, which is a thing that has happened several times, I fear, in my experience. Success as measured by money never came to my share. Miss Muloch in this way attained more with a few books than I with my many. I don't know why. I don't pretend to think that it was because of their superior quality.

On Miss Mulock's marriage to Craik—she was thirty-nine at the time and he twenty-eight—Mrs. Oliphant observed tartly to Alexander Macmillan: "I hope she may be happy in her marriage— though, to tell the truth, I have denied so strenuously to everybody who has spoken of it that such a marriage was possible, that I feel taken in a little." Nevertheless, the Craiks and Mrs. Oliphant remained friends. They took a holiday together in Scotland in

1882, and when the Craiks made their first trip to Italy in 1884, Mrs. Oliphant gave them letters of introduction to friends there and got one for them from William Blackwood to the American sculptor W. W. Story. She felt close enough to Mrs. Craik to ask her to visit Maggie's grave in Rome: "Only to make a little pilgrimage out to the sacred place where my darling lies by her father's side—that is all. You knew him too. Yes, I remember as if it were yesterday you sitting by my bedside, holding that miracle of Heaven, my firstborn. What dark waters since then one has waded through!"[71]

From Macmillan's as from Blackwood's Mrs. Oliphant constantly sought the security of a steady income. In 1880 she wrote to Craik:

> I wonder if you, who are in the world and hear of everything that is going on, think it at all possible that I could get something to do of a permanent character, which would relieve me a little from the necessity of perpetual writing. I don't mean to say that I am tired of writing or that it exhausts me, or that I don't like it better than any other occupation, for these assertions would not be true. But as I am growing old I have more and more desire for a regular quarter day, a regular occupation, and so much money coming in.[72]

Macmillan had briefly entertained the prospect of publishing a weekly paper or magazine which Mrs. Oliphant might edit. She seized on the idea eagerly. In 1878 she offered a definite and detailed plan to Craik:

> Principal Tulloch has been with me lately, and he and I have been having some conversation on literary subjects. I told him you had once suggested to me a weekly paper as a likely enterprise and he is very anxious to get a medium for keeping (without too much of it) the ordinary public here acquainted with the sad state of Scotch affairs. Thinking it over it has occurred to me that a weekly publication, more like a magazine than a newspaper, would be a likely form for such an undertaking—to be called 'The Three Kingdoms' and to have a portion of its space set apart for Scotch news of the more important kinds, great subjects—Principal Tulloch taking charge of that—and a similar portion for Ireland in the hands of an equally trustworthy authority. 'The Three Kingdoms' would have their spiritual side in Literature, Science, and

History and would embrace reviews, criticisms of all kinds, and biographical essays, with the necessary sweetening in the way of fiction. What do you think of this idea?[73]

Nothing came of this project, but a year later Mrs. Oliphant offered another:

I wonder how it would answer if a (I do not say *the*) projected new paper were got to be somehow under the patronage of the Queen? The idea has just shot across my mind, and I don't know if anything could be made of it, or if even that patronage could be secured. But I am sure her Majesty must feel (as she is one of the chief sufferers) the iniquity of these society papers which we would essay to combat on their own ground.

I should like very much to attempt some social sketches of an impersonal kind in the style *(con respetto parlando)* of the 'Spectator,' by which one might do all (I think) that the gossip papers pretend to do, without the gossip. How I might succeed is another question, but I should like to try.

And, I think, that a sort of creaming of the foreign press might be done, so as to give the public a chance of seeing what different parties say abroad of themselves, which is what it is most difficult for dwellers at home to know.[74]

None of these schemes came to anything, and Mrs. Oliphant's quest for financial security continued. On July 28, 1882 she wrote Craik suggesting an arrangement by which she should receive a fixed income for her fiction:

I propose that you should make an agreement with me for two years to pay me quarterly an income, I should like to say of a thousand a year, I in the meanwhile giving you in return three novels—one for use in the Magazine, the others to be published in the usual way. . . . The three novels would, according to my usual prices, mean two thousand pounds—and I should pledge myself to publish nothing else during the time that would in the least interfere with them. It would relieve me of the uncertainties and negotiations which always annoy me, and it would divide my money into regular payments.

Her proposal was apparently rejected. A year later she repeated her request for "something like an editorship where there would be steady income without perpetual strain—such as his friends have found more than once for Leslie Stephen—but then he is a man."[75]

Mrs. Oliphant's friendly relations with Macmillan were broken several times by quarrels, but none was so lengthy and so bitter as those she had with Blackwood. One source of friction was the firm's editor, John Morley. She accepted his editorial judgments with humility but not without complaint. She was fully aware of his downright disapproval of her book on Sheridan for the English Men of Letters series. It was a poor book, as she was obliged to admit to Craik: "I don't think it particularly well done, and the subject was one that never tempted me." She even offered to make up with other work the £100 that Macmillan had paid her for it if they decided to cancel publication. But she could not conceal her bitterness toward Morley. He might revise the book as he saw fit, she told Craik, but she would not see him personally: "Can anything be more accommodating? . . . The mistake was to ask me, a very ordinary person, to take a commission of this kind among the very most superior beings of the time. Don't be offended. It is quite true."[76] She also complained to Craik that Morley was cutting her manuscript of *The Wizard's Son* which was running serially in *Macmillan's Magazine*. She was still smarting from her wounds two years later when she wrote to William Blackwood about disposing of one of her "Little Pilgrim" stories. She had decided to offer this one to Principal Tulloch for a new magazine he was hoping to publish—"having an inveterate disinclination to offer such a thing to Mr. John Morley and yet not wishing to offend the Macmillans by sending a new portion of what has been done so well in their hands to any other established medium of publication."[77]

Only twice in the Macmillan correspondence are there any expressions of serious anger. Both occur in 1889 when Mrs. Oliphant's personal problems—finances and the health of her sons—were critical. One was over the novel *Kirsteen* which Macmillan had accepted after Blackwood's had rejected it. Although the original arrangement had been solely for book publication, they decided to publish it also in the Magazine, neglecting first to seek Mrs. Oliphant's permission. "Don't you think this is a little *brusque* on your part? . . . This is treating me rather cavalierly, I think.

. . . Have I done anything rude or disagreeable that your tone towards me is so dry and peremptory? I am quite unconscious of it."[78] The other occasion was provoked by illustrations done by George Reid for Mrs. Oliphant's article "Margaret of Scotland," which appeared in the *English Illustrated Magazine* (VII, 1889–90), published by Macmillan. The article was a chapter from her work-in-progress, one of the travel series which Macmillan published—*Royal Edinburgh: Her Saints, Kings, Prophets, and Poets* (1890). When the plans were first made, she had agreed with Craik that the illustrations should be chosen for their beauty rather than for their exact relation to her text. When the article was published, however, she was highly indignant because of what she considered their inappropriateness. They were mainly scenes of modern-day Edinburgh, giving no suggestion of the eleventh-century Edinburgh in which Queen Margaret lived:

> I am dreadfully disappointed by the extraordinary selection of illustrations given with my St. Margaret in the Illustrated Magazine. I hope that these are only collected at random from among the illustrations. . . . In the previous books I was consulted and had something to say in the matter of illustration. Mr. Delamotte came to me repeatedly about the Florence books and attended to my hints. I cannot think of any reason why I should be left entirely out of this. I might at least surely be allowed to see proofs of the engravings before the public has them since they are at least supposed to be in illustration of what I have written. . . . As a matter of courtesy I might at least have been permitted to see them.[79]

One of Mrs. Oliphant's last letters was written to Craik from her deathbed. She died owing the firm £150, but the debt was paid by the posthumous publication of two collections of stories. Craik was the prime mover in the effort to erect a memorial to her and in getting a Civil List pension for her niece Denny Oliphant. Like Blackwood he had, no doubt, had his trying moments with Mrs. Oliphant, but in the long-range view of her lifetime of association with Macmillan he must have recognized that her industry and loyalty far out-weighed her occasional outbursts of temperament and temper.

Her relations with other publishers must be dismissed briefly for lack of records. Passing references in the Blackwood letters indicate that she had both practical and temperamental difficulties with several of them. She had nothing but bitterness and scorn for most of her American publishers, mainly because some of her works were pirated and some were paid far less generously than she had expected.[80] Early in her career she sought eagerly to have her novels reprinted in the Tauchnitz series. In 1865 she wrote to Blackwood: "By the way do you ever have any dealings with Mr. Tauchnitz and his Continental Editions? I don't suppose he gives any money worth speaking of—but people ask me why my books are not in his series, and as everybody else is, I am afraid I look foolish now and then. If it should come in my way would you object to my arranging with him for the publication of the Carlingford series—or would you make the suggestion yourself for the sake of my *amour-propre?*"[81] Blackwood was cooperative, and Baron Tauchnitz published reprints of a large number of her novels and of her biography of Montalembert (his 1884 advertisement lists twenty-eight of her novels including the earliest, *Margaret Maitland,* and the whole Carlingford series). As the years passed she realized at least "some little profit" on them. But she grew dissatisfied with Tauchnitz' payments. In 1885 she complained to Blackwood:

> Tauchnitz has written to me saying that you have offered him the 'Stories of the Seen and the Unseen' for his edition. Now I don't want him to have these as I am not pleased with his dealings with me lately. Nothing was said in our bargain about that little book of Tauchnitz—nor in short of anything in particular—that I always in all my dealings reserve the right so far as the Continental edition is concerned. You will see that this has always been the case in all previous arrangements. Do you hear anything of Asher, the other continental man? I hear he has tumbled down again. An opposition to the Baron is much wanted—otherwise his monopoly is too strong for us.[82]

Another publisher with whom she quarreled was Hurst and Blackett. Her association with this firm was as long-standing as her connection with Blackwood's. In fact, it began the same year, 1852, with *Adam Graeme of Mossgray;* it has endured far longer, for Hurst and Blackett published a re-issue of *It Was a Lover and*

His Lass as recently as 1950. Most of the twenty-nine of her books that they published were undistinguished, but two of them— *Phoebe, Junior* and *The Life of Edward Irving,* are among her best work. The files of the correspondence were destroyed in the bombings of World War II, an especially unfortunate loss since Mrs. Oliphant, during the 1860's, was very friendly with the Blackett family and no doubt revealed herself frankly in her letters. It was not, however, as close a relationship as the one she had with Blackwood's. Furthermore, although a neighbor of the Blacketts in Ealing from 1861 to 1863 and a close friend of Mrs. Blackett's (to whom she had dedicated her novel *Agnes*), she did not hold Blackett himself in very high regard and probably never confided in him or sought his advice as she did with John and William Blackwood. "He is no genius," she wrote to John Blackwood in 1861, "but by no means of the London tradesman school." On another occasion she confided, "Even my excellent friend Blackett, however, is not exactly what you understand by a gentleman. . . . He is thoroughly good, friendly . . . but not exactly on the level from which *you* view affairs in general."[83] After Blackett's death her relations with the firm deteriorated. In 1875 she wrote Blackwood:

> I am going to ask you to do me a great favor. I have arranged everything for one of my usual three-volume publications with Hurst and Blackett which ought to have been finished and in their hands by this time but has been delayed by various reasons. And what I want to ask of you is whether you would kindly lend me so large a sum as £200 until this book is completed and the money paid for it. This can scarcely be a longer period than two months. In ordinary circumstances I should have got this from Hurst and Blackett themselves, but their business is in the hands of an old clerk whose chief qualities are caution and thickheadedness and I don't want to make any requests to him. I will send you if you please one of my life policies as security.[84]

Blackett's sons, whom she had known as children, took over the management of the firm, but Mrs. Oliphant's relations with them were strained. In 1882 she offered—and Blackwood rejected—a novel which she had originally intended for Hurst and Blackett:

The management of their business has lately passed into the hands of the young Blacketts, and I was offended by the manner of the eldest, an underbred and uneducated young man, whom I have been very kind to all his life but whom I should now prefer to have no further dealings with, as I perceive I shall not be able to support him. These are the circumstances which give me this work to dispose of, as I do not wish to let them have it. (It is no question about price but mere personal feeling.) . . . I would rather modify my price and have it published by you. They have lost their father just when they have need of guidance, but Arthur was always a cub and has given me much trouble as a boy. So that I have no disposition to submit myself to him in any way.[85]

It is noteworthy that fewer of her books were published by Hurst and Blackett after this time (there were twenty-three through 1881, only six from 1883 to 1897), but Mrs. Oliphant was not able to indulge her pride to the point of breaking off the association completely.

Some forty-nine letters to William Isbister of the magazine *Good Words* indicate that here again Mrs. Oliphant pursued an uneven and often stormy course with a publisher. She began publishing in *Good Words* in 1866, receiving the handsome sum of £1,000 for her serialized novel *Madonna Mary*. Over the years she published four other novels (*At His Gates,* 1872; *Whiteladies,* 1875; *Lady Jane,* 1882; and *The Marriage of Elinor,* 1891), some travel sketches and miscellaneous articles, and some short stories in the magazine. Although she was not a close personal friend of Isbister, she did not conceal her financial problems from him, and many of the letters echo the same appeals for more and prompter payment:

Have you paid in the money I asked for to my bankers? Please reply by return of post as it is of serious importance to me. I hope if it is not already done that you will be good enough to do it at once.

I do not really think that £150 is adequate pay for the Christmas story. . . . I do not really think (and I am sure you will agree with me) that £200 is a penny more than I should get for this story. . . . At the same time I have always an objection to exacting [?] and much prefer to trust myself to the honourable feeling

of my publisher. Shall we say £175 with a stipulation that if the
sale is very large (you to fix the rate) you will give me something
more—a royalty or what you please. Will this suit you? You remember that you promised to let me have a hundred pounds now
on account—today or tomorrow. Would you please pay this in for
me to my account at Messrs Cocks Biddulphs . . . as I have special
occasion for it. May I trust you for this? It is of importance to
me.[86]

She also approached Isbister for assistance to personal friends and
relatives—Mrs. Macpherson, Principal Tulloch's son Frank, Annie
Walker, and Denny Oliphant. And finally, with Isbister as with
her other publishers, there were the same flare-ups of irritation:

What do you mean by reprinting 'The Fugitives'? You know you
have no right to do so. I was petrified by finding it on a railway
stall the other day. It was given to you for your Christmas number without any ulterior bargain or view. Why did you republish
it? and without a word to me. You know I could get you into
trouble about it if I chose. Take care with the others. I cannot
permit such republications.

I do not find your enclosure in the least satisfactory, nor can I
accept it as payment of my story. You cannot surely expect that
I will make over to you what is in reality a one-volume novel for
such a price. It is entirely out of the question. I return the receipt
unsigned therefore and request that you will be good enough to
arrange the matter in a manner more befitting my reputation and
yours. Had you dealt frankly with me and told me what you
wanted this story for, I should have either consented or refused,—
at least settled what the terms were to be. Therefore the additional trouble you have in this matter is entirely your own doing,
not mine.

Here is the last number of Lady Jane. It is too long I know but
you must not meddle with it. *It cannot be cut down.* It has been
very hard to get the story squeezed into the small dimensions afforded me and it cannot spare a word. This time you must oper-
ate upon other people and leave me alone.[87]

The association, however, continued more or less smoothly until
Mrs. Oliphant's death, her last contribution to *Good Words* being
an article on the Queen's Diamond Jubilee.

A study of Mrs. Oliphant's relations with her publishers reveals more, probably, about her own personality than about Victorian publishing in general. Nevertheless, it also casts light upon certain practices and policies of the time. We see the writer gradually emerging into professional and economic, as well as artistic, status: his struggle for some determining hand in such matters as editions, reprints, illustrations; for standardization of payment and copyright policy. He remained, however, essentially dependent—dependent upon his pen alone, for the residuals of publishing were neither fixed nor profitable, and the income always uncertain unless he could find an editorship or some other journalistic outlets to fall back upon. With no "middle man" in the person of a literary agent, the writer worked more closely and directly with his publisher. There was less delegation of labor and responsibility and therefore greater rapport between them. The influence of the Victorian publisher was considerable, not only in what he chose to publish but in what was actually written—its subject, length, revision, and so on. The commercial aspects of publishing were perhaps not too strikingly different from what they are today. The development of a mass reading population in the nineteenth century created a market, and publishers rushed to supply that demand at the greatest possible profit to themselves. Some exploited authors and the reading public outrageously, but a survey of Mrs. Oliphant's career suggests that her publishers treated her on the whole fairly and sometimes generously.[88]

The pressures upon Mrs. Oliphant were greater than those upon many of her contemporaries, especially among women novelists. Yet in reviewing her tremendous output, we cannot overlook the fact that she was a writer as well as a breadwinner. She could not afford the leisure that art demands for its cultivation and development. She had constantly to seek and woo a mass reading public which she disdained. Strangely enough, in spite of this she managed to grind out her work with at least a measure of freshness and vitality. And even when inventiveness of plot and the niceties of style eluded her, her vigorous intelligence and her good taste rarely flagged. Her publishers were keenly aware of this fact. Eminent and established firms like Blackwood's and Macmillan did not continue to publish her out of mere charity and pity for her desperate financial needs. If she did not, except once, provide them with the profits of a best seller, she was nevertheless a competent and steady source of income for them. Her indefatigable pen supported her and her family for a lifetime, but it also helped to support her publishers.

Chapter VI

Literary Jack-Of-All-Trades

Paradoxical as it may sound, Mrs. Oliphant was a practicing novelist who did not like novel writing. Although she wrote a small number of very good novels and a large number of reasonably competent and readable ones, although she also wrote some very shrewd criticism of her fellow novelists, and as a critic for *Maga* read a staggering amount of fiction good and bad, she never overcame a personal distaste for a considerable amount of the fiction of her age and a personal preference for what she regarded as the more solid tasks of writing literary criticism, literary history, and biography. "I like biography," she wrote Isabella Blackwood in 1861. "I have a great mind to set up that as my future trade and tout for orders. Do you know anybody that wants his or her life taken?"[1] She was being facetious of course, but there was more than a little truth in her remark. Thirty-five years later, old, sick, and lonely, she confessed to William Blackwood that she infinitely preferred the compiling of his company's history to the writing of fiction: "But my heart sickens at novel-writing and the traffic . . . and the position of a seller of goods which perhaps no longer command the market. All this seems inappropriate to my age and to my standing, and to my total indifference to anything that life can bring me."[2]

Her gifts as a writer—unlimited energy and industry, a capacity for enormous reading, adaptability to almost any subject-matter, and a shrewd critical sense—were indeed better suited to non-fiction than to fiction. These talents were especially suited to biography, a literary form which served her in many ways as well as

183

she served it. No matter what emotional and family problems beset her, she could discipline her mind to the hard, attention-absorbing demands of writing biography. This she regarded as adult work, while fiction came increasingly to be associated in her mind with youth and frivolity. Biography, she argued, has all the attractions of fiction—its drama and excitement, its irony and suspense—with the additional advantage of reality: "its moral is worked out before our eyes with that solidity of experience which is more telling than any logical deduction." Fiction is at its best when it impresses us with its reality. "But the actual chronicle itself, when simply set forth, is more impressive."[3] As a practicing critic as well as a biographer, she early developed high standards by which to measure biography. She wrote no classic of biography herself, but she thought long and seriously about the form. Her own works varied in type and quality from serious, carefully researched full-length biographies like *The Life of Edward Irving* (1862), *Memoirs of the Count de Montalembert* (1872), *Memoir of the Life of John Tulloch* (1888), *Memoir of the Life of Laurence Oliphant, and Alice Oliphant, His Wife* (1891)—to hasty surveys based on secondary material like *Saint Francis of Assisi* (1868) for Macmillan's Sunday Library Series; *Cervantes, Dante,* and *Molière* (all three 1877) in Blackwood's Foreign Classics for English Readers series; *Sheridan* (1883) for Macmillan's English Men of Letters series; and *Thomas Chalmers, Preacher, Philosopher, and Statesman* (1893) for the Methuen Leaders of Religion series—to mere extended sketches of hack work like *Jeanne d'Arc: Her Life and Death,* published by Putnam (1896), and *Queen Victoria, a Personal Sketch,* published by Cassell (1900).

Most of these works give ample evidence of Mrs. Oliphant's integrity as a biographer and of her keen understanding of the demands of the form. Her research was careful and conscientious. She knew the value of working from original source materials and wherever available she used them heavily. The subjects of her major biographies, Irving, Montalembert, Tulloch, and Laurence Oliphant, were all close to her; with the exception of Irving she knew them personally. Though hesitating to intrude herself into the writing, she leaned upon personal recollections, feeling that they gave her work authority and interest. Planning the Laurence

Oliphant biography, she wrote to Blackwood: "I think I could do this piece of work best by writing in the first person and with my own name, unless you have any objection. I object to it on principle myself, but, as a point of fact, it would be less easy to make any interesting portrait of him in any other way."[4] Actually, there is very little personal detail in that book, since she knew him only slightly; but when she came to write the life of her friend Principal Tulloch, and still later the history of her publisher Blackwood, she frequently injected personal recollections. Most of her contemporaries appear to have condoned the practice. An anonymous writer in *Maga,* summing up her achievement as a biographer, observed: "No part of Mrs. Oliphant's biographies, as a rule, are more pleasant reading than those in which she herself appears on the scene . . . She neither obtrudes herself, nor, when her presence is essential, does she affect coyness and hang back."[5]

Valuable as such personal knowledge was to her, Mrs. Oliphant displayed considerable reluctance about exploiting it. She was ever sensitive to the importance of individual privacy. Indeed, her only reservation about biography was her dislike of its intrusion upon personal life. In reviews of other biographies she frequently condemned any invasion of privacy, any "strain upon the modesty of nature," any "unnecessary betrayal of private lives." The biographer of a contemporary, she points out, must be especially alert to "the occasional difficulty of saying all that ought to be said while there are still many persons living, liable to be deeply wounded or injured by some sidelight thrown upon them, or revelation of unknown events in their history." Equally objectionable to her was the sentimental approach. Hero-worshipping, romanticizing, and glamorizing of the subject were violations of the criteria of balance and proportion: "We should say to the young writer—never mind what is your idea of the man; nobody cares what you think of him; let him show us himself what he was; if he is not capable of doing that, he is not a man whose life needs to be written." Nowhere does she criticize the sentimentalizing biographer more sharply than in her review of Mrs. Sutherland Orr's *Life and Letters of Robert Browning.* When that biographer suggested romantically that "only a delicate woman could have been the mother of Robert Browning," and that his father *had* to have "placid intellectual powers," Mrs. Oliphant drily observes: "The reader will see from this that when a bank clerk who is fond of books marries a woman with no health to speak of, a poet is likely to be the result."[6]

Mrs. Oliphant practiced her art of biography vigorously, conscientiously, and intelligently. Like almost everything else she wrote, her biographies failed in the long run to realize their potentialities. With the exceptions of *Irving, Montalembert,* and *Tulloch,* they suffer the faults of much of her fiction—haste, superficiality, lack of intellectual or emotional involvement with her subject. One feels in reading many of them, as one does with the novels, that she was giving this phase of her writing only part of her attention —her mind leaping ahead even as she wrote, to the myriad of other writing projects on which she was simultaneously engaged. Nevertheless, as with her fiction again, one cannot help marvelling at her competence. In our age of subject specialization her versatility appears extraordinary. There was no subject she would not tackle. The remarkable thing is how often and how successfully she met the challenge. Her lively mind, her industry, and her basic understanding of the technique of good biography on the whole served her well.

They served her equally well in her lifetime of work as a literary critic. In the course of regular reviewing for *Maga* and other journals, and subsequently as a literary historian, she passed judgment on a goodly portion of the great imaginative and intellectual writing of the Victorian Age, and inevitably on much of the less great too. Hasty and superficial as they necessarily had to be, her journalistic reviewing and popular criticism were shrewd rather than profound. But they are not to be ignored. Considered as part of the history of literary opinion, as distinguished from literary criticism, her contribution is of value to a student of the period. Her judgments, to be sure, reflect her convictions—not infrequently her peculiar prejudices and crotchets—her intelligence, her sense of values, at times her obtuseness and certain blind spots in her imagination. Mrs. Oliphant's critical writing tends to bring her own literary values into focus, but because of her essential conservatism it may be taken as representative of the cultivated taste of her day. Posing simply as one who knew what she liked, she was not given to critical theories. Nevertheless, she did express something of a credo in one of her omnibus reviews for *Maga,* where, in assessing Richard Holt Hutton's *Essays Theological and Literary,* she defined the ideal critic:

> He must have the power of close observation—the eye to see, the skill to analyse; he must combine much positive knowledge, and confidence in his own power and judicial authority, with so much intellectual modesty as will make him ready to perceive excellence, even outside the laws which usually regulate its manifestation; and, above all, he must have true sympathetic insight, such as will lay open to him the meanings, not always clearly expressed, the *motif,* not always clearly indicated, of his subjects. The true critic should see more than the book before him—he should see the mind that produced it.[7]

To the extent of her powers and within the limits imposed by the treadmill pace at which she both read and wrote, Mrs. Oliphant may be said to have worked by this model. One characteristic of her ideal critic she most certainly had—one that must have enhanced her position as a literary guide to readers of *Maga*—a catholicity of interest. Next to Matthew Arnold, no critic worked harder than she did to remove British literary insularity and provincialism. She covered not only English literature, but contributed as well substantial articles on such major continental writers as Béranger, Goldoni, Leopardi, Hugo, Goethe, Schiller, Dumas *père,* Lamartine, Molière, Voltaire, de Musset, Daudet, and Turgenev (whom she read in French), and the Greek and Latin classics (which she read in translation). She took on heady tomes of history, philosophy, and theology with the alacrity, if not the penetration, characteristic of George Eliot during her *Westminster Review* days. Her essays on Macaulay and Froude, Berkeley and Hume, Savonarola and Lacordaire, to choose a few examples, are excellent introductions to these complex figures for the uninitiated reader. The extent of her command over the books of the day is conveyed by one series rather misleadingly titled "Modern Light Literature," subdivided into: Theology; Science; History; Travellers' Tales; Art; Poetry. A typical *omnium gatherum,* and only one of many, takes up *Orissa,* a part of Sir William Wilson Hunter's *Annals of Rural Bengal; Lectures on the History of the Church of Scotland,* by

Dean Stanley; *Miscellaneous Writings of J. Conington, M. A.;* *Goethe and Mendelssohn,* translated from the German by M. G. von Glehn, and *Olrig Grange,* a once popular pastoral poem by Walter C. Smith.[8] Such omnivorousness exposes one inevitably to a charge of dilettantism, but this was before the heyday of the academic specialist. Without benefit of any formal education, Mrs. Oliphant made all humanistic learning her province. "Positive knowledge" she stood ready to acquire; "judicial authority" she took it on herself to assert; but she knew her limitations sufficiently to exercise "intellectual modesty." Above all, her open-mindedness made her disposed "to perceive excellence" wherever she could find it.

Her faculty for "sympathetic insight" reveals itself many times. De Quincey she sees as one who "thought, dreamt and wandered, often stumbling by the way, about the 'world not realized'—the great mystic universe which his temperament and strange experience kept always wonderful and mysterious to him as a child." Of Charles and Mary Lamb she writes: "Never were two people more dearly consecrated to humanity by love and misery, and sacred patience and pain." On Jane Austen's attitude towards her characters she comments: "She sympathises with the sufferers, yet she can scarcely be said to be sorry for them; giving them unconsciously a share in her own sense of the covert fun of the scene, and gentle disdain of the possibility that meanness and folly and stupidity could ever really wound any rational creature." The genius of Charlotte Brontë, to Mrs. Oliphant, lay in the vividness with which she "intensifies the sensations of solitude and the vacancy of the heart, into a force with which perhaps no woman, either before or since, has expressed [such emotions]. . . ."[9]

These characteristic passages bear out Mrs. Oliphant's conviction that "the true critic should see more than the book before him —he should see the mind that produced it." Her criticism for the most part leans towards the psychological rather than the aesthetic mode, concentrating attention more on the personality and temperament of the writer than on his artistry or style. Wordsworth, to her, is "a poet of feeling, never of passion. Reflection and contemplation are his natural atmosphere. . . . His genius is essentially reflective, not dramatic." She penetrates to the core of Keats' frustration: "This wonderful passion, so hectic and feverish, so devouring and unsatisfied, was the only human influence that helped to kill the young poet. Love, and not Mr. Gifford in the *Quarterly.*" Byron's *Don Juan* is to her "spontaneous as running water, rapid, eloquent, extraordinary, full of the vulgarities and pettinesses of the meanest mind, and of sentiments and perceptions worthy of the highest . . . a web of reckless and heartless licentiousness from beginning to end." Among the great novelists of her time, Dickens was preeminent to her as a humorist. She refused to take him seriously: "His highest ideal has a quiver, as of semi-intoxication, in its voice, its virtue is smug, self-conscious, surrounded by twittering choruses of praise." Thackeray, on the other hand, "had the variety, the changeableness, the power of rapid transformation which is to be found only in the highest intelligences. He was by turns humorous, contemptuous, tender—a moralist, a jester, a laughing philosopher, a cynic; yet with a vein of pathos infinitely touching and true, which went to the hearts of his readers."[10] Mrs. Oliphant's efforts to trace what she called the "mental influences" which produced literary masterpieces resolved themselves sometimes into impressionistic sketches, but rose not infrequently to sound intuitions into the psychology of imagination. She rarely provided any extended analysis or interpretation of a work, but the general reader could gain from her a good sense of the effect of a writer and some idea of his literary milieu.

In her estimates of contemporary novelists, Mrs. Oliphant tended to speak for *l'homme moyen sensuel,* with her affinity for the healthy-minded and the wholesome, avoiding the extremes of coarseness on the one hand and of over-refinement on the other, repelled alike by cold detachment or intense passion in an author. Within this middle range of taste and sensibility she moved with ease and her instinct was sure. Beyond it she was often blind, or at least short-sighted. She acknowledged Charlotte Brontë's genius, but at the same time considered her intellectually naive and lacking in emotional reserve. *Wuthering Heights* was, in her estimation, an "unlovely book," and Heathcliff completely without appeal as a hero.[11] Like a number of her contemporaries, she thought that Dickens went into a decline after *David Copperfield.* Thackeray was to her the noblest of writers and *Henry Esmond* his best book, yet she thought that the love of Lady Castlewood for the hero was in poor taste. Trollope's importance as a writer rested for her on the Barsetshire novels. She ignored all his other work. George Eliot's novels after *Silas Marner* were in her estimation (as well as that of many another reader of her time) "injured by too much philosophy and the consciousness of being considered a public instructor"; *Middlemarch,* while she admired some of its characterization (notably Rosamond Vincy), was to her overly pedantic. The only novelists she overrated were Bulwer-Lytton (whom she ranked immediately below Thackeray and Dickens) and Charles Reade (whom she considered on a level with Trollope). While all these judgments place her four-square within the Victorian mould, it should be pointed out that she praised George Meredith's *The Adventures of Harry Richmond,* which baffled most of its first readers, and she found much to like in Hardy's *Tess of the d'Urbervilles,* despite its sordidness.[12] She was alternately impressed, overwhelmed, perplexed and annoyed by "the champion and exponent of the New World," Henry James. Outside of England, she recognized the greatness of *Crime and Punishment* when its author's name was barely known across the Channel. But, all in all, Mrs. Oliphant stood by her conviction, first voiced in disparagement of Hawthorne, that "the novelist's true audience is the common people of ordinary comprehension and everyday sympathies, whatever their rank may be."[13]

The swelling numbers of fiction writers in the Victorian Age disturbed Mrs. Oliphant. She was concerned with preserving both the prestige and the popularity of the novel. In an omnibus review article, "Novels," in 1863, she observed: "It is difficult to account by any natural law for the vast development attained by fiction within the last twenty or thirty years." Since serious literature also flourished in this period, the rise of fiction is not necessarily a sign of frivolity, "but at no age, so far as we are aware, has there existed anything resembling the extraordinary flood of novels which is now pouring over the land—certainly with fertilizing results, so far as the manufacture itself is concerned." As a result, she writes, the author has suffered something of a fall from eminence in society; he is no longer regarded as the phenomenon he once was. "The same art which once glorified Fanny Burney into a celebrity all but historical is now contemptuously treated by witty critics as a branch of female industry not much more important than Berlin wool."[14] Clearly, Mrs. Oliphant was alarmed by this descent in status now threatening fiction because of the emergence of a new race of female "scribblers." While she all too often wrote her own novels casually and carelessly, she upheld the novel as a serious form worthy of mature readers and deplored the feeling of so many that they were wasting their time by reading any novel of later vintage than Scott.

Queen Gertrude's admonition to Polonius, "More matter, with less art," sums up what Mrs. Oliphant urged upon her fellow novelists. In her evaluations of individual writers, as well as in her *obiter dicta* on the novel in general, she consistently rated substance over style. At its best, she believed, the novel had the truth of history, the exemplary influence of biography, and the moral force of religious writing. Both her emphasis on realism and her ethical preoccupation led her to subordinate plot to character. She tended to judge a novel by its recognizable humanity. No amount of brilliant description could compensate for the lack of characters with whom she could identify herself. "The fact is that readers prefer people to trees" she once wrote facetiously. In a more serious mood, she conceded that "this power of landscape-painting is no small gift," but, she added, "it is only the setting of the gem, the frame of the picture. The art of fiction requires that the human figures in the scene should always be first and greatest, more important even than the sweetest scene of morning freshness, or the most magnificent of storms."[15] Obviously her predilection for what Matthew Arnold called "the personal estimate" sometimes got in the way of her full understanding and appreciation of imaginative literature. At her best she could display a remarkable power of empathy, but she could also prove obtuse and narrow-minded. Both her strength and her weakness as a critic lay in her habit of seeing novels and novelists alike in her own image.

Mrs. Oliphant's literary journalism represents her passing judgments on writers. Her more considered judgments are to be found in the two literary histories which she published during the latter part of her career. The first and by far the better of these is *The*

Literary History of England in the End of the Eighteenth and Beginning of the Nineteenth Century (3 vols., Macmillan, 1882). Here she speaks for herself and not as part of the collective voice of *Maga* or any other periodical. In one chapter of the *Literary History,* tracing the history of the *Edinburgh Review,* she defends the policy of anonymity of that journal, linking its tradition with that of *Maga:*

> The principle lingers still in some regions, and specially in the only great literary organ which still has its headquarters in Edin- burgh. In our own days a different canon has begun to be su- preme; but we cannot help reverting with approval to the earlier idea. It is true that in the chief circles of literature there is never any great uncertainty as to whose is the hand that admin- isters chastisement, but we believe that criticism is always most free for praise or blame, when it is anonymous, and that the ver- dict, of an important publication, whether it be review as in those days, or newspaper as in our own, is more telling as well as more dignified than that of an individual, whose opinion, in nine cases out of ten, becomes of inferior importance to us the moment we are acquainted with his name.

So willingly did Mrs. Oliphant merge her own identity with that of the journal that much of her criticism was faceless and brought her no esteem. *The Literary History of England,* on the contrary, is stamped with her signature and irradiated with her personality. Because of its special character, certain allowances must be made in assessing it. As critics of the day were quick to point out, its title is something of a misnomer. It is not really a history of literature in either the documentary or the developmen- tal sense. Mrs. Oliphant left out far too much to make her work of value as a chronicle or record, and she lacked the theoretical mind and synthesizing faculty to give it much conceptual struc- ture. Like her travel books and her *Historical Sketches of the Reign of George Second,* which are fundamentally series of pro- files of great figures, her *Literary History of England* surveys the literatures of the periods under consideration through the leading personalities of the age. Scaled down from its pretentious title, however, this book remains one of her finest accomplishments. If not precisely a *history* of English literature, it holds our attention as the *story* of English literature. As one of the severest critics of the book asserted, after pointing out her many limitations for the task she had undertaken: "She has, however, produced a readable and even a fascinating book. Few more critical students could have vitalized their portraits in the way that hers are vitalized, and her bright insight into character and her knowledge of human life are most refreshing in this branch of literature."[16]

Vitality certainly is one of the virtues of the work. Its pages abound with character, as her fiction often does not, real people more frequently inspiring her to better writing than her imagined characters. She shows here that ability so well demonstrated in her *Autobiography* of striking off the essences of people quickly and sharply: Joanna Baillie is "one of those maiden princesses about whom there always breathes a soft and exquisite perfume, too delicate for common appreciation, of that reserved and high virginity, which, never reaching to any second chapter of life, involves an endless youth"; Theodore Hook is a "Yorick of infinite fancy and frolic, whose existence was good to nobody, not even to himself"; John Galt is an "odd and vulgar Scot, pushing his devious way about the world"; Leigh Hunt's "enthusiasm for everything that was green and moving has a tone of exaggeration in it which sounds like that of a man whose garden was a flower-box in a window." She revels in paradoxes of character. She observes of Shelley, for example, that "his intellect tangled him in theories of political justice, in fantastic schemes for the amelioration of the race, and his child's heart of pity and tenderness made him incapable of denying kindness or help to any supplicant—save those who had a lawful claim upon his service"; William Godwin was "one of those unusual, though not altogether singular men, who are able to set forth and reason out to its logical (however impossible) end, the most deeply reaching and universally applicable philosophy, without feeling themselves under any practical necessity either to embrace it themselves or to apply it to others." As for Jeremy Bentham: "The prophet was one of the oddest that ever moved humanity, a strange little being full of quips and cranks, in mind a sort of thinking machine . . . in habits a recluse, though surrounded by an endless flow of society, and incapable of existing without a little court of dependents and admirers; in all studies but his own destitute of so much as the capacity to understand."

Obviously Mrs. Oliphant was no dispassionate literary historian. Her tendency to enter into the minds of her subjects (conjecturing, for example, what went through Sir Walter Scott's mind as a boy musing on the side of Arthur's Seat), invests her work with human drama and emotion, even if at times her intrusions may seem gratuitous, wrong-headed, or mean-spirited. One delight of her approach to writers is that crackling common sense with which she whips pretension and pomposity. Of a once celebrated religious poet she recalls: "In the dearth of writers properly marked with the sign-manual of the Universities, it ought to be noted that Heber gained the prize of poetry at Oxford, fulfilled all his studies there with distinction, and became a fellow of All-Souls. So much for so little! But it has never ceased to be true that poets must be born and cannot be made." Praise for Joanna Baillie's fine delicacy and gentility is followed by this shaft: "Perhaps, however, we must add, such a one is very inadequately qualified for the composition of tragedies, especially those that deal with the passions." She expresses mock compassion for Southey, disappointed at receiving less than four pounds for *Madoc,* "which had cost him so much labour, for which he had collected waggon-loads of material, and weighed every word and verified every landscape," while Scott made a thousand pounds for the relatively effortless *Lay of the Last Minstrel.*

Mrs. Oliphant's barbs were not reserved for little fish. She disposes summarily of Coleridge's "twenty-year plan" for an epic poem: "It is fine to see the desponding poet forget himself and those little troubles about the bread and cheese, and rise to this great climax. No one yet, so far as we are aware, has ever prepared a great epic after this prescription; even Wordsworth, who has approached it most nearly, can scarcely be said to 'have warmed his mind with universal science.' " But she is no less biting on his friend's preface to "The Excursion": "The artificial solemnity of this scheme, given forth with a sublime unconsciousness of all possibilities of derision, is not, perhaps, more remarkable than the arrogant humility of the theories with which the Lyrical Ballads were issued to the world . . . Poetry blew away his systems like the mere foam of fancy they were. No one, even among his worshippers, has thought of his work as of a 'Gothic church.' " Here and there she plays the anti-sentimentalist, as when she describes Shelley and Byron reading Rousseau together in Geneva while strolling "through 'the bosquet de Julie,' moved almost to tears, glad that no vulgar spectator was by to see their emotion . . . It is to be feared that most of us nowadays find the Lake Leman somewhat prosaic, remembering little and caring less about Julie and St. Preux, unwholesome lovers, but to Byron and Shelley they were divine."

Apart from these incidental felicities, *The Literary History of England* is distinguished by a point of view which gives the work a unity and a rationale. Through the whole runs the theme of *tempora mutantur*—the sifting process of time. For her own generation she was evoking the memory of contemporaries, or recalling the books of their childhood. To the new generation some of these writers were known by reputation, some were but names, others were entirely forgotten. "Wordsworth has for the present, perhaps, passed the height of his fame. He is less universally appreciated, less beloved, than he was twenty years ago," she observes from the vantage point of the early 1880's. The phrase "another poet celebrated in his own immediate days with an admiration which has much failed him now," by which she describes Thomas Campbell, recurs with variants throughout the book. The novels of Thomas Holcroft "have dropped out of recollection altogether"; Hazlitt's essays and criticism, "though often brilliant, have fallen into that limbo which alas! is the natural place even of the ablest commentaries upon other men's works and lives." She remarks of the once-popular *Canterbury Tales* of Sophia and Harriet Lee, "These tales have fallen out of the knowledge of the present generation." A central concern of the book, as these passages suggest, is the fickleness of fame—a subject to which, by the early 1880's, Mrs. Oliphant was herself keenly and even painfully sensitive.

On the positive side, her *Literary History* is an inquiry into the *durability* of fame. Time may be ruthless, but it performs a rough justice. Wordsworth's eclipse at this time, as Mrs. Oliphant correctly predicted, was only temporary. Now that the historical novel was taken so much for granted, she realized that Sir Walter Scott was no longer as striking for novelty and freshness as he had been to his first readers, but she felt that he would always find readers because of the humanity that breathes from his books. Many now unread authors, she was convinced, deserved their obscurity. Their writing had been too topical, local, or temporal. Sheer quantity of writing was no guarantee either of lasting reputation, as witnessed by the decline of Southey's fame, with his enormous output, alongside the continuing fame of Keats and Coleridge, despite the slimness of their production. To account for the permanence of reputation Mrs. Oliphant refers to such collective intangibles as "the general heart," "the public ear," "popular sympathy," and "universal memory." To stir up the forgotten past and to keep memory fresh are her dual functions as literary historian. But in the long run she puts her trust in the judgment of the common reader—"the true reader," she calls him—the man or woman of taste and sensitivity somewhat above that of the populace but beneath that of the educated specialist. And it is this "true reader" who must be reached, if a writer's name is to live.

Above all, in giving her book the title *The Literary History of England in the End of the Eighteenth and Beginning of the Nineteenth Century,* Mrs. Oliphant was making a pioneering effort at defining an epoch in literature. She sensed that the period which she called "the age of George" had developed a literature of such distinctive quality as to merit equal consideration with the age of Elizabeth and the age of Anne. "Our present object," she announces in her introduction, "is to trace the awakening of the new epoch in literature which dawned in the end of the eighteenth century, stretching forward into our own, and not only creating a new code and new laws, but changing the very atmosphere, the scene, the firmament, and bringing in a purer moral, and a higher soul." She recognized that the movement of literary history cannot be compared to that of the history of a nation; while a nation may advance by gradual and orderly progression, literature experiences sudden upheavals followed by declines. Neither is the growth of literature to be compared to the evolution of man, for it is by its nature unpredictable and fortuitous: "Nothing is more remarkable in the history of humanity, or less capable of reduction of rule, than are the waves of literary impulse." It is these "waves of literary impulse" which Mrs. Oliphant endeavors to record in her literary history. She therefore emphasizes the impact of original geniuses on their times and on literature in general, and tries to recover for a new generation of readers the shock of recognition with which readers at the beginning of the century greeted the advent of such figures as Wordsworth, Scott, Byron, and Keats.

The Literary History of England is one of the few books by Mrs. Oliphant that seem to have been written as a labor of love rather than merely as a breadwinner. Whatever its limitations and deficiencies, as one reviewer declared, "It does not contain a dull page . . . it has much in it to charm as well as to instruct the reader."[17] Its sequel, The Victorian Age of English Literature (2 vols., Rivington, 1892), seems by comparison a tired and perfunctory work. Much undoubtedly of its failure is to be imputed to Mrs. Oliphant's advanced age and to her difficult family circumstances at the time. But the main fault of The Victorian Age of English Literature, as Mrs. Oliphant herself was quick to acknowledge, was that she attempted to encompass a period still not closed, over which she did not have adequate grasp to make any useful generalizations. "It is always somewhat rash to attempt to determine the final place in literature of contemporary writers," she observes in the preface by way of apology. "There is nothing in which the generations make greater mistakes." She justifies herself by making clear that "what is written here is for the reader of to-day, and not for the eventual judge whose verdict will ultimately prevail, let us say what we will." For the "eventual judge" there is a certain interest in Mrs. Oliphant's last words on her contemporaries, her second thoughts on writers treated earlier and at greater length in Maga articles. Apart from these, one gets some idea of the number of popular writers of the age who have since passed into eclipse, but only the barest of ideas inasmuch as the more detailed chapters tend to deteriorate into mere directories of names and titles. Her attempts at all-inclusiveness within limited space make her treatment little more than bibliographical name-dropping. But the last chapter, devoted to periodicals and newspapers, always a particular interest of hers, is of genuine reference value. (In this connection it is interesting to see her observing that

the magazine is threatening to crowd out the book in reader interest
and implying that illustrations may well in time displace news-
print.)

On the whole the writing throughout the book is flat and humdrum, but here and there is a touch of the old sting: "It has, we
fear, . . . been proved by many years' experience that Mr. Swin-
burne has not very much to say to us. He has said it in the most
exquisite manner and at the greatest length"; Rossetti, in his
"Blessed Damozel," "sets heaven before us in a succession, or maze,
of lovers' walks, where the presumably re-united pairs stroll about
together in a perfect but somewhat banal bliss." There is a quaint
charm in her encouragement of the new generation of novelists.
In one instance a note of poignancy creeps in: "With this marvellous range of capacity it is impossible to predict or even to attempt
a prognostic of the direction which his next effort may take," she
writes of Robert Louis Stevenson, who died two years later with
a work unfinished that some think would have been his masterpiece. Her catalogue of fiction writers ends with "two names of
young men . . . who have made so remarkable a beginning and
possess such unquestionable power, that we take leave of our subject with them in all the brightness and satisfaction of a noble
prospect as well as an already admirable record." She was referring
to Rudyard Kipling and James M. Barrie. The book also has
moments of sensitive interpretation, notably in the pages devoted
to *In Memoriam,* which affected her deeply. Tennyson's death
occurred just as the book was about to go to press, and its preface
served as a kind of dedication to him, "full of years and honours."
The passing of the Poet Laureate, in effect, marked the close of
the era for Mrs. Oliphant. She wrote in tribute: "He has gone in
a noble tranquility and faith which is one of the greatest lessons
he has ever given to the country he so much loved; and his death
puts back this record almost as by the end of the epoch which it
treats."

As a literary critic and historian Mrs. Oliphant worked faithfully in the service of the general reader at perhaps the last period
in our cultural history when that group was both substantial and
readily identifiable. A reviewer of her *Literary History of England,* writing in the *Athenaeum,* pinpointed just the audience at
which she aimed:

The taste for reading in these days is universal, and it must be borne in mind that between the absolutely illiterate classes and those who have the genuine taste for literature there has sprung up within the last half century a vast number who are able to take pleasure in books, and to whom the main facts of our literary history are not only interesting but new, while criticism such as Mrs. Oliphant's, though it is second-hand, is in the majority of cases sensible, temperate and judicious . . . [It] has a piquancy and freshness which no amount of critical ability could give.[18]

A "pre-digester" of literature, aiding in the general education of the burgeoning reading public, Mrs. Oliphant was one of that "race of middlemen" she refers to in her *Literary History of England,* practicing what she modestly styled a "secondary art." In this capacity she revealed a remarkable facility for "telling the old, but ever new, story . . . with a marvellous freshness and vivacity."

To the same audience for which she wrote her literary criticism she also directed a large, unwieldy bulk of miscellaneous journalism—observations on her times, on art, on music, on theatre. There was almost literally nothing on which Mrs. Oliphant did not at some time or other speak her mind (including even the subject of swimming; a non-swimmer herself, she wrote a preface in 1875 to Sergeant Leahy's *The Art of Swimming in the Eton Style*). A rumor once circulated that she had written an entire number of *Maga*.[19] Like most rumors this one exaggerated what was actually a small grain of truth. She never wrote a whole number, but she did, more than once, contribute as many as three substantial pieces to a single issue, and on numerous occasions she had two contributions in an issue. Since most of the work she published there was unsigned, she wrote as much as the Blackwoods would take—and often more, many of her articles being cut down before publication. She was their good reliable "right-hand," from the early days when they called her "Katie" to the trying last days when, in spite of her ill-health and irritability, she could still be relied upon to turn out a hasty obituary article or a review of an important new book just as the magazine was going to press. The Blackwoods were duly impressed not only with her industry and efficiency but also with her versatility and virtuosity in handling the widest variety of subject matter and in shifting rapidly and gracefully into whatever tone, vocabulary and idiom her subject demanded. She could cheer the achievements of Queen Victoria's reign with jingoistic fervor, lament the passing of old traditions, generously hail a new author, savagely needle another, write solemn obituaries, serious if not distinguished poetry, conscientious reviews of works of literature, philosophy and theology, witty observations on fashions and home furnishings, sentimental tributes to family life, and sophisticated reports of the London season. What is most remarkable is that she could do all this almost simultaneously and that she could do it with intelligence and felicity of style. "Perhaps we must go back to Goldsmith for a similar versatility, and for a similar genius for adorning all she touched," wrote the editors of *Maga* in their obituary article on her.[20]

It is impossible to list all the periodicals to which Mrs. Oliphant contributed during her lifetime. Since most of the articles were unsigned, we can know only those which she claimed, either in her letters and autobiography, or which are attributed to her in the records of the periodicals themselves. Mrs. Coghill printed a list of the articles she published in *Maga* in the *Autobiography and Letters,* and most of her anonymous contributions to the *Spectator* have been identified.[21] Beyond that we know that she published non-fiction in *Fraser's, Macmillan's,* the *New Review,* the *Edinburgh Review,* the *St. James Gazette,* and probably others. She enjoyed her periodical writing. Like biography and literary criticism, it proved more stimulating to her than the writing of novels. Furthermore, she had a relatively free hand here, not confined by the formulas of popular fiction. The Blackwoods and the editors of the *Spectator,* Richard Holt Hutton and Meredith Townsend, were her friends and admirers. She embarrassed them occasionally with her tactlessness or inaccuracy. The *Spectator* was obliged to add a dissenting "Editor's Note" once or twice to her articles.[22] But generally her personal views reflected those of the editors and their readers, and as a journalist and critic she maintained an independence and integrity denied to her as a novelist.

In forty-five years of writing periodical journalism Mrs. Oliphant inevitably showed development, a certain changing and enlarging of views, and differences in tone. Yet the most striking impression a survey of this work leaves is one of consistency. At the basis of all her writing, regardless of its enormous variety, is always the personal estimate. Whether creating a purely imaginary character in a novel, writing a biography, evaluating the achievement of a poet or a painter, reviewing a current book or play, or commenting upon a topical social problem, Mrs. Oliphant usually managed, like George Eliot's Dorothea Brooke, to resolve all complexities with her feelings. In many ways this very limitation worked to her advantage. It gave her fiction realistic color and detail; it gave vitality to her biographies; it brought a sense of sincerity and immediacy to her reviewing. In brief, although she had many literary gifts and was intellectually far superior to the average, she nevertheless managed to put herself on the same level with the middle-class reader of journals like *Maga* and the *Spectator*. She never pretended to intellectual eminence. In fact, she sometimes posed as an anti-intellectual, indifferent to the profundities of scholarship and aesthetics, impatient with theorizing. This was a pose, for Mrs. Oliphant was actually fascinated by learning, scholarship, and ideas. Her impatience with excessive intellectualism was nevertheless completely genuine. She was practical and pragmatic, essentially unimaginative, with a no-nonsense approach to all matters. Moreover, she had a lively, rather cynical sense of humor which prevented her from taking an overly solemn view of any intellectual subject. That sense of humor emerges occasionally in her journalism as it does in her fiction. She lightened her touch whenever she could—especially in reviews of current fiction and in the easy, rambling departments she wrote for *Maga* in later years like "The Old Saloon" and "The Looker-on," and in the thirty-three columns she wrote for the *Spectator* under the title "A Commentary in an Easy Chair" (December 7, 1889 to November 8, 1890).

Her characteristic approach to political and social problems was one of skepticism and cynicism. Public charity and social welfare, the newly emerging "social science," idealistic slum-visiting social workers, trade unions—she discussed and dismissed them all with a note of faint mockery. No number of institutions and organizations, no amount of theory, would reform man or society. She looked to her own life and struggles and concluded that only hard work and private charity were the answers. Shorter working hours, easier working conditions, security, and protection against economic disaster—she had had none of these and by 1890 she had a grim certainty that she would never have them. The increasing bitterness of her tone as the years passed is striking. Domestic servants are demanding two free hours a day: what mistress of a household has that much leisure Mrs. Oliphant asks sourly.[23] Everyone complains of overwork: whoever heard such a complaint thirty years ago? "But now it is rather a common, vulgar sort of thing not to have been prostrated by it, proving either that the non-sufferer has done no work to speak of, or has so rude and insensible an organisation as to be incapable of human nature's more delicate distresses." She even ridicules the current complaint of "writer's cramp": "This is a complaint of which the last generation was quite unconscious. Scott never heard of it, one may be sure; no, nor even Dickens, who was not averse to pose a little; nor our excellent Anthony of the Trollopes, who wrote enough, one may well believe, to wear out twenty right arms."[24]

Always short-tempered and sharp-tongued, she grew increasingly crotchety with the years and with the burden of sorrows and disappointments which almost crushed her. Willie Tulloch recalled her fondly, yet he recorded her irritability in the last years: "Somehow it seemed to me she could never quite understand and sympathise with those who took views differing from her own, and she was not slow to pour ridicule on you and your favourites if they were not hers."[25] Increasingly with the years she sharpened her attacks. Special butts of her contempt were America—which she never visited—and the feminist cause. The basis for her anti-Americanism was evidently the literary piracy flourishing during most of her career and a feeling that she had never been properly compensated for the American publication of her works. Her opposition to the women's rights movement was to a degree less personal and less bitter, but it too was barbed. Few women of the Victorian Age better demonstrated their ability to live independently than Mrs. Oliphant. Nevertheless, she scorned the fight for women's suffrage and equal rights as unfeminine and demeaning to the sex. Personally dignified, reticent and aloof, she deplored speech-making and other public activity for her sex. A devoted mother who was fortunate enough to have a career which she could pursue within her home, she opposed any activity which would take women outside the domestic circle. Faintly contemptuous of the male sex, she disliked seeing her sex compete with men on any economic or social level.

In her journalistic pieces Mrs. Oliphant no doubt echoed the proper, conventional, conservative sentiments of her publishers and her readers. Yet there was an element of complexity in all her views. She swallowed nothing whole, examining everything analytically and independently. True, she arrived at popular conclusions, but whether through expediency, conformity, or simply her own judgment, it is not always easy to say. She was independent in spirit and candid in expressing her ideas. Nowhere is this freedom better demonstrated than in her miscellaneous reviewing of art, theatre, and London life in general for *Maga* and the *Spectator*. Unhampered by strong emotional involvement and free to wander as casually as she pleased, she reveals freshness, wit, and sophistication as in no other writing. No expert in any of these fields, she simply reported on what stimulated and amused her. In art, of course, Mrs. Oliphant had a certain amount of expertise, largely due to the influence of her husband. She ridiculed Ruskin because Francis Oliphant had been bitterly disappointed with the Gothic Revival, also because Ruskin's idealistic schemes for social reform appeared foolish to her: "Society, we fear, can never be trained into those fine and tapering lines which regulate the leaves of our trees, the petals of our flowers."[26] She disliked Turner because, in her view, his was "a polluted life and a contracted soul."[27] Even when this personal estimate does not completely distort her vision, it is restricting and narrowing. Her passions for children and motherhood made her sensitive to the beauties of Italian religious painting, especially Raphael, but she was curiously unable to respond to art which did not immediately appeal to those emotions. She could duly acknowledge Michelangelo's genius, although she confesses that his David "touches our heart individually in no wise and is absolutely indifferent to us."[28]

Mrs. Oliphant regularly reviewed the Royal Academy shows

for *Maga*. Her reviews were simple and straight-forward reports on what she saw—faithful descriptions of the paintings, crisp, cautious evaluations in terms of the beauty of the work, the conviction of its theme or subject, and the general effect upon the viewer. In three decades or more of reviewing, she witnessed and reported the passing of old trends and the coming of new developments. Not surprisingly she took a dim view of the Philistine *verismo* so popular in the latter part of the century but she was equally cynical about the earlier Pre-Raphaelite school. Where are they now she asked in 1876:

> The vulgar splendour which lingers about that brilliant array of portraits with which Mr. Millais covers so much wall, is all that remains of them inside the Academy. Outside there are Mr. Holman Hunt's elaborate and far-fetched compositions, trifling, and tedious from over-care, and those choice and recondite marvels of art which Mr. Rossetti and his school show to the initiated in the half-light of their studios, scorning the homely day and the common light. And this is all . . . The Pre-Raphaelites have gone out like a sputtering taper.[29]

In place of the gauzy mysticism of the Pre-Raphaelites, Mrs. Oliphant detects in 1876 a new Philistinism—"gaudy paintings of the tea-board species." She describes two of these with relish, beginning with

> the "Honeymoon" . . . where a florid young Philistine in his new marriage-clothes is pointing out to a flounced and decorated young woman in all the shine of the *trousseau* the (apparent) announcement of their marriage in the morning paper; the "First-born," a similar young woman, got up with equal elaboration, though the glories of the *trousseau* might be supposed a little dimmed by that time, and contemplating with imbecile gratification a fat baby on the floor which leers up at her like a little satyr.[30]

Whatever her deficiencies as an art critic, Mrs. Oliphant was never taken in by vulgarity. She rightly sensed that hers was not a great age of art, and that English painting was largely innocuous and decorative: "Perhaps we ought not to seek sensation of any marked kind, sensation, emotion, in a picture, but only calm images, tranquillising scenes, which go no deeper than the canvas, without any moral perspective nor even too much of the other kind. This is what our greatest painters certainly seem to aim at, and it is, of course, much more probable that they are right than we are right."[31] The only paintings in demand, she concluded sadly but realistically, are those which are "adapted for the domestic interior . . . scenes from Shakespeare in which the costume was much more important than the meaning, and historical subjects of the same kind, and scenes from the Vicar of Wakefield conspicuous for their clean and thin smoothness, and illustrations of country schools and impossible *fêtes* and weddings, and Sir Edwin Landseer."[32]

These are the observations of a witty, worldly woman. Mrs. Oliphant did not take herself very seriously as an art critic. In a letter to George Lillie Craik in 1882 she admitted, à la Zuleika Dobson, that she knew little about painting: "I know what I like but not why I like it, nor am I quite certain whether I ought to like it or not."[33] She was indifferent to the technical, impatient with the abstract. Essentially she looked for the *story* in a work of art. If it was "told" beautifully and tastefully she was pleased. Her attitude toward painting was better informed than but not unlike her attitude toward music:

> My own sensations at a concert of the more elevated kind are, in fact, humbling. I love what I vulgarly call a tune . . . when the human voice comes in, I am always interested, especially when I can hear "the words" (which, by the way, are usually not at all worth hearing). But when there is neither tune or words, and it (the music) lasts very long, I generally take refuge in contemplation of the fiddlers . . . It is the instinctive resource of the listener whose mind is warped by the literary sense, and who prefers the play of human character and meaning to that of the most exquisite strings.[34]

Her highly developed literary sense apparently narrowed Mrs. Oliphant's vision in art and music, but it heightened her appreciation of the theatre, in which she had a distinct and discriminating taste. At home she and her sons and their friends enjoyed amateur theatricals. She even, very briefly, entertained the idea of dramatizing some of her own work for the stage.[35] Her play reviewing for *Maga* was informal—usually remarks introduced into her rambling comments in the "Old Saloon" and "Looker-on." Her taste in drama, though conventional, was marked with a degree of sophistication superior to that of the average theatre-goer. Thus, while she admired Sardou's *Diplomacy* ("about which everybody is raving"), she was quick to spot its structural weaknesses, writing of it to Blackwood: "It has so much excited me—that is the cleverness and suggestiveness of the piece generally and the complete failure in art of the last act—that I am bent upon taking the story for my personal use with the intention of entirely changing the conclusion."[36] She was as much interested in production and performance as in the plays themselves. At the root of all her criticism was her practical good sense. Writing of Lytton's play *Money,* she observes: "How droll it is to see a respectable young man ranting about a stage and delivering high-flown sentiments which read extremely well in a book, but want a good deal of skill and arrangement to sound well in a shooting-coat and a modern drawing room." She was impatient of sentimentality, melodramatic plots, exaggeration of any detail, and especially of overacting. Coquelin in *Fourchambault* was her ideal: "There is no strain, no struggle for effect." Henry Irving, on the other hand, while fascinating, was too flamboyant a personality for her taste, having "attained his successes more by sheer force of character than by genius." She was delighted, late in her career, to find her opinion of Irving shared by a impudent young critic on the *Saturday Review,* one Mr. G. B. S., whose "contempt for everybody and everything" she found quite exhilarating. Quoting his attack on Irving with complete approval she could not resist confessing that she was reminded of Dr. Johnson's "At her, little Burney" in her patronizing of this promising young writer.[37]

Informed, intelligent, but essentially dilettante in her approach to these subjects, Mrs. Oliphant described her role well in the title "Looker-on," which she used for her articles in *Maga* from August 1894 to October 1896. Like the eighteenth-century Spectator she observed from the outside, curious, detached, amused, sometimes censorious. Because she observed over so long a period, her miscellaneous journalism offers a revealing index of her age. Possessed of a keen sense of history and drama, she identified herself with the Victorian Age. The last decade of her writing career coincided with the last decade of the nineteenth century and with the Diamond Jubilee of Queen Victoria. The last article she wrote for *Maga* was appropriately a retrospective review of the Queen's reign, " 'Tis Sixty Years Since," published in May 1897, a month before her own death and the celebration of the Jubilee. It is a personal article, full of her recollections of her childhood. She had been six when Victoria ascended the throne. Her whole life, from its humble origins in Scotland and the early days in Liverpool to her genteel but bitterly unhappy final days, was spanned by Victoria's reign. She was proud of her country and her queen, the "mother-queen"—of the expansion of empire, trade and industry, of the railroad, of public education. But there is also an echo of regret, a sense of something lost from that quiet earlier age when life was simple. It is a fitting article to conclude Mrs. Oliphant's long career in periodical jouralism. Over nearly half a century of observing her society and reporting on it her thinking changed very little. Yet her mind remained constantly open to new ideas and new challenges. She traveled, she read, she met people of vastly different opinions and beliefs from her own; she never stopped moving, physically or mentally. But she remained solidly and consistently conservative. The London *Times* obituary on her observed: "No woman, and perhaps no writer of either sex, has been so long and so intimately associated with the literature of the Victorian era."[38]

Chapter VII

The Later Years

At one point in the *Autobiography* Mrs. Oliphant describes herself as having "a spirit almost criminally elastic." Her ability to bounce back after every crisis was little less than extraordinary. Her life records are a dreary chronicle. Yet in reading her letters and in attempting to reconstruct the normal pattern of her existence, one is struck by her unflagging resiliency. In her last years she was sustained largely by a deep personal religious faith, but during most of her life she drew her resources rather from a remarkable ability to survive from day to day. "The real philosophy of life," she wrote to William Blackwood, "is, I believe, to store up one's strength while all is prosperous for the inevitable reverse and work through the dark moment in confidence that there is something better beyond."[1]

Even at her peak of literary productivity she never knew real financial security. In 1872, for example, with a family of eight to support, she found herself in desperate financial straits. The letters to Blackwood are a series of frantic appeals—"Forgive me asking like Oliver Twist for more in the very face of your great liberality. It gives me a horrible pinch to do so . . . I am afraid you will think me terribly grasping, but it is necessity and not will that makes me so . . . Pray pardon me for writing to you so. It is the *want* of money I think rather than the love of it that is the root of all evil."[2] She had the manuscript of a novel which she had been trying unsuccessfully to publish, making discouraging trips up to London to offer it to publishers. Then, providentially, an editor of a newly established newspaper, *The Graphic,* appeared and offered her £1,300 for a novel. "I was absolutely without hope or help. I did not know where to turn, and here, in a moment, all was clear again—the road free in the sunshine, the cloud in a moment rolled away."[3]

Providentially or otherwise, Mrs. Oliphant was always able to procure the comforts of life. There were late summer holidays in Scotland, where she usually stayed near the Blackwoods' country house, Strathtyrum, in St. Andrews, convenient to the golf links and gay with the society of old friends and new ones. These were literary people—Anthony Trollope, Charles Reade, Arthur Kinglake—and also a large number of statesmen, scholars, clergymen, that host of energetic, public-spirited people who contributed to *Maga*—W. Lucas Collins, Colonel Lockhart, Edward Hamley. There were also more ambitious trips abroad. Most of these she financed with writing assignments. In 1867 she went to Paris to see Montalembert and traveled on from there to Germany and Bohemia. In 1871 she returned to France to collect material for her biography of Montalembert (who had died in 1870), taking Cecco, then too young for Eton, with her. In June 1873 she opened negotiations with Alexander Macmillan for a book on Florence which became the first of a series of highly profitable travel books published by Macmillan: *The Makers of Florence* (1876), *The Makers of Venice* (1877), *Royal Edinburgh* (1890), *Jerusalem: Its History and Hope* (1891), and *The Makers of Modern Rome* (1895). She persuaded her publisher to give her an advance of £300, with which she took a trip to Florence with her sons in 1874, "to retrieve my recollections and give the book a more perfect local colour," admitting candidly to Macmillan a few years later when she was working on the book on Venice that "this is the only way of giving my boys foreign trips."[4]

Not all the foreign trips, however, were conceived in so commercial a fashion. In 1875, to celebrate Cyril's completion of his Eton studies and his entrance into Oxford, and also to provide a pleasant farewell for her nephew Frank who was going off to work in India, she took her family to Switzerland. They were a large and happy party. Frank and Cyril delivered the two younger Wilson girls, Madge and Denny, to school in Germany, while Mrs. Oliphant, Nelly Wilson, and Cecco waited for them in Interlaken.

Mrs. Oliphant with her sons Francis Romano ("Cecco") and Cyril ("Tiddy"), and her nephew Frank Wilson, in front of the family home at Windsor (1874).

Reproduced from "The Autobiography and Letters," by permission of William Blackwood and Sons, Ltd.

There she met the ebullient Annie Thackeray, who was to become a lifelong friend. They moved on to Grindelwald where Miss Thackeray was joined by her sister Minnie and her husband Leslie Stephen, then editor of *Cornhill*. The meeting had practical as well as social value. Stephen, who was kind to her boys and went on walks with them, also bought two of her stories for his magazine. Annie Thackeray has left a little sketch of Mrs. Oliphant at this period, busily at work even while holidaying:

> I used to see her at her daily task, steadily continuing notwithstanding all the interruptions of nature and human nature—the changing lights on the mountains, the exclaiming of youthful excursionists, the many temptations to leave her desk. I was always struck, when I saw her writing, by her concentration and the perfect neatness of her arrangements—the tiny inkstand of prepared ink, into which she poured a few drops of water, enough for each day's work, the orderly manuscript, her delicate, fine pen. . . . When she had finished, she would come out in the evening for a saunter along the valley with Leslie Stephen and the rest of us. She was one of those people whose presence is ever more than a *pleasure,* it is a stimulus; she was kindly, sympathetic, and yet answering with that chord of intelligent antagonism which is so suggestive and makes for such good talk.[5]

The education of her nephew Frank Wilson was a burden Mrs. Oliphant had assumed willingly but not without a certain amount of complaint. She had great affection for him—"the most trustworthy and satisfactory boy in the world, loving home, fond of amusement and diversion, but only in the right ways—such a one as is a stand-by and tower of strength in a family." But educating a young man for a career was expensive. He did not receive the "gentleman's" education at Eton and Oxford that she gave her sons. Instead he prepared for a career in engineering. On August 1, 1871 she wrote Blackwood: "I am pushing on my nephew for the Forest Exam for India which takes place in November, and these horrible coaches are a perfect deep sea for money. I have great hopes that he will pass, but the preparation takes a good deal out of me. Of course if one succeeds it is a provision for life, and the boy is a good boy and will I am sure lighten my burdens as soon as he is in a position to do so." But the burden was not lifted as soon as she had hoped. Frank came out seventh in the examination and there were only five vacancies. She sent him on to engineering school at Cooper's Hill for another three years of training. In 1874 she wrote: "I am looking forward with more eagerness and hope than, perhaps, in the uncertainty of human affairs should be entertained, to the time when I shall be, I hope, considerably relieved of my expenses, but this blessed period is still eighteen months off and in the meantime I am going through the labours of Hercules—and am under a continual strain."[6]

Frank completed his work with a first-class in July 1875, just about the time his father died. He elected to go out to the Punjab and sailed for India in October. "Thus one of my anxieties is disposed of," Mrs. Oliphant wrote happily to Blackwood on July 27. "Death has taken away another, and I trust my life may be less burdened in the future; but in the meantime this is a somewhat tremendous moment." Frank's career in India was successful and happy, but it and he were short-lived. In the autumn of 1879 he died of typhoid fever, a terrible blow to Mrs. Oliphant: "I had trained him with pain and trouble, and sent him out to India with every hope and blessing four years ago, and here is the end, so far as this sad world is concerned"[7]

The year before Frank went to India a photograph was taken of Mrs. Oliphant and her three boys, posed with studied casualness on the steps of their Windsor home. It is a touching and revealing picture. Mrs. Oliphant stands in the background in her widow's dress and a neat cap, with something of a wistful smile in her eyes. Cyril lounges elegantly, elbow propped against the stair rail. Seated below are Cecco, an impish-looking, handsome boy, and a stalwart Frank Wilson with a fine moustache. The pride that Mrs. Oliphant felt is amply evident in the picture:

> I think often if all had gone well, as might then have been so confidently expected,—had Frank been a prosperous man in India, perhaps sending home his children to be educated, and Cyril been a rising lawyer as was hoped, and Cecco, if delicate, still able with care to keep on, it would all have been so natural, not anything wonderful, just the commonplace of life for which other fathers and mothers would scarcely pause to give thanks, it being all so usual, exactly what might have been expected. And ah, the difference to me! But, thank God! we did not know what was coming in these days.

Twenty years later when she wrote these lines in her *Autobiography* all three boys were dead. The sense of total waste—of so much youth and vitality in them and of so much hope and futile labor in her—is more moving, perhaps, than even the fact of their deaths.

Her own sons, she did not hesitate to admit, were disappointments to her. There was no failure at any time in her love and devotion for them. Indeed, Mrs. Oliphant herself recognized that it may have been the very excess of this love which caused the trouble, especially for Cyril: "I had so accustomed them to the easy going on of all things, never letting them see my anxieties or know that there was a difficulty about anything, that their minds were formed to that habit, that it took all thought of necessity out of my Cyril's mind, who had always, I am sure, the feeling that a little exertion (always so easy *to-morrow*) would at any time set everything right, and that nothing was ever likely to go far wrong so long as I was there."

Cyril was a thriving boy, a healthy baby, and, until only a few years before his death at thirty-four, apparently untroubled by serious illness. He was poised, good-looking, sociable—a character that seemed to have been shaped more by his easy-going father than by his earnest, industrious mother. His record at Eton was good; he was third in his graduating class, an honor rare for an Oppidan (a student who lived away from the college). His record at Oxford was less distinguished, though by no means poor. It failed to reach his mother's expectations, but these were probably too high. Following the traditional Eton pattern, he selected Balliol, matriculating in October 1875. He had tried since 1873 for a scholarship. "He passed a very creditable examination," his mother wrote proudly to Blackwood, "and . . . his English essay was the second in order of merit."[8] Being "second" seemed indeed to be Cyril's fate. He did not receive the hoped for scholarship but a smaller one, the Bryant, of £60-80 a year.[9] When he came home on his first Christmas holiday, his mother wrote hopefully to Frank in India:

> Tids has come back from Oxford since I wrote you last, and I think in my last letter to you I talked to you of the anxiety I could not help feeling about his first start in independent life.

Thank God, in everything he seems to have acted so as to put my fears all to flight and to give me confidence for the future, and has come home not only quite unchanged but even more completely Tids than he was before—as fresh, as boyish, and as good as a boy can be. I can't tell you how thankful and how happy I am in this. I was very much frightened for the ordeal, and he seems to have come through it scatheless. He has not succeeded about the exhibition, but that is a very much lesser matter. There is some talk at present about standing for the Cowper Scholarship, but this is not yet decided—you shall hear about it after.

Her hopes were frustrated. In December 1876 she wrote: "My boys are very well and all that I could wish them, though Cyril disappointed me and himself (horribly) by getting only second class in Mods. We felt terribly cast down for a while, but the Master of Balliol cheered me up again, which was a wonder, as he is not too genial generally on the subject."[10]

What troubled Mrs. Oliphant especially about her older son was his frequent failure to make the necessary effort, his lack of the discipline and industry with which she herself was so amply endowed. Throughout Cyril's university career there are references in her letters to his indolence: "Tids is by way of working tolerably hard," she wrote Frank in the summer of 1877. "He also does a tolerable amount of cricket, and it is very pleasant to have him at home. You say I used to say you had no energy: I suppose we elder people are inclined to think so with all boys. I can only hope Tiddy will take heart o'grace as you have done as soon as he gets real work in hand." She detected and was alarmed by a similar trait in Cecco who at seventeen showed some literary ambitions—"But I fear he is less good at steady study of the plodding kind than I supposed. How curiously appearances deceive. I believe now that he is right in what he always said, that he does less work than Tiddy, but I fear, I fear he does not 'plod,' that grand necessity of scholastic success, any more than his brother."[11] She had good reason for anxiety. She had given her sons gentlemen's educations without a gentleman's income for them to live on. Her own financial insecurity made it imperative they become self-supporting. Moreover, the decline in her literary reputation and her natural weariness with hack work and the grubbing which made up so large a part of her career led her to count heavily on the boys' making something of themselves. On Cyril's twenty-first birthday she wrote to Blackwood comparing her son with his own more fortunate son Jack:

> Jack has more to come of age for than my poor Tids, who is "lord of his presence and no land beside." He is a very good sweet-hearted boy, and very tender to me, but I can't help feeling doubtful whether he has enough of the sterner stuff in him to get success in those thorny ways of law (not to say life) which he is bound for. I am going to enter him directly at the Inner Temple. If all these boys of ours had but ten thousand a-year what delightful fellows they would be! I fear that is what our modern education trains them for, more than anything else.[12]

Cyril entered the Inner Temple in 1878, reading law desultorily. In 1879 he took a second class in classics and left Oxford. His mother was bitterly disappointed, writing to Blackwood: "I am sure you would sympathise with me in my mortification over Cyril's 2d class. He has been very unwell during this last most important year which is some sort of excuse—but idleness is at the bottom of it." She made efforts to get him some public office or a school inspectorship, applying to the Duke of Richmond and Lord Salisbury, while acknowledging that the bar would be the best career for him. "But two or three years more of study and fees and an uncertain prospect at the end appals me." As she feared, his legal studies came to nothing. By 1882 she had given up hope, and by this time too she was beginning to suspect that Cecco's future prospects were no more brilliant than his brother's. She offered their services rather desperately to Blackwood:

> I wonder whether one of my boys could not be utilized in your great concerns which must want so many workers. At the best Cyril is likely to be a briefless barrister. I should be very glad to hear of anything he could do that would give him a prospect of being settled in life. And Mr. Langford [manager of the London office in Paternoster Row] is getting an old man. If you thought there might be an opening for one of them I should be glad to send them to Baron Tauchnitz in Leipzig or my American friend [Mr. Roswell-Smith, president of the Century Company] to get an insight into foreign publishing—or indeed do anything else you thought necessary to qualify our aspirant.[13]

The *Autobiography* and the letters published by Mrs. Coghill reveal Mrs. Oliphant's fears concerning Cyril's future, but they fail to show the extent of her bitterness, or the growing rift between mother and son. To release her deeper tensions Mrs. Oliphant again turned to fiction, as she had so often before. In a curious novel which attempts to combine the supernatural with homely domestic realism, *The Wizard's Son,* she introduced herself and her son and described her personal trouble in great detail. She began it in 1882, at the very time she was thrashing about for an occupation for Cyril; the novel was published in *Macmillan's Magazine* in 1883 and in book form in 1884. The greater part of it concerns the exorcising by the hero of a corrupt spirit who has been haunting the family estate for generations. But the opening sections portray the hero as an idle, feckless young man living at home on the bounty of a widowed mother:

> The fact remained that at twenty-four, Walter, evidently a clever fellow, with a great many endowments, had got nothing to do; and, what was worse,—a thing which his mother, indeed, pretended to be unconscious of, but which everybody else in the town remarked upon—he was not in the least concerned about the fact, but took his doing nothing quite calmly as the course of nature, and neither suffered from it, nor made any effort to place himself in a different position. He 'went in for' an examination when it was put before him as a thing to do, and took his failure more than philosophically when he failed as, as yet, he had always done: and, in the meantime, contentedly lived on, without disturbing himself, and tranquilly let the time go by—the golden time which should have shaped his life.

Mrs. Oliphant draws a painfully realistic picture of the tensions in the household generated by the boy's indolence and his mother's nagging criticism of him. Her sympathy is with the mother who, she writes, "saw her son's faults almost too clearly, and they gave her the most poignant pain." *The Wizard's Son,* however, turns into a happy fairy tale. The boy inherits an estate in Scotland and in the process of facing the family ghost matures into a fine and solid man, much to his mother's delight.[14]

Cyril Oliphant had no such fairy tale wonders in store. To add to his mother's worries, his health began to fail in 1883. He recovered sufficiently to take advantage of the first really promising opportunity that had offered itself—a secretaryship to Sir Arthur Gordon, governor of Ceylon, at a salary of between £200 and £300 a year. Possibly because of the tension between them, Mrs. Oliphant welcomed the chance, although she saw him off with misgivings. On January 29, 1884, the day before he sailed, she wrote to Blackwood: "I hope the new start will do him good. Whether it ever comes to much is another matter."[15] Less than six months later Cyril was back in England, ill, declared unfit for the climate of Ceylon. He had tried to spare his mother the news of his illness and did not let her know of his return until the last moment. Traveling in Venice with Cecco that spring to collect material for *The Makers of Venice,* she came back to England in July to receive the news that Cyril was returning in a few days. When she met his ship at Gravesend, she found him looking better than she had expected but still showing the signs of tropical fever. They spent the remainder of the summer in St. Andrews. It was very costly, but, she wrote Mrs. Coghill, "I think St. Andrews is the best place for Cyril to get up his strength, which is the first thing for me to think of. It is a great disappointment, but that seems my lot in life."[16]

Cyril's lot for the six years of life left him was sheer dilettantism. Mrs. Oliphant remained unsuccessful in her efforts to find him a position. In August 1887 she wrote to Blackwood: "I have wearied Heaven, or rather the Education department, with my prayers on Cyril's account for years past." There was now an opening in the department, but by the new regulations only a schoolmaster could be appointed. "I would give my ears to get a chance for it for Cyril." She asked Blackwood to intercede with Lord Cranbrook. "I am ready to humble myself to anyone and have done so in all quarters with no result. People say to me that *of course* other people will take pleasure in helping me, and that my name will be enough, etc. But I have not hitherto found the smallest advantage in anything I have tried." Meanwhile Cyril occupied himself with golf and minor literary and secretarial jobs for his mother. He had a brief flurry of activity when, with a college friend, he attempted to launch a "society" paper—*Court and Society Review.* The venture involved no financial investment, his function being largely to use his mother's literary connections for the paper's advantage. Thus he wrote to Blackwood asking for some books to review—"of a lighter description than those which you send to my mother. . . . You can, you know, depend upon the mother to see that my notices are not contemptible, even if you have no faith in—Yours sincerely, Cyril F. Oliphant." Evidently his mother held the reins tightly, for she wrote a supporting letter to Blackwood, pointing out that "In many cases Cyril will be the reviewer and I will have a sort of supervision." Not surprisingly, the paper failed after a very brief existence. On September 20, 1888 Mrs. Oliphant wrote Blackwood: "Cyril's paper, I am sorry to say, has come to an end. His foolish friend who was the proprietor and editor would take no advice about it and the result was inevitable."[17] The remainder of Cyril's literary career was brief. He assisted his mother in her biography of Laurence Oliphant, mainly by arranging the notes. He wrote a little book on Alfred de Musset published by Blackwood in the Foreign Classics series which his mother edited. Work on the book proceeded slowly and it appeared only a few weeks before his death in 1890. He received £60 for it.[18]

Since 1887 Cecco had been showing alarming signs of tuberculosis, and Mrs. Oliphant managed to send him away every year to escape the rigors of English winters. In January 1889 she, Cyril, Cecco, and her friend Miss FitzMaurice set out for the south of France. To meet her expenses she took along two young ladies, acting as a kind of chaperone-cicerone for them. The expedition was a total disaster. Just as they were leaving Paris for Beaulieu, Cyril collapsed in the railway station. She sent the girls ahead with Miss FitzMaurice and remained behind with her sons. "You may imagine what a dreadful business this has been," she wrote to Blackwood—"the terrible shock and alarm to begin with and the expense which will be a dreadful addition to my carefully calculated expenses which I had just enough to cover creditably—and then the embarrassment of having two girls under my charge whom I ought not to have left." A few days later Mrs. Oliphant went on to Beaulieu leaving Cyril better but by no means recovered. She wrote desperately to Blackwood for additional money: "I had hoped that all was safe and smooth for the next four months—but, God help me, so many things are against me. This was like the falling of a thunderbolt, and the anxiety I have gone through is embittered by this constant accompaniment of financial need." Beaulieu proved more costly than she had anticipated. The once cheap little French town had had a tourist boom and living costs had soared. The fact that she had paying guests with her made it necessary to take a large house and hire several servants. "I do not know how I am to get out of it," she wrote to Black-wood on April 2, asking for £250 for future work, "unless you will be so good as to come to my aid." Two days later she wrote again, repeating her request and asking him to telegraph his an-swer. On April 11 she received a check from him for £100. She replied with thanks but urged him to send her more: "It is really a question of life and death."[19]

Cyril recovered from this attack. Though never well again, he improved sufficiently in health to accompany his mother, his brother, and Madge Wilson on a strenuous trip to Jerusalem in the spring of 1890. He suffered no ill effects from the trip, but during the summer at Windsor he was not well. His mother was at this time more anxious about Cecco's health, for in spite of his long stays in Switzerland he was showing little improvement. In November Cyril caught a heavy cold. After only a few days of illness he died, of what was diagnosed as lung congestion, quite suddenly and peacefully on the night of November 8. Once again came the cry of anguish. At 3 A.M. on November 9, Mrs. Oli-phant wrote to Mrs. Coghill: "My boy, my Tiddy is gone!—a few hours ago—dead! You will not believe it, nor can I. You will won-der at my writing to you myself, but I can't sleep or rest, and I can only talk of him—my bonny boy—my darling! I am like stone —I can't feel it—but it is true." Some years later, when the acute grief had subsided, she summed up his futile life: "He went out of the world, leaving a love-song or two behind him and the little volume of 'De Musset,' of which much was so well done, and yet some so badly done, and nothing more to show for his life. And I to watch it all going on day by day and year by year."[20]

Cecco's fate was in some respects even more pathetic than his brother's, and his early death was an even more crushing blow to Mrs. Oliphant. Her attachment to him was far greater than her attachment to Cyril. Her last child, born in Rome six weeks after his father's death, he remained her baby, "my bonnie rosy baby," longest of her children. As he grew into manhood his delicate health kept him even closer to her. Although he showed some of the same signs of idleness that had so distressed her in Cyril, she was quicker to make excuses for him. And Cecco proved ultimately more talented and industrious than his brother. He had some literary gift, though probably not enough to assure a successful career in literature, and a real affinity for scholarly research. In short, he had more of his mother than his father in him—or so Mrs. Oliphant believed. He was shy, yet in the intimate home circle warm and gay.[21] His only fault, she wrote when he was about fifteen, was that he was too fond of home "and prefers my society to that of other boys, which I don't think quite good for him." But no serious alarm is reflected in such a complaint. In fact she took great satisfaction in his devotion to her. Their letters, during his absences from home while he was at Oxford and later traveling abroad for his health, are deeply affectionate. She could speak to him more freely than she could to Cyril. When Maggie died she had grieved not only for the loss of a child but for a daughter-companion in whom she might confide. To a degree at least Cecco provided that outlet. "God bless you, my dearest boy," she wrote him in 1886. "I thank Him every day of my life that I can have full trust in my Cecco."[22]

Soured perhaps by her disappointments in Cyril's school career, Mrs. Oliphant expected less of her younger son and was cheered by any success. His Eton record was good. On his leaving the school in 1878 she wrote to Blackwood: "He is the steadiest fellow in the world and full of intelligence and brains, though not much of a winner of prizes. He is however Prince Consort's prizeman for this year as his brother was." Bad health and bad luck combined to prevent his achieving academic distinction. He worked hard to prepare himself for the Newcastle scholarship at Eton, but fell ill with gastric fever the day before the examination and could not compete.[23] He followed his brother up to Balliol, but again illness, this time a mild case of typhoid, struck just as he was preparing himself for "Mods." "Alas," she wrote to Mrs. Craik in 1880, "the examination began yesterday, and here he is in bed tearing his hair."[24]

Soon after Cecco matriculated at Oxford in October 1878 Mrs.

Oliphant rented her Windsor house and moved to be near her
sons: "I see no good in staying here when both the bits of my
heart will be in another place." In February 1879 she took a
house in Crick Road and settled down comfortably in Oxford
society where she was very well received. She wrote to Frank in
India:

> Many of the great persons at Oxford have already called on me,
> and I have been asked to several solemn dinners, to one of which
> I am going to-night and to another to-morrow. The people are all
> very civil, but I am sometimes doubtful whether I have been wise
> in coming. Cecco seems to have begun very well indeed. It is
> difficult to realise him as a Balliol man, but such he is, and has
> taken to smoking, which I never thought he would do, and talks
> about "other men" as if he had not been the baby a very little
> while ago. He has a good many friends, and seems to be quite
> cheery and happy, which is a great satisfaction to me, for I was
> always a little nervous about his start.[25]

At Oxford she met a number of literary people ranging from
Rhoda Broughton to Mark Pattison and his wife Frances Emilia
Strong, Professor Max Müller, the philologist, and the novelist
Turgenev, who had come to Oxford to receive an honorary degree
and was Max Müller's house-guest. Turgenev visited Mrs. Oliphant, who left a brief description of him as "a great giant with
much melancholy, much gentleness of expression. He was not to
be hurried, not given to talking much when he had come ex-
pressly to converse, but contemplative—oh, a very contemplative,
very gentle big man."[26]

Cecco took his degree in 1883, passing creditably but with no
academic distinction. The problem of his settling into a career
was as urgent, though less vexing to his mother, as his brother's.
He hoped to get an appointment in the Heralds' College, heraldry
and genealogy being his special interests, but he failed. In 1885
Mrs. Oliphant applied to Blackwood for assistance in getting him
the post of Secretary to the Society of Antiquaries. She had little
hope since it was highly competitive and Cecco was younger than
most of the other candidates: "Still it can do no harm to try.
Cecco was rather idle in his Oxford career, and did not do so well
as he ought to have done; but I am happy to say he sees the

folly of that sort of thing now, and is as determined to get work and to get on as I could desire, as well as being my most constant companion and the greatest help and comfort to me."[27] He had his heart set on this appointment and his mother did everything in her power to help him. She even asked Madame de Montalembert to apply to the Duke of Norfolk in his behalf. Meanwhile, however, Cecco was practical enough to explore other possibilities, including a less attractive job in the British Museum. To prepare him for the competitive examination, his mother sent him to Göttingen to brush up on his German. He took the examination in 1887 and "passed brilliantly." Much elated, he waited eagerly to be assigned, but he and his mother were doomed to bitter disappointment. A final prerequisite for the appointment was the passing of a physical examination, and this he failed. His examiner was the distinguished physician Sir Andrew Clark whom Mrs. Oliphant knew only too well, having consulted him earlier for Cyril.

Cecco was not content to settle into a life of easy semi-invalidism as apparently his brother had. His mother's connections in Windsor finally got him an appointment in 1889 to the royal library at Windsor Castle, where he assisted the librarian R. R. Holmes, but this was not a full-time position. As late as 1893, the year before his death, he applied unsuccessfully for a librarianship in the London Library. During this whole period he had been writing for both the *Spectator* (to which he had access by his mother's friendship with its editor Richard Holt Hutton) and for *Maga*. He began reviewing books for the *Spectator* in July 1884; his first contribution to *Maga,* a short story "The Grateful Ghosts," appeared in January 1886. He had a light, pleasant, easy style, some wit and whimsy, and a conscientiousness which compensated perhaps for his lack of real talent. He worked hard, as hard at least as his health would permit. The Blackwood files contain many letters from him recording a fairly large amount of writing. In June 1886 he published an article on John Guillim, the seventeenth century herald. In 1887 he translated from the Italian a series of articles on Cesare Borgia by Charles Yriarte; in March 1889 he published a review-essay on current political affairs called "France and her Neighbours"; and in March 1889 Blackwood accepted another story, "The Ghost Baby," which, Cecco writes, "I have corrected in the best way I could according to the ideas both of my mother and myself."[28] He also submitted a prospectus for a series of small volumes on the early history of Scotland to be about the size of the Ancient Classics and Foreign Classics series Blackwood had published. The publisher turned down the project but accepted two rather substantial articles on Scotch literary history—one on Henryson and one on Dunbar.[29] Blackwood also published his only book, *Notes of a Pilgrimage to Jerusalem and the Holy Land,* in 1891, an expansion of a series of articles which he wrote for the *Spectator* in the summer of 1890. It is a practical sort of travel-guidebook written in a breezy style: "This [tour of Egypt] will give time for a glance at Cairo, the Pyramids of Gizeh—which are disappointing—and the Sphinx—which is not." He writes of hotel accommodations, problems of travel by horse and mule, and takes a generally pleasant but superficial view of the region. Only in the last chapter, "The Balance of Power in Palestine," does he become more serious, arguing the advantages of a British protectorate there.

In all his literary activities Cecco worked closely with his mother. Much of his work was mere routine indexing, copying and sorting notes for her. She respected his talents enough to allow him to collaborate with her in 1892 on *The Victorian Age of English Literature.* One doubts if the collaboration was a strictly equal one. Mrs. Oliphant was far too rapid a worker for anyone to keep pace with her. But Cecco evidently did a large part of the research for the book, even if he did not participate in the actual writing. They planned to collaborate again on a guidebook to the Riviera where they spent so much time during Cecco's annual winter flights from England. She proposed it to Blackwood as the first of a series of travel books that she would write with her son. Blackwood was not especially receptive, and all that ever saw publication was an article by Cecco in *Maga,* December 1892, "A Bird's-Eye View of the Riviera." Undaunted by Blackwood's refusal, he continued to work on the book. He and his mother considered publishing it themselves, but they finally settled with "one of these new young publishers." In the summer of 1894 he was hurrying to finish six more chapters, involving considerable research in the British Museum, in order to have the book ready for the tourist season in October. "I only go into these details," he wrote Mrs. Coghill, "to show you that there is no humbug about it, because, as a general rule, I find my friends have a healthy disbelief in my having anything to do, or doing it if I have, perhaps on account of my not concealing the fact that I regard work of any kind with a cordial detestation, and would never do any if I could help it."[30]

Less than three months after he wrote this light-hearted letter to his cousin he was dead, at the age of thirty-four. The long, costly, wearying pursuit of health had failed. From the moment Mrs. Oliphant received the news in 1887 that he showed definite symptoms of tuberculosis she had faced the ultimate prospect with dread. "My mind jumps at everything that is worst and most dreadful," she wrote Mrs. Coghill. She took him to Pau that winter, looking for every hopeful sign but also seeing every discouraging one:

> He is a little better, I think, eating better, and his cough variable, sometimes not troublesome at all. God grant that the move may do him good. You know how anxiety of this kind acts upon me. I am in a suppressed fever, and can think of nothing else day and night. I watch every morsel he eats, each varying look and change of colour. How strange it is! All my troubles, and God knows they have been neither few nor small, have been repetitions —always one phase or another coming back, and that makes it all the worse, for I know how far my anguish can go.[31]

When they returned to England in May, after traveling home via Spain, he was much improved. The doctors still warned him to seek more healthful climates in winter, which accordingly he did. In 1888 he wintered on the Riviera and in Spain, this time alone. He wrote his mother lively and charming letters during his absence. In 1889 he was part of the ill-fated expedition to Beaulieu during which Cyril fell so ill. Immediately after his brother's death in 1890 he went to Davos, in Switzerland, taking his mother with him. Here the doctors gave them a cheering verdict—"He will not be as strong as other men for a while, but eventually he will be so . . . This is, you may suppose, balm to my heart, as much as I am capable of, and I hope I shall live a year or two more to make things as smooth as I can for my Cecco." They remained in Davos until March, then went south to San Remo for the spring. They were in the south of France again in 1892–93. But there was little basis for optimism by this time. Friends who saw Cecco at the wedding of Mrs. Oliphant's niece Madge Wilson in July 1893 were alarmed by his appearance. Their winter on the Riviera in 1893–94 produced little change: "He is tolerably well, but still much troubled with his breathing; and he has not gained much strength, I fear," she wrote to Mrs. Coghill in March 1894. His death came peacefully, back home in Windsor, after a brief siege of tonsilitis, on October 1, 1894: "My Cecco died last night. He is gone from me, my last, my dearest, and I am left here a desolate woman with the strength of a giant in me, and may live for years and years. Pity me,—it seems as if even God did not, and yet no doubt He had a higher reason than pity for me. The dreadful thing is that I can't go too: I am forced to live, though everything in life is gone."[32]

Mrs. Oliphant survived her younger son for three years. Her spirit had by now lost all its elasticity—no more cycles of optimism and hope, only a weary resignation, broken now and then in the *Autobiography* and in a few personal letters by outbursts of despair. But these were quickly controlled. Lifelong habits of industry and self-discipline remained unchanged. Mrs. Oliphant continued to write until a few weeks before her death, and she died apparently as impecunious as she had lived. Her last years were saddened not only by personal tragedy but by a bitter sense of failure and frustration in her literary work. She had outlived her children, her friends, and her reputation as a writer.

Nowhere is this sense of failure more movingly expressed than in "Mr. Sandford," a short novel written in 1888 with a grim foreboding of her future. "I am afraid you will not like it, or at least that it will vex you," she wrote to Cecco.[33] Certainly Cecco would not have liked a story which bared so frankly his mother's inmost fears and disappointments. Mr. Sandford is a painter who, most of his life, has enjoyed a reasonable amount of prosperity and success. He has supported his loving but extravagant family comfortably. His sons are charming and talented, but unemployed. There is a familiar echo of her own life in her description of one of them—"one of those agreeable do-nothings who are more prevalent nowadays than ever before, a very clever fellow, who had just not succeeded as he ought at the University or elsewhere, but had plenty of brains for anything, and only wanted the opportunity to distinguish himself." As he grows older, Mr. Sandford becomes painfully aware that his work is out of date; the art dealers can no longer sell his canvasses. Since his career had always been precarious and he had lived from day to day, providentially selling his paintings when he most desperately needed money, he now faces the prospect of ruin for himself and his family. His life, however, is insured, and he realizes that only by dying can he save his family. Providence intervenes once again when he is killed in a carriage accident. His widow and children grieve but soon adjust themselves to his absence. Ironically, even his paintings begin to sell again: "And all went well. Perhaps with some of us, too, that dying which is a terror to look forward to, seeing that it means the destruction of a home, may prove, like the painter's, a better thing than living even for those who love us best. But it is not to everyone that it is given to die at the right moment as Mr. Sandford had the happiness to do."

In the last year of her life Mrs. Oliphant published "Mr. Sandford" and another story, "Mr. Robert Dalyell," in a volume called *The Ways of Life*. To this she supplied a preface, "On the Ebb Tide," in which she described both stories as treating of an experience of life which she called the "ebb"—"they were at least produced under the strange discovery which a man makes when he finds himself carried away by the retiring waters, no longer coming in upon the top of the wave, but going out." She associated the ebb not so much with old age as with something even more poignant—"the wonderful and overwhelming revelation which one time or another comes to most people, that their career, whatever it may have been, has come to a stop; that such successes as they may have achieved are over, and that henceforward they must accustom themselves to the thought of going out with the tide." Mrs. Oliphant had been aware of the ebb in her own career for many years. She frequently contrasted the money she received for her novels with the much larger sums sometimes given to novelists whom she regarded as inferior, like Mrs. Henry Wood, Miss Mulock, Mrs. Humphry Ward. Only by constant industry had she been able to earn the fairly large income she had most of her life. As early as 1868, writing to Blackwood of her disappointment in the poor sale of *Brownlows,* she said: "the prospect of dropping into the shade is doubly painful—not to say that it is bitter to see any kind of folly noticed and not a word given to one's best efforts." Fifteen years later she observed bitterly of another novel: "It is very tiresome about the Ladies Lindores— especially as the papers (even the Saturday!) have been kind. I suppose the public thinks it has a little too much of me."[34] By the end of her life this bitterness turned into total indifference: "And now that there are no children to whom to leave any memory" she wrote in the *Autobiography,* "and the friends drop day by day, what is the reputation of a circulating library to me? Nothing, and less than nothing—a thing the thought of which now makes one angry, that anyone should for a moment imagine I cared for that, or that it made up for any loss."

Though much of Mrs. Oliphant's correspondence and writing during these later years indicates a state of extreme despondency and a decline in her creative powers, one of her best stories, "The Library Window," also belongs to this period and testifies to the endurance of her talent. Published in *Maga,* January 1896, it is usually grouped with her Stories of the Seen and Unseen because it deals with hallucination. It stands apart from others of this genre, however, in that it is not religious in subject or tone. A journey back into the past, it is the story of a widow who recalls an episode from her youth, a visit she paid while recuperating from illness, to her aunt in the little Scottish town of St. Rule's. Imaginative and given to introspection, the girl enjoys retiring with her books and sewing basket to the recessed window of her aunt's drawing room which faces a window of the College Library across the road. The window fascinates her strangely. One evening she suddenly notices a light in it and an escritoire at which a man is busily writing. Just as suddenly the vision disappears. She sees this vision repeatedly on succeeding nights, but nobody of her acquaintance shares the impression. Her aunt, who prides herself on her own unimpaired sight despite advanced age, considers the girl, as the Scotch say, "far ben." The girl meanwhile makes unsuccessful attempts to locate and identify the man whom she has seen. When she visits the library itself she discovers that what she thought was a window was merely a blocked-up wall. Nevertheless, once back in her aunt's drawing room, she sees the illuminated chamber across the way just as before, with the writer working away at his desk. " 'Oh . . . say something to me!' " she cries out. " 'I don't know who you are, or what you are; but you're lonely and so am I; and I only—feel for you. Say something to me!' " Apparently the man hears her, for he rises, comes to the window, and looks out at her. But he only waves what seems to be a farewell and disappears.

Its hints of necromancy and dark deeds from the past have kept "The Library Window" glimmeringly alive among mystery story enthusiasts, but its power and beauty transcend the sensational.[35] Perhaps the girl's shrewd old aunt sums up the significance of the story when she suggests, in trying to account for the light in the window: " 'It is a longing all your life after—it is a looking—for what never comes.' " Another character, the sybilline Lady Carnbee, warns the girl: " 'The eye is deceitful as well as the heart . . . the imagination is a great deceiver.' " Undoubtedly something of the mystery is to be ascribed to the girl's age and temperament, her delicate health, and the time of the year when the adventure occurs—Midsummer Day, a season, she indicates, when "the world was full of that strange day which was night, that light without colour, in which everything was so clearly visible, and there were no shadows," and a time " 'when the fairy folk have power.' " It may well be that in this intensely subjective tale Mrs. Oliphant utilized her native folklore to suggest something of the workings of the imagination itself. Like the widow whose story this is, Mrs. Oliphant herself could have been looking back on her own early dedication to the romancer's art—creating characters out of thin air. The heroine tells us at the end that although she has not returned to St. Rule's, she continues to see her vision of the library window when she is lonely. The gift of imagination then remains with her through the years, and if it deceives, it also consoles. For Mrs. Oliphant the crowning irony is the heroine's strong bond of sympathy with an unfulfilled writer.

While her faith in her literary powers waned, Mrs. Oliphant's religious faith grew stronger in her last years, becoming her prin-

cipal spiritual mainstay. It was an intensely personal faith, one
in which she found identification with God as the bereaved Father,
as she was a bereaved mother. The more profound aspects of
theology eluded her, or she ignored them. The function of her
faith was not to explain but to reconcile her to the tragedy of the
loss of her children. In a deeply personal essay she wrote for
Maga in February 1895, "The Fancies of a Believer," she commented on the many young men who are snatched away in the
prime of life: "Are they perhaps more to Him, more unutterably
attached to Him, being of His age, young men as He is, with
deepest reverence, be it spoken, in the eternal prime. I have reasons for loving to think it is so, and trying to picture it where
everything is so hard to realize." This was not faith which brought
hope and cheer, but only patience to endure. Mrs. Oliphant regarded her last years as simply a temporary waiting period until
she might join her loved ones in the afterlife. Yet she was denied
complete serenity even in such a faith. The bitter sense of the
futility of Cyril's life was always with her. Cecco's death, though
more terrible to her, she learned to accept fatalistically. The
memory of Cyril, however, continued to plague her.

Just six months before her death she published in *Maga* (January, 1897) one of her many stories of the afterlife—in the spirit
of her beautiful Stories of the Seen and the Unseen and her Little
Pilgrim series—"The Land of Suspense," unquestionably the most
personal, the most deeply felt of all her work in this genre—
written, she said, "not from the head but from the heart." Publishing so intimate an expression of her feelings was not easy. "It
hurt me to publish anything so personal, but if there is any comfort in the communion of sorrowful souls it was perhaps worth
doing—and one's personality will so soon be blotted out."[36] The
story had probably been conceived a year earlier in "The Verdict
of Old Age," her review for *Maga* (October 1896) of Gladstone's
Studies Subsidiary to Butler's Works. Here she cites Gladstone on
the subject of universal salvation, an idea which struck her as beautiful and consoling:

> Could we take it as established, what lights of heaven would break
> upon the mourner's eyes! Let us imagine an erring but notwith-
> standing loving child, perverse on earth, building his house upon
> the sand, coming suddenly as it seems to us, to the great calamity,

to death itself, 'unhousel'd, disappointed, unanel'd'; but startled
by that shock, and stepping straight into the arms of a radiant
father or mother spirit, in that great world, no longer dim or
shadowy, where goodness has every enlargement, and offence and
temptation none. Alas! we fear that nothing, even this glorious
possibility, could lighten permanently the longing yearning sur-
vivor to whom earth has become all blank, and heaven dim in the
greatness of present desolation. Yet this dream, if it is but a
dream, is at least nobler and more beautiful than all the other
devices of the soul of sorrow to reconcile itself to the absolute
deprivation which death brings to the living. *The world of suspense!* it is indeed, as Mr. Gladstone says, a world and an interval
of which little is thought—perhaps a world in which life will flow
in no unfamiliar channels, the greatest of all worlds, constantly
added to, owning no decline.

"The Land of Suspense" is Mrs. Oliphant's Purgatory. It is a
calm, lovely country, no different physically from heaven. The
story begins with a young man walking toward a distant city. He
meets people along the way who speak to him courteously but
never look at him directly—because, as he later learns, he is invisible. He does not know where he is. He has a feeling that he is
going home, but also a dim recollection "that his former goings
home had not been always happy. There had been certain things
in which he was to blame." At last he reaches a gateway where
a family—brothers, sisters, and a father—is waiting. They recognize his presence, but because he is invisible, he cannot join them.
His sister tells him that he must wait for God's forgiveness—
"then your spirit will be no longer unclothed, and all will be well."
From a fellow spirit he learns that he is in the Land of Suspense,
"where we all are until a day which no one knows—a visionary
day which, perhaps, may never come." He waits then for that day,
and as he waits he remembers his mother, alive and alone now on
earth:

> "God! the mother! the mother!" And the far distant earth
> seemed to roll up under his vision and open, and show a house
> desolate and a woman who sat within. And he who was himself
> desolate, yet within sight of the joy, forgot himself and every-
> thing that was his, to think of her . . .
> "For now she is alone," he cried. And then in his trouble he
> reproached the Most High God, and cried out, "Thou are not

alone; Thou hast Thy Son." And he forgot all his trouble and
complaining, and became all one prayer, one cry for another,
for one who was desolate and now had no child.

He prays then for his mother: "You who are together, leave not
her alone"—and falls asleep. When he wakes he is no longer
"unclothed" but is saved and reunited with his family. The story
does not end with his salvation, but with the despairing mother
on earth: "As for the prayer which he made, and which was
answered in a way he asked not, it is still unfulfilled; yet they know
it is not forgotten, for nothing is forgotten before God."

Desolate as she was, Mrs. Oliphant nevertheless crowded her
last years with activity. Her main occupation, one which gave her
much stimulation and satisfaction, was the ambitious history of
Blackwood's, *Annals of a Publishing House,* which she did not live
to complete. She was committed to many other projects as well.
Her financial burdens were not lightened by the deaths of her
sons. For thirty years she had struggled for financial security. In
the early days there had been greater urgency, but the demands
never ceased. While the boys were little she had provided a
measure of security for them with life insurance. In 1871, writing
to Blackwood of the sudden death of Henry Blackett, she asked
him to be her executor, "and a kind of guardian to my boys in
case of my death before they are grown up." She made the same
request of Principal Tulloch. At that time she calculated her
estate upon the continuation of her royal pension while the boys
were minors, her life insurance of £1,000 for each boy, and about
£500 in savings, "which probably might be wanted to pay debts
and wind up everything—and besides my small personal posses-
sions in the way of furniture, plate, etc."[37]

During the 1870's she counted heavily upon scholarships for
her sons' educations and on her nephew Frank's success in a lu-
crative position, but mainly she relied upon herself. "For the next
three years," she wrote in 1872, "during which I shall have all
three at work, I can look forward to nothing but a fight *à outrance*
for money: however, it is to be honestly come by. I don't care how
much or how hard I work, and fortunately my sanguine temperament and excellent health save me from the gnawing of anxiety
which would kill many people."[38] Her optimistic expectations

were doomed. There was never enough money. In 1877 the house in Windsor which she rented for £105 a year went up for sale for £1,600. "I should like very much to buy it, but I have no money," she wrote to Blackwood, asking for a £1,000 advance on a yet unwritten novel. "If I were to die the said novel would be a little more rather than a little less valuable (Mr. Trollope tells me he has more than one thus prepared for posthumous issue)." The house was sold, but not to Mrs. Oliphant. She continued to rent until March 1886 when apparently she scraped together enough money to buy it, writing hastily to Blackwood in pencil on the top of a letter—"I have just been signing and sealing my purchase of the house." A year later Cecco became ill and she was once more in urgent need of money to take him abroad. She refused to ask for a personal loan: "I do not like the dangerous privilege of borrowing from private friends and have never done it in all my burdened career. When business relations exist as well it is more legitimate I think and more safe." Instead she asked Blackwood if he knew anyone in Edinburgh who would lend her £1000. She offered to re-insure her life as security and pay five per cent interest, or to turn over her Civil List pension to pay the high insurance premium that would be required at her age. Blackwood helped to arrange this loan, with her pension as security.[39]

With the growing realization that both her sons were doomed to idleness, she made even more desperate attempts to find money. The ill-fated expedition to Beaulieu in 1889 was financed by taking two young ladies along for a fee. That same year she asked Blackwood to introduce her to the executives of the North British Railways. She had gotten the idea from her travels in France of renting pillows to passengers and thought that this might be a profitable business. The Northwestern Railway, she told him, had already rejected her offer on the grounds that they admitted no business concessions to their stations but the railway libraries of W. H. Smith. Such business schemes were hardly in accord with her determination to lead a genteel life, but she appears to have had no choice: "You know that literature ceases to be very productive to me and that any means of securing an income in less precarious ways would be of the utmost importance to my comfort, not to say my life."[40]

Pride was a luxury Mrs. Oliphant could no longer afford. In 1894 she again issued an urgent call to Blackwood for an advance of £200. "I am afraid that I shall die as poor as I lived." Her son's illness, the marriage of her niece Madge, drainage and repairs on her house—these were the demands of the moment. "I do not neglect the fact that my age is a good reason for making a loan to me less likely—but I have in my hands literary property quite safe and worth much more than this from which or by which you would be repaid if anything soon happened to me." One of these pieces of property was the *Autobiography* on which she was working at this time: "it will be more adapted perhaps for the public and will be something to make up deficiencies when I am gone. It is premature to speak of it in its present state, but I think it well to let you know that there is such a thing to be calculated upon."[41] On May 4, 1896 she wrote a pathetic plea to Blackwood for a steadier income. Mr. Allardyce, a chief editor of the firm, had just died:

> I wished to speak to you when I saw you on business matters but was shy of beginning and feel that I can say what I wanted to say better with a pen in my hand. It was simply this—that as you will probably have to make some changes in consequence of your sad loss in Mr. Allardyce which no one can regret more than I do, I should be very glad if you could make use of my services in almost any systematic way. I need not tell you how entirely my life has changed of late and lost so to speak its *raison d'être* altogether —but still according to God's will, not mine, I have to live on, and supply the means of living by work in which there is little savour or meaning for me. It seems a hard necessity, but I do not complain of it for I should be much more miserable than I am if I had not to work, and of course it is my own fault that I have spent my past earnings in other ways than securing a provision for my old age. Anyhow age is here with very few of its consequences, for I am, God keep me, as strong and fit for work as ever, though I hope this unnatural vitality cannot go on forever . . . You would be doing me the greatest favour if you could trust me with the duties of a regular post, insuring a certain income. I would not mind in the least what I turned my hand to. To escape the chances of an uncertain profession and the necessity of struggling for a place, or to keep my place, would be the greatest of advantages to me . . . If you could find any way of making me useful in the work of the Magazine you could rely I think on my devotion to

the work and on my discretion . . . I have no hesitation in saying
that a steady engagement would be the one thing that as long as
my faculties last, and they show no signs of failing, could give a
little faint comfort to my end of life. I do not want, you will
understand, to trade upon your sympathy for me, but I think I
have it in me to be of use.[42]

So serious was Mrs. Oliphant's financial plight at this time that her
cousin Mrs. Coghill and Mr. Blackwood began to discuss the possibility of buying an annuity for her. This was to be arranged without her knowledge and presented to her as a kind of tribute for
her forty or more years of service to literature. Mrs. Coghill's husband made inquiries and learned that for the sum of £1,050 an
annuity of £100 could be purchased. Mrs. Coghill also sent to
Blackwood a list of people who might be interested in the scheme.
These included the Bishop of Winchester, the Provost of Eton,
R. H. Hutton, Hamilton Aidé, Henry James, and Andrew Lang.[43]
The plans were dropped, however.

Old age did not in any appreciable way limit her physical activity. Hardly a year of her life after 1859 did not see at least one
expedition—to Scotland or abroad. She traveled for pleasure, to
gather material for her books, and to seek better climates, first for
her ailing husband, then for her sons. She always traveled well
and expensively, hiring private carriages, stopping at the best
hotels, scorning petty economies. When her sons were still young
and healthy she also traveled with zest and delight. When their
health failed she traveled restlessly, almost desperately, in search
of cures—Scotland, Italy, the south of France, Spain, Switzerland.
She wrote steadily as she traveled, utilizing every scene in novels,
in articles for *Maga* and *Good Words,* or in the travel series she
wrote for Macmillan. The most ambitious of her trips was to Jerusalem in the spring of 1890. She was no longer young, she was a
bad sailor, she was stout, short of breath, and troubled by rheumatism which made walking difficult. Nevertheless she undertook a
strenuous journey, accompanied by her sons and her niece Madge.
In Jerusalem she insisted on walking the Via Dolorosa on Good
Friday. "I don't know how I could have done it had it not been
for the boys, who took me by the elbows, one on each side, and
almost carried me along." They spent twelve days in Jerusalem,

then went on to Haifa by boat, from where they traveled to Damascus in a caravan—the young people on horseback, Mrs. Oliphant in a palanquin. She was badly shaken up in an accident on Mount Carmel when a pole of her chair broke and she was thrown to the ground, but she returned to England in May with no visible ill effects. After Cecco's death the desire and incentive for travel were gone but she made two more trips abroad. One was to Paris in October 1895 with her niece Denny. The girl had shown some artistic talent (her engraving of Mrs. Oliphant, made that year, and reproduced in the *Autobiography,* is a sensitive piece of work); and she took her to France for further training. The last trip, only three months before her death, was to Siena to gather material for another travel book to be published by J. M. Dent. She went reluctantly: "It is a very long and expensive journey, and I am not perhaps in strong enough health to risk it, but I fear it is quite indispensable." She asked Blackwood to lend her £100 for the trip, although she was doing the book for another publisher, "to be repaid, if not in work, from the price of the book which I promised to have ready in August." Not surprisingly, Blackwood refused, although a month later he sent her a liberal check, evidently for articles she had written for *Maga.*[44] She left for Siena in April, accompanied by Denny and by Fanny Tulloch, the Principal's daughter. It was a fatiguing trip, interrupted by illness, but she managed to complete her research before the end of the month. The book on Siena was never finished. Her last article in *Maga* (July 1898) was an essay on that city.

Although Mrs. Oliphant suffered some physical decline in her last years, her mental faculties remained as powerful as ever. Old age itself held no terrors for her. Early in life she had created an attractive image of it, and, in spite of the tragic losses in the last decade of her life, she lived up to that image remarkably. She saw it not as a period of decline, but as one of quiet strength and serenity. Her elderly characters, especially her old ladies, are unfailingly charming and appealing. For a number of years she had before her the real-life model of the elderly lady of fashion, Mrs. Duncan Stewart, who had been the inspiration for her story "Old Lady Mary." Mrs. Oliphant often speculated on why novelists devoted so much of their attention to youth, though she knew the

answer well enough—"the monotonous demand for a love-story
which crushes out of court all the rest of life." For herself she
found many compensations in being old—chief among them of
course the proximity of death and reunion with her loved ones:
"I find a great quiet invading the mind that once was restless with
many thinkings, a power of being silent yet not consuming the
heart, a capacity of content that was not in earlier days."[45]

Whatever her inner sufferings, friends who visited her were
struck by her calm, steady control. "You felt somehow," wrote
J. M. Dent, who saw her in 1896, "that no suffering would break
her spirit, and that her body must obey to the last ounce of its
strength her indomitable will. This I felt although I did not know
her story until afterwards."[46] James M. Barrie, who met her first
in about 1888, described her at that period as regal, gracious,
something of the *grande dame,* witty and sharp-tongued. When
he saw her almost ten years later, very shortly before her death,
he was struck by the change:

> The wit had all gone out of her eyes, though not quite from her
> talk; her face had grown very sweet and soft, and what had started
> to be the old laugh often ended pitifully. The two sons who had
> been so much to her were gone, and for the rest of her days she
> never forgot it, I think, for the length of a smile. She was less
> the novelist now than a pathetic figure in a novel. She was as
> brave as ever, but she had less self-control; and so, I suppose it
> was, that the most exquisite part of her, which the Scotswoman's
> reserve had kept hidden, came to the surface and dwelt for that
> last year in her face, as if to let all those who looked on Mrs.
> Oliphant know what she was before she bade them goodbye.[47]

It may well have cost a struggle, but Mrs. Oliphant retained the
image of graceful, genteel old age until the very end. The adjective
"regal" with which Barrie described her would have pleased her.
All her life she had a queenly contempt for petty economies. Although she slaved in her writing and swallowed her pride many
times to beg for help from her publishers, the figure she presented
to the public was an elegant one. It might have been wiser, she
once acknowledged to Blackwood, in the early years when she had
the boys to educate, to have lived more cheaply and simply: "I
hold myself ready to do this should the necessity absolutely arise;

but you will understand that while still in the full tide of middle life I shrink from such a sacrifice and would rather work to the utmost of my powers than withdraw from all that makes existence agreeable."[48] Such habits, once acquired, are not easily broken. In 1894, a grim year both personally and financially, she planned a trip to Scotland and wrote to Archie Smith of Blackwood's to find lodgings for her in Edinburgh: "I am so thoroughly sick of hotels that I should very much like if possible to get rooms in a nice place where there would be a view like the view from Charlotte Square, or else in Princes Street. . . . I should want a good sitting room, two bedrooms and room for a maid or rather for two maids."[49] She dressed simply but expensively, mainly in black and grey, wore no jewelry, but had a taste for the finest old lace. An expert needlewoman herself, she had contempt for cheap, machine-made clothes: "when she was shown or heard of any 'bargain' she fired up at once, calling the material 'coarse and rough,' and the work either 'abominably bad or shamefully underpaid and in either case not fit for any gentlewoman to wear.' "[50]

Like so many women of her generation, as she grew older Mrs. Oliphant modelled herself more and more upon the Queen. Her attitude toward her sovereign softened considerably from the scorn and cynicism of her first reactions to Blackwood's request that she review the Queen's books in 1868. In later years she was not only Queen Victoria's neighbor in Windsor but also her friend. However little respect she had for the Queen's literary efforts, she was deeply flattered by her admiration for her own writing. It must have been consoling indeed to know, on the testimony of Mr. Holmes, the librarian at Windsor Castle, that hers were "the only books of which Her Majesty insisted that a complete series should be placed in the Royal Library. The Queen wished to show (we may believe) her recognition of the purity of her work and something perhaps of fellow-feeling in industry. 'I also work hard, Mrs. Oliphant,' the Queen said to her, in a conversation of which Mrs. Oliphant only permitted herself to say that it touched upon politics."[51] Of their private meetings there is, of course, no record, only a few reticent remarks in Mrs. Oliphant's letters. The first presentation, when she received her pension in 1868, had been strictly formal. In 1886 she had a private audience mainly to discuss Prin-

cipal Tulloch who, until his death a short time before, had been
one of the Queen's chaplains. Mrs. Oliphant reported to Mrs. Coghill: "She spoke to me a great deal about the Tullochs and also
about myself, and was very sweet and friendly, hoping to see more
of me. It alters one's ideas of her when she is pleasant to oneself."
A few days after this meeting the Queen sent Mrs. Oliphant a copy
of her *Journals of the Highlands* with a note written by Sir Henry
Ponsonby saying that "she is well aware how humble her efforts
are at authorship, but as a true Scotchwoman the Queen ventures
to send them to you."[52] In 1887 she attended the Queen's garden
party in celebration of the Golden Jubilee, at Buckingham Palace.
Cecco wrote proudly to Blackwood:

> The Queen has been very kind lately. My mother having sent her
> a letter of congratulation on her jubilee, she sent down, first, while
> she was too busy to do anything else, one of the silver medals
> which she has had struck in commemoration of her jubilee. (This
> my mother is to wear today.) Then, when her hands were freer,
> a very kind and pretty little letter and finally this invitation to the
> garden party, which is in itself perhaps rather a nuisance for the
> moment, but no doubt a great honour.[53]

Royal recognition like this suggests the vast distance Mrs. Oliphant had traveled from her humble origins. Whatever success she
achieved was the result entirely of her own industry, her physical
energy, and her resiliency of spirit. In 1885 she wrote:

> I have lived a laborious life, incessant work, incessant anxiety—
> and yet so strange, so capricious in this human being, that I would
> not say I have had an unhappy life . . . Sometimes I am miserable
> —always there is in me the sense that I may have active cause to
> be at any moment—always the gnawing pangs of anxiety, and
> deep despair. And yet there are times when my heart jumps up
> in the old reasonable way, and I am, yes, happy—though the word
> seems so inappropriate—without any cause for it, with so many
> causes the other way.[54]

A large measure of this remarkable power to bounce back was the
result of that vigorous good health of which Mrs. Oliphant so often
boasted. She also had cause to despise it—yearning in moments
of crisis for the release of illness, unconsciousness, and death.

But without the health, as she well knew, she would have faced financial ruin. Until her final illness she knew hardly a moment of serious sickness. In May 1875 she had a siege of neuralgia which left her suffering from shortness of breath but did not interfere with her work. "I am still far from well, but as I see no reasonable prospect of being better I am contenting myself as well as I can in being not very well—which is rather a complicated sentence, though perhaps not more complicated than the feelings with which one seems oneself condemned to take a lower place in the ranks of health. All the same I have had a long spell of robustiousness and have every inducement to make the best of it now."[55] A few years later she developed rheumatism and in August 1886 went to Wiesbaden for the baths with her friend Miss FitzMaurice, who was suffering even more severely from the same complaint. The first really alarming attack of illness came a few months after Cyril's death. She was in Davos with Cecco at the time. Ironically, the high altitude which was assumed to be so beneficial for his lung trouble proved very harmful to her. She wrote to Blackwood in February 1891: "It appears that the High Alps are not good for elder people, and almost always produce a collapse of some kind. Mine has been attended by very severe internal pain, of which I have had a few attacks before, but none so repeated and continued." Rheumatism continued to plague her periodically. In 1894 she wrote to Mrs. Coghill from Mentone: "I have been rather a cripple ever since I came here, very much taken up about my knees, which gave way in the most ridiculous manner when I attempted to walk, and gave me great pain; and though this of course did not prevent me from writing, it hampered me in many ways."[56] Not until a few weeks before her death, however, did she give any real sign of failing health. "I am not any great things in the way of health," she wrote to Blackwood on May 7, 1897, "and I begin to think will never be any more—which considering that I entered my seventieth year the other day is not wonderful, nor do I grumble at it in the least, though I don't like pain, but I feel quite able to work which is a fortunate thing."[57]

The three years between her younger son's death and her own were lonely and bitter, but not perhaps as lonely and bitter as the *Autobiography* suggests. She did not want for companionship. Her two nieces, Frank Wilson's daughters whom she had adopted and educated, were devoted to her. Madge, the elder, married a Mr. Valentine in July 1893 and went to live in Dundee. Denny (Janet Mary) was her aunt's constant companion during her last years. "I thank God for my dear little Denny, to whom I seem to do wrong by speaking as if she were not mine, which she is by every tenderest tie." Fanny Tulloch also made her home with her from 1895 and was considered a member of the family. Mrs. Oliphant wrote just after Cecco's death that she "has made herself so one with us in our calamity that we are never likely to part." Denny shared her aunt's sad lot very closely. A shy, sensitive girl, she seems to have been deeply affected by the melancholy atmosphere of the household. Mrs. Oliphant confided her fears about her in a letter to Mrs. Coghill: "I think it is very bad for her being continually under my shadow. She gets more undecided, more hesitating, and has less confidence in herself every day. This troubles me very much. I don't know what would be best for her. I have even thought of going to Paris, that she might get to work there, but I can't make sure of anything." She took Denny to Paris later that year, but the trip did not solve the problem. In 1896 she wrote again to Mrs. Coghill: "I so often find myself silenced by the young people, unable to say what is in my heart, because it saddens Denny."[58]

Mrs. Oliphant moved to a house on the Common in Wimbledon in April 1896. Unable to bear the memories it had for her, she had rented the Windsor house. Leaving her home of so many years was not easy: "It is hard going and it is hard staying. I don't know which is worse," she wrote Archie Smith. The new house was not so fine as the Windsor house: "We are just on the edge of the fine and fashionable, but quite out of it unfortunately. I have begun to say that we are like the Peri at the gate. It is really a very tumble-down and shabby house but comfortable enough inside, and with the Common outside there is abundant space and freer air."[59] Her health failed rapidly now. In July 1896 Denny wrote to Blackwood: "She has had internal inflamation, and though the acute pain is gone, she still suffers a good deal, and is very weak and pulled down—unlike herself in every way; and the doctor evidently thinks it will be some time before she is well again. I can't help feeling very anxious about her, and the doctor has absolutely forbidden work or even talking; but she must be kept quiet, and she is too weak to wish for anything else."[60]

She recovered sufficiently to undertake the trip to Siena, but about a month after her return went into a decline. In early June 1897 her doctor told her that her case was hopeless—news she received with great serenity. She continued to work at the Blackwood history, and only a few weeks before her death wrote a poem celebrating the Diamond Jubilee, "2nd June 1897" (*Maga,* June 1897). She expressed a wish to live to see that great day, which she did, dying just three days later. Her last letters were to the two publishers who had worked most closely with her—William Blackwood and George Lillie Craik of Macmillan. Her main concern at the end, characteristically, was money—paying off her debts and making some provision for Denny's future. The letter to Blackwood, which is not dated, she dictated to Denny. The letter to Craik was written in her own hand:

16 June [1897]
Wimbledon

Dear Mr. Craik,

I want to write a few words to you while I am able about the remnant of debt which I owe you. The child's story [unidentified] has somehow got lost, but I would like you to take two of those published in magazines which have never been republished and which would form a volume of the size of the Ways of Life published by Mssrs. Smith Elder. They gave £250 for that with its new preface. What I owe you is about one hundred and fifty. Perhaps someone could write a short preface of my life to enable you to add a hundred. I am anxious to leave everything as smooth as possible for my child [Denny].

I am dying but not suffering much. I am sorry there has been a cloud on the end of our long friendship—but no unkind feeling on my part. Goodbye.

Very truly yours,
M. O. W. Oliphant[61]

Dear Mr. Blackwood,

I have looked at the title page [of *Annals of a Publishing House*] and made the last correction of the press that I shall ever be able to do. I can't tell you how sorry I am not to be able to revise the second volume. I hope you and Mr. [J. H.] Lobban will go over it with great care. Your grandfather's letters to your father are all admirable, but perhaps you may think I have quoted too many. . . .

I am now dying, all possibility of work over, awaiting a very speedy end. You know that I have been working for a long time for daily bread. I will leave enough behind me to clear off everything, besides the literary remains, autobiographical, etc. I wish therefore to ask you as a last kindness to pay my bankers £100 to meet the expenses of the time, which will either be repaid to you by Denny as soon as my affairs are settled, or else subtracted from the price you may offer to her for these unpublished fragments. We are very old friends and have always I think worked along very comfortably together. Except for these matters I am very grateful to get away to 'the rest that remaineth,' and very comfortable in my mind reposing on Our Dear Lord. Goodbye—my love to you all.

M. O. W. Oliphant[62]

Most of her close friends were dead—Geddie Macpherson, Mrs. Tulloch, Isabella Blackwood, Emma FitzMaurice, Lady Cloncurry. Anne Thackeray Ritchie saw her on her death-bed and wrote to her son: "I am out of spirits and very sad, for my dear Mrs. Oliphant is too ill ever to get well again. She sent for me and kissed me and sent you and Hester her love. I think she is longing to go. They sent to borrow Alfred Tennyson's poems last night. There was one that she wanted. In it he says Death should have another name and this is 'Onward.' "[63] Another visitor was her old friend Robert Story. They had not met often in the last years, but she had once written to him: "I am glad you don't altogether forget me; there must be some little thread of immortality in a friendship which, with as little intercourse to keep it up, still holds fast." Story recorded the last visit in his memoirs:

Hearing she was very ill, I went down on Sunday week to Wimbledon, and found her on her death-bed. Her voice was still strong with its old, familiar tone; her wonderful eyes were as lambent as ever; and her mind was as calm and clear as a summer's sea. "I am dying," she said. "I do not think I can last through the night." Thinking of the "Little Pilgrim" and the "Seen and Unseen," and the many touching efforts her eager imagination had made to lift the impenetrable veil, I said, "The world to which you are going is a familiar world to you." "I have no thoughts," she replied, "not even of my boys; but only of my Saviour waiting to receive me, and of the Father."[64]

She died peacefully at twenty-five minutes to twelve on the night of Friday, June 25. On the following day Denny wrote to Blackwood:

> The doctors had told us last Tuesday week that it could only last a few days, but her strength and constitution were so great that she has lived much longer, and I wish now very much you had been able to see her. It was her only trouble at the end that she had not been able to revise the second volume nor written any of the third. Also the little book she had begun about Siena is only just begun—not that that troubled her.
>
> The house and all seems very desolate, and we all seem to me such poor creatures now she is not there, all the world seems to me less worthy, less capable of good now she is out of it.[65]

The funeral was held on June 29 and burial was in the Eton Parish Cemetery. She is buried between her two sons. A large Celtic cross stands for Cyril, two smaller ones for herself and Cecco. Moss and mildew have now almost obliterated her name, but the names of her sons stand out clearly. There is no indication anywhere of her literary career. An inscription runs round the small white marble rectangle enclosing the three graves:

In their death they are not divided

M. O. W. O.   C. F. O.   F. R. O.

Cyril's grave is inscribed significantly: "He hath delivered my soul in peace from the battle that was against me"; Cecco's, "Beholding with open face the glory of the Lord"; and hers, "I shall be satisfied when I awake with Thy likeness." On the top of her headstone are these words: "Thou wilt keep him in perfect peace whose mind is stayed on Thee because he trusteth in Thee."

A few days after the funeral George Lillie Craik initiated a movement to erect a public memorial to Mrs. Oliphant. He wrote William Blackwood suggesting that he issue an appeal for funds. Blackwood was reluctant to push arrangements. He recalled his recent frustrations in an attempt to launch a drive for a memorial to Robert Louis Stevenson. That effort had collapsed—much to the embarrassment of its promoters. Craik, however, was persistent: "I fear if you hesitate to be the active agent in arranging about a memorial to Mrs. Oliphant that it will be difficult to get anyone to take it up. As I said when I wrote to you, I feel that you are the fittest person to move in the matter. Mrs. Oliphant was personally connected with you and your house in a special way, and I do not like anyone taking the task of honouring her out of your hands. To tell the truth, I do not believe anyone would attempt if you decline." Blackwood then assumed the honorary secretaryship of a committee to establish the memorial.[66] A call for support was issued in the *Times* and in many of the journals in which she had been published. Eleven years after her death a plaque to her was at last unveiled in St. Giles Cathedral in Edinburgh, on July 16, 1908. A large portrait medallion by Pittendrigh Macgillivray, set in green marble, it is located in the west end of the Albany aisle facing a monument to John Knox and adjacent to the large memorial to Stevenson. Inscribed underneath the portrait are her dates of birth and death and the words: "That we may remember her genius and power as a novelist, biographer, essayist and historian."

The dedicatory services were well attended, although it was a wet day. The invocation was spoken by Dr. Cameron Lees, and there was an address by Lord Dunedin, who called Mrs. Oliphant "the greatest Scottish female writer since the days of Miss Ferrier." The principal speaker was James M. Barrie, who unveiled the monument and eulogized her "as a woman and as a writer"— "The woman was the greater part of her. Throughout her life she had other things and better things to do than write, and she was doing them all the time; they were the things that made her heart glad or depressed—never her books." Barrie emphasized the practical nature of her literary career: "She took to literature for the most honourable of all reasons—to make a livelihood; but she took to it as some finely equipped ship slips for the first time into the water." And he did not underestimate her significant and considerable contribution to her age: "We know that she was the most distinguished Scotswoman of her time, and a steady light among the band of writers who helped to make the Victorian reign illustrious."[67]

Chronology
of Mrs. Oliphant's Principal Works

This list includes only books which can positively be attributed to Mrs. Oliphant. The dates indicate the first publication in book form. Many of these works, however, appeared earlier in periodicals.

1849. *Passages in the Life of Mrs. Margaret Maitland of Sunnyside. written by Herself.* 3 vols. Colburn.

1851. *Caleb Field, A Tale of the Puritans.* Colburn.
Merkland, A Story of Scottish Life. Colburn.

1852. *Memoirs and Resolutions of Adam Graeme of Mossgray.* 3 vols. Hurst and Blackett.

1853. *Katie Stewart, A True Story.* Blackwood.
Harry Muir, A Story of Scottish Life. Hurst and Blackett.

1854. *The Quiet Heart, A Story.* Blackwood.
Magdalen Hepburn, A Story of the Scottish Reformation. 3 vols. Hurst and Blackett.

1855. *Lilliesleaf. Being a Concluding Series of Passages in the Life of Mrs. Margaret Maitland.* 3 vols. Hurst and Blackett.

1856. *Zaidee, A Romance.* 3 vols. Blackwood.

1857. *The Athelings: or, The Three Gifts.* 3 vols. Blackwood.
The Days of My Life, An Autobiography. 3 vols. Hurst and Blackett.

1858. *Sundays.* Nisbet.
The Laird of Norlaw, A Scottish Story. 3 vols. Hurst and Blackett.
Orphans, A Chapter in Life. Hurst and Blackett.

1859. *Agnes Hopetoun's Schools and Holidays.* Macmillan.

1860. *Lucy Crofton.* Hurst and Blackett.

1861. *The House on the Moor.* Hurst and Blackett.
(trans.) Montalembert (Charles Forbes René de) Count. *The Monks of the West from St. Benedict to St. Bernard.* 7 vols. (1861–1879). Blackwood.

245

1862. *The Last of the Mortimers, A Story in Two Voices.* 3 vols. Hurst and Blackett.
The Life of Edward Irving, Minister of the National Scotch Church, London. Illustrated by his Journals and Correspondence. 2 vols. Hurst and Blackett.

1863. *The Rector, and The Doctor's Family.* 3 vols. Blackwood.
Salem Chapel. 2 vols. Blackwood.
Heart and Cross. Chapman and Hall.

1864. *The Perpetual Curate.* 3 vols. Blackwood.

1866. *Agnes.* 3 vols. Hurst and Blackett.
Miss Marjoribanks. 3 vols. Blackwood.
A Son of the Soil. 2 vols. Macmillan.

1867. *Madonna Mary.* 3 vols. Hurst and Blackett.

1868. *Brownlows.* 3 vols. Blackwood.
Francis of Assisi (The Sunday Library). Macmillan.

1869. *Historical Sketches of the Reign of George Second.* 2 vols. Blackwood.
The Minister's Wife. 3 vols. Hurst and Blackett.

1870. *John, A Love Story.* 2 vols. Blackwood.
The Three Brothers. 3 vols. Hurst and Blackett.

1871. *Squire Arden.* 3 vols. Hurst and Blackett.

1872. *At His Gates.* 3 vols. Tinsley.
Ombra. 3 vols. Chapman and Hall.
Memoirs of the Count de Montalembert, A Chapter of Recent French History. 2 vols. Blackwood.

1873. *May.* 3 vols. Chapman and Hall.
Innocent, A Tale of Modern Life. 3 vols. Sampson Low.

1874. *A Rose in June.* 2 vols. Hurst and Blackett.
For Love and Life. 3 vols. Hurst and Blackett.

1875. *The Story of Valentine and his Brother.* 3 vols. Blackwood.
Whiteladies. 3 vols. Chatto.

1876. *The Curate in Charge.* 2 vols. Macmillan.
Phoebe, Junior, A Last Chronicle of Carlingford. 3 vols. Hurst and Blackett.
Dress (Art at Home Series). Macmillan.
The Makers of Florence: Dante, Giotto, Savonarola, and their City. Macmillan.

1877. Foreign Classics for English Readers. Blackwood.
Cervantes.
Dante.
Molière. (With Francis B. C. Tarver)
Young Musgrave. 3 vols. Macmillan.
Mrs. Arthur. 3 vols. Hurst and Blackett.
Carità. 3 vols. Smith, Elder.

1878. *The Primrose Path, A Chapter in the Annals of the Kingdom of Fife.* 3 vols. Hurst and Blackett.

1879. *Within the Precincts.* 3 vols. Smith, Elder.
The Greatest Heiress in England. 3 vols. Hurst and Blackett.

1880. *A Beleaguered City, being a Narrative of certain Recent Events in the City of Semur, A Story of the Seen and the Unseen.* Macmillan.
He that Will Not when He May. 3 vols. Macmillan.

1881. *Harry Joscelyn.* 3 vols. Hurst and Blackett.

1882. *In Trust, The Story of a Lady and her Lover.* 3 vols. Longmans.
The Literary History of England in the End of the Eighteenth and Beginning of the Nineteenth Century. 3 vols. Macmillan.
A Little Pilgrim in the Unseen. Macmillan.

1883. *Sheridan* (English Men of Letters). Macmillan.
Hester, A Story of Contemporary Life. 3 vols. Macmillan.
It Was a Lover and his Lass. 3 vols. Hurst and Blackett.
The Ladies Lindores. 3 vols. Blackwood.

1884. *Sir Tom.* 3 vols. Macmillan.
The Wizard's Son. 3 vols. Macmillan.

1885. *Two Stories of the Seen and the Unseen* ["Old Lady Mary"; "The Open Door"]. Blackwood.
Madam. 3 vols. Longmans.

1886. *Oliver's Bride, A True Story.* Ward and Downey.
A Country Gentleman and his family. 3 vols. Macmillan.
Effie Ogilvie, The Story of a Young Life. 2 vols. Maclehose.
A House Divided against Itself. 3 vols. Blackwood.

1887. *The Makers of Venice: Doges, Conquerors, Painters, and Men of Letters.* Macmillan.
The Son of his Father. 3 vols. Hurst and Blackett.

1888. *The Land of Darkness, along with Some Further Chapters in the Experience of the Little Pilgrim.* Macmillan.
Joyce. 3 vols. Macmillan.
The Second Son. 3 vols. Macmillan.
Memoir of the Life of John Tulloch. Blackwood.
Cousin Mary. S. W. Partridge.

1889. *Neighbours on the Green, A Collection of Stories.* Macmillan.
A Poor Gentleman. 3 vols. Hurst and Blackett.
Lady Car, The Sequel of a Life. Longmans.

1890. *Kirsteen, A Story of a Scottish Family Seventy Years Ago.* 3 vols. Macmillan.

The Duke's Daughter; and The Fugitives. 3 vols. Blackwood.

Sons and Daughters. Blackwood.

Royal Edinburgh: Her Saints, Kings, Prophets, and Poets. Macmillan.

The Mystery of Mrs. Blencarrow. Hurst and Blackett.

1891. *The Railwayman and his Children.* 3 vols. Macmillan.

Janet. 3 vols. Hurst and Blackett.

Jerusalem: Its History and Hope. Macmillan.

A Memoir of the Life of Laurence Oliphant, and of Alice Oliphant, His Wife. 2 vols. Blackwood.

1892. *The Cuckoo in the Nest.* 3 vols. Hutchinson.

Diana Trelawney, The History of a Great Mistake. 2 vols. Blackwood.

The Marriage of Elinor. 3 vols. Macmillan.

The Victorian Age of English Literature. (With F. R. Oliphant) 2 vols. Rivington.

The Heir Presumptive and the Heir Apparent. 3 vols. Macmillan.

1893. *Lady William.* 3 vols. Macmillan.

The Sorceress. 3 vols. F. V. White.

Thomas Chalmers, Preacher, Philosopher, and Statesman (English Leaders of Religion). Methuen.

1894. *A House in Bloomsbury.* 2 vols. Hutchinson.

Historical Sketches of the Reign of Queen Anne. Macmillan.

Who Was Lost and Is Found. Blackwood.

The Prodigals and their Inheritance. 2 vols. Methuen.

1895. *A Child's History of Scotland.* Fisher Unwin.

Two Strangers. Fisher Unwin.

Sir Robert's Fortune, The Story of a Scotch Moor. Methuen.

The Makers of Modern Rome. Macmillan.

"Dies Irae," The Story of a Spirit in Prison. Blackwood.

1896. *Jeanne d'Arc: Her Life and Death* (Heroes of the Nations Series). Putnam.

The Unjust Steward; or, the Minister's Debt. W. and R. Chambers.

The Two Marys (and Grove Road, Hampstead): Tales. Methuen.

Old Mr. Tredgold. Longmans.

1897. *The Lady's Walk, A Tale.* Methuen.

The Ways of Life, Two Stories ["Mr. Sandford"; "Mr. Robert Dalyell"]. Smith, Elder.

Annals of a Publishing House: William Blackwood and his Sons, their Magazine and Friends. Vols. I, II. Blackwood.

1898. *A Widow's Tale, and other Stories.* With an Introductory
Note by J. M. Barrie. Blackwood.
*That Little Cutty, and Two Other Stories: Dr. Barrère; Isabel
Dysart.* Macmillan.
The Autobiography and Letters of Mrs. M. O. W. Oliphant,
Arranged and Edited by Mrs. Harry Coghill. Blackwood.

1900. *Queen Victoria, A Personal Sketch.* Cassell.

1902. *Stories of the Seen and the Unseen* ["The Open Door"; "Old
Lady Mary"; "The Portrait"; "The Library Window"]. Blackwood.

Novels by Mrs. Oliphant attributed to William Wilson:

1851. *John Drayton, the Liverpool Engineer.* 2 vols. Bentley.

1852. *The Melvilles.* By the author of "John Drayton." 3 vols.
Bentley.

1853. *Ailieford, a Family History.* By the author of "John Drayton."
3 vols. Hurst and Blackett.

1856. *Christian Melville.* By the author of "Matthew Paxton."
Bogue.

Notes

1. See her letters in the Macmillan MSS., especially January 10 [1866]; also *The Life and Letters of Alexander Macmillan,* edited by Charles L. Graves (London, 1910), p. 33; and *The Letters of Alexander Macmillan,* edited by George A. Macmillan (Privately printed, 1908), pp. 187–88.

2. *Memoir of the Life of Laurence Oliphant and of Alice Oliphant, His Wife* (Edinburgh and London, New Edition, 1892). pp. 2–3. Mrs. Oliphant disclaimed any real relationship to Laurence Oliphant: "There was a pleasant superstition of kindred between us, which had no existence save in the far and misty distance of centuries, beyond the reach of even a Scottish genealogist" ("Laurence Oliphant," *Maga,* February 1889, p. 281). "The Heirs of Kellie: An Episode of Family History" was first published in *Maga,* March 1896, pp. 325–63, later reprinted in her posthumous collection *A Widow's Tale and Other Stories* (Edinburgh and London, 1898).

3. " 'Tis Sixty Years Since," *Maga,* May 1897, p. 602.

4. Blackwood MSS. 4111 [1855].

5. Mrs. Oliphant refers to her childhood reading only briefly in various critical articles in *Maga:* "The Letters of Sir Walter Scott," January 1894, p. 26; "Mary Russell Mitford," June 1854, p. 661; "Charles Dickens," April 1855, p. 458. See also *Annals,* II, 429.

6. *A & L,* pp. 158–59. Nine novels are attributed to William Wilson in the British Museum Catalogue and in Halkett and Laing's *Dictionary of Anonymous and Pseudonymous Literature.* For a discussion of Mrs. Oliphant's share in the composition of some of these, see Vineta Colby, "Wiliam Wilson, Novelist," *Notes & Queries,* N.S. xiii (Feb. 1966).

7. George M'Guffie, *The Priests of Etal, or Annals of Tillside,* Fourth edition (Edinburgh, 1902). See Ch. XI, "Rev. William Wilson, or 'The Literary Priest,' " pp. 63–69.

8. Blackwood MSS. 4476.

9. The novel went into three editions within the first year of its publication—a not extraordinary practice among Victorian publishers who kept single editions small and made a strong selling point of each "new" edition—but still unusual for a first novel as modest as *Margaret Maitland.* It was still being read widely in 1869 when a reviewer

in the *British Quarterly Review* (April 1869, p. 305) described it as "a book that charmed and soothed us when we were young, and which we can read over still on summer days and winter nights with undiminished satisfaction."

10. Probably the soundest critical evaluation of Mrs. Oliphant's early fiction was made by George Meredith, who reviewed her *The Athelings* along with Trollope's *Barchester Towers* in the *Westminster Review*, October 1857. Needless to say, *The Athelings* looked very pale beside Trollope's masterpiece, yet, surprisingly enough, Meredith had some slight praise for the book:

> Now, Mr. Trollope has a distinct intrigue on foot, which the reader never loses sight of, and the characters successively help to unfold it; but the authoress of the 'Athelings' has nothing of the sort, and we have to look through her three volumes again and again to discover how she can possibly have contrived to spin out dreary conversation to such an extent as to fill them, and preserve a vestige of interest. The secret is that the novel is addressed to the British Home, and it seems that we may prose everlastingly to the republic of the fireside . . . The authoress is clever; she can describe society . . . Her main fault has killed the most charmingly written book, and this lady has only to practice compression to become an excellent novelist.

(Quoted in Gordon S. Haight's "George Meredith and the Westminster Review," *Modern Language Review*, LIII [January 1958], p. 11.)

11. *A & L*, pp. 153–54.

12. *Annals*, I, 316.

13. Blackwood MSS. 4119. The letter is included in the 1856 volume of the Blackwood MSS., but obviously was written in 1851. Similar evidence of Mrs. Oliphant's keen business sense, even this early in her career, is afforded by her letters to the publishing firm of Richard Bentley, cited by Royal A. Gettmann in his *A Victorian Publisher* (Cambridge, England, 1960).

14. Blackwood MSS. 4099, February 11 [1852].

15. For example, William Bell Scott, who was personally acquainted with Frank Oliphant, wrote a quite prejudiced account of him in his memoirs, suggesting that he was "not an artist by natural gift as she was a writer . . . His wife's literary success was sufficient to make him an idle and aimless man; they went to Rome and there he died" (*Autobiographical Notes of the Life of William Bell Scott and Notices of his Artistic and Poetic Circle of Friends, 1830–1882,* edited by W. Minto, 2 vols. [New York, 1892], I, 188.) Equally misleading is the assumption by Lucy Poate Stebbins that Mrs. Oliphant married her cousin simply to escape an unhappy home life (*A Victorian Album* [London, 1946], p. 167).

16. *A & L*, p. 34. Mrs. Oliphant evidently forgot, or preferred to forget, that she had introduced the distinguished scholar Benjamin

Jowett into her novel *A Son of the Soil* when it first appeared serially in *Macmillan's Magazine* in February 1865. Alexander Macmillan wrote to her on February 14 in some consternation: "But why did you put Jowett—a live man—in? Mr. [Frederick Denison] Maurice was remarking on it. I said it was the wonted audacity of woman, and the wonted cowardice of man that I did not mutter a remonstrance—indeed did not even think of one. See how the coarser sex cower before you—Oh, ye tyrannesses" (*Letters of Alexander Macmillan*, pp. 187–88). She heeded his complaint, and when the novel appeared in book form in 1866 the name "Heward" was substituted for Jowett, and she omitted an incident in which Jowett had actually appeared as a character.

17. Blackwood MSS. 4119, March 26 [1856]. According to the DNB sketch, the famous choristers' window at Ely "was the joint work of Oliphant and William Dyce, R.A., the former being responsible for the original design."

18. *Annals*, II, 472.

19. Blackwood MSS. 4099, n.d. [1852].

20. Blackwood MSS. 4103

21. Blackwood MSS. 4106.

22. Blackwood MSS. 4099, August 13 and October 21 [1852].

23. Blackwood MSS. 4103.

24. Blackwood MSS. 4119, October 27 [1856].

25. Blackwood MSS. 4099, October 8 [1852].

26. *Haps and Mishaps of a Tour to Europe* (Boston, 1854), p. 53.

27. *Annals*, II, 470–71. The article on Sydney Smith was published in *Maga*, April 1856, pp. 350–61.

28. *Annals*, II, 475.

29. An announcement of the birth appears in *Gentleman's Magazine*, July 1854.

30. Blackwood MSS. 4111, February 9 [1855].

31. Blackwood MSS. 4119.

32. See her letter to John Blackwood, n.d., 1855: "I am afraid what you say about my labours is scarcely complimentary, but a naturally restless temperament makes it almost a necessary of life for me to be constantly occupied, and Providence has added just such an amount of pressure as makes it desirable for me to do what I can" (*A & L*, p. 160). As early as 1852, in its review of her *Adam Graeme of Mossgray*, the *Athenaeum* had warned: "It may be feared that a promising author runs some danger of being tempted to produce too rapidly—without sufficient meditation or experience of life" (May 1, 1852, p. 487). In 1854, reviewing *The Quiet Heart*, the same journal observed: "The author seems to have written herself quite out for the present at least" (December 23, 1854, p. 1557).

33. Blackwood MSS. 4725, February 5 and April 25 [1859], from Casa Grazzini, Via Maggio.

34. Blackwood MSS. 4141, from Rome.

35. They met the Brownings later in Rome. All that Mrs. Oliphant recalled of the meeting was Mrs. Browning's intense, searching look— a form of scrutiny she rather disliked both in her and in Miss Mulock who had the same habit (*A & L*, p. 38).

36. Blackwood MSS. 4725.

37. In *A & L*, p. 59, Mrs. Oliphant remembered Macpherson kindly: "I could not bear him at first, poor Robert,—we used to quarrel on almost every subject; but in the end I got to be almost fond of him, as he was, I believe of me, though we were absolutely so unlike." Elizabeth Barrett Browning who had met him in 1847 described him with mock horror and passionate punctuation as "a bad artist! an unrefined gentleman! a Roman Catholic (converted from Protestantism!), a poor man!! with a red beard!!!" (*Elizabeth Barrett Browning: Letters to her Sister, 1846–1859*, edited by Leonard Huxley [London, 1929], p. 63).

38. Blackwood MSS. 4141, June 9 [1859].

39. Blackwood MSS. 4725, from 56 Via Balbuino, Rome.

CHAPTER II

1. Blackwood MSS. 4152, June 9 and March 6 [1860].

2. *A & L*, p. 169. The residences at Hampton Court were set aside for the widows and close relatives of army officers and government officials. Mrs. Oliphant did not actually qualify for such a grant.

3. Blackwood MSS. 4152.

4. *Ibid.*, n.d. When the work was finished, Mrs. Oliphant later recalled, Montalembert "bore witness to the scrupulous and most conscientious fidelity of the text" and "the good faith and straight-forward equity of a most literal translation" (*Memoir of Count de Montalembert*, 2 vols., Leipzig: Tauchnitz Ed., 1872, II, 247).

5. See the *Spectator's* enthusiastic comment: "Tozer, the butterman, is such a character as we should have thought scarcely anyone but George Eliot could have drawn" (February 14, 1863, p. 1639).

6. Mrs. Oliphant changed his name to Beecham in *Phoebe, Junior*. She is often careless about her characters' names. Frank Wentworth was originally Cyril in *The Rector*. Mr. Brown of *The Executor* becomes Mr. Brownlow in the novel *Brownlows* (1868). Lady Western in *Salem Chapel* is referred to as Lady Weston in *Phoebe, Junior*.

7. Blackwood MSS. 4163, n.d. Parts of this letter are printed in *A & L*, p. 179, but Mrs. Coghill omitted the entire section following the first sentence quoted here.

8. Since both authors were published anonymously in *Maga* there were some grounds for confusion. George Eliot, however, hotly denied the authorship: "I am NOT the author of 'The Chronicles of Carling-

ford. They were written by Mrs. Oliphant author of 'Margaret Maitland,' etc. ect. etc. . . . I have not read 'The Chronicles of Carlingford' but from what Mr. Lewes tells me, they must represent the Dissenters in a very different spirit from anything that has appeared in
my books." In the same letter she adds a comment which reveals the
extent of her personal knowledge of Mrs. Oliphant: "And I should
tell you by way of interesting you in Mrs. Oliphant that she is a
widow with a family of six children, and does a perfectly stupendous
amount of work of all sorts—translation and article writing and everything literary" (Letter to Sara Sophia Hennell, 23 April [1862], *The
George Eliot Letters,* edited by Gordon S. Haight [New Haven, 1955],
IV, 25). Mrs. Oliphant, for her part, showned no indignation when Mr.
Langford, Blackwood's editor, suspected her of being the author of
"Amos Barton" (*Ibid.,* II, 435, n. 5).

9. To the Victorians he was "a self-satisfied, smug, and sanctimo-
nious person, a fellow, to use Hurrel Froude's phrase, 'who turned up
the whites of his eyes and said *Lawd.*' He was of no importance
socially and he and his chapel and minister were all a trifle ridiculous
as well as schismatic" (Amy Cruse, *The Victorian and Their Books,*
London, 1935, p. 71).

10. Although widely praised by contemporary reviewers for her
portraits of clerical life, Mrs. Oliphant received some criticism for
inaccuracy of details. See a letter signed "C. G." in the *Athenaeum,*
December 31, 1864, p. 901, and W. Robertson Nicoll's introduction
to the Everyman edition of *Salem Chapel,* p. x.

11. See her article "Edward Irving," *Maga,* November 1858, pp.
573–74.

12. Blackwood MSS. 4172, n.d. [1862].

13. Blackwood MSS. 4731, n.d. [1862].

14. Blackwood MSS. 4184, n.d. [1863], 4189 [1863], 4725, June
18 [1864].

15. *A & L,* p. 191.

16. Mrs. Oliphant is of course alluding to Newman's *Apologia,*
published in the same year as this novel.

17. Blackwood MSS. 4184, n.d. [1863].

18. In his brief discussion of *The Perpetual Curate* in *The Novel
and the Oxford Movement* (Princeton Studies in English # 8, 1932,
p. 178), Joseph Ellis Baker states that Mrs. Oliphant used religious
divisions "merely for the psychological situations they produce" and
adds: "The author is interested in religious problems and practices
entirely as a matter of story." He seems to have ignored the passages
cited here and, indeed, the entire purpose of the introduction of Gerald
into the novel.

19. She was writing about two numbers ahead of publication at this
time. The January, February, and March numbers of *The Perpetual
Curate* appeared in *Maga* without interruption; but there was a gap in

April, and the novel was resumed in the May issue. In April also there was an interruption in the monthly numbers of *A Son of the Soil* in *Macmillan's Magazine*.

20. *A & L,* pp. 196–97. This letter is not dated, but the first mention of *Miss Marjoribanks* is in an unpublished letter from Paris, December 5, 1864 (Blackwood MSS. 4191).

21. Blackwood MSS. 4204, August 2 [1865]. Written from St. Addresse. Her underlining.

22. *A & L,* p. 198.

23. *Ibid.,* pp. 204–5.

24. Blackwood MSS. 4213, March 20 [1866].

25. Blackwood MSS. 4213, April 3 [1866] and n.d.

26. Even her name remains unchanged by her marriage to her cousin: " 'And yet it is odd to think that, after all, I never shall be anything but Lucilla Marjoribanks.' " It is probably not accidental that Mrs. Oliphant named her Lucilla. Very likely she took the name from that paragon of female virtue, Lucilla Stanley, heroine of Hannah More's *Coelebs in Search of a Wife*.

27. *Annals,* II, 487.

28. The firm's reluctance to publish fiction was not confined to Mrs. Oliphant's work, although her sales especially had dropped off. *Brownlows* (1868), on which she had counted heavily, was a disappointment. By 1870 John Blackwood was beginning to doubt the future of the three-decker format. He wrote to his nephew William: "I am worried excessively about the non-sale of the 'Brownlows,' but I know not what more a man can do. The days of the three-volume novel are over for profit, but what is to be the substitute?" (*Annals,* III, 175).

CHAPTER III

1. *Memoir of the Life of John Tulloch* (Edinburgh and London, 1888), p. 162.

2. *Memoir of Robert Herbert Story*. By his Daughters (Glasgow, 1909), p. 43.

3. *Ibid.,* p. 54.

4. Blackwood MSS. 4163, n.d. [1861]; Macmillan MSS.

5. *Memoirs of R. H. Story,* p. 70.

6. Blackwood MSS. 4725, n.d.

7. *A & L,* pp. 172, 186–7.

8. Macmillan MSS.

9. Blackwood MSS. 4725 [1864].

10. "The Poet—Dante," *The Makers of Florence* (London, 3rd edition, 1881), p. 4.

11. Mrs. Oliphant did attempt the tale of terror at least twice. In

"A Christmas Tale" (*Maga,* January 1857) the narrator is entertained
by a country squire who announces that since his estate is too small
to be shared, he will cease to exist on the very next day when his son
and heir will come of age. On the next day, to the narrator's horror,
the host has indeed disappeared, but the narrator awakens to find that
it has all been a dream. In "The Secret Chamber" (*Maga,* December
1876; reprinted in *Tales from Blackwood,* Second Series) a young
man who has just come of age must survive the ordeal of spending a
night in an ancestral mansion haunted by the spirits of his forbears.
Mrs. Oliphant repeated this theme, with some variations, in her novel
The Wizard's Son (1884).

12. She visited the real Semur while spending some time with the
Montalemberts in nearby La Roche-en-Breny. The visit was reported
by her little son Cecco in a letter to Mrs. Coghill (*A & L,* pp. 233–
34). His description indicates that there were actual counterparts for
the wall, river, dark wood, and cathedral which serve symbolic purposes in the tale.

13. For a detailed study of its sources and genesis see Robert and
Vineta Colby, *"A Beleaguered City:* A Fable for the Victorian Age,"
Nineteenth-Century Fiction, March 1962, pp. 283–301.

14. As early as January 1878, a year before its first publication,
Mrs. Oliphant submitted a draft of the story to John Blackwood. Six
months later she wrote that "it wants a good deal done to it" (Blackwood MSS, 4380, January 21, 1878; July 2, 1878). Originally she had
intended to make it just long enough to fill two numbers in *Maga,* but
the story grew as she proceeded. "It is very much enlarged and altered,
you will perceive," she wrote apologetically to Blackwood in her covering letter of December 4, 1878 (*A & L,* p. 276). Ironically, for reasons which remain obscure, the story did not appear in *Maga* after all,
but in the Christmas number of the *New Quarterly Magazine* (January 1879). Her frantic letters at this time suggest that Blackwood
procrastinated, leading her to accept the immediate offer of another
editor, eager as she was for Christmas publication. Nor do we know
why she offered it as a book to Macmillan rather than to Blackwood.
The book contains a narrative, that of Madame Veuve Dupin, which
is not in the magazine version and has other additional passages.

15. It was reprinted in 1881, 1889, 1897, 1910, and 1930. The most
recent publication in the United States is in *Six Novels of the Supernatural,* edited by Edward Wagenknecht (New York: Viking Press,
1944). It was translated into French as *La Ville Enchantée,* by Henri
Bremond, with an introduction by Maurice Barrès (Paris, 1911; reprinted 1925).

16. "Old Lady Mary" originally appeared in *Maga,* January 1884.
It was again joined to "The Open Door," this time with the addition
of "The Portrait" and "The Library Window" in the posthumously
published *Stories of the Seen and the Unseen* (1902).

17. Mrs. Stewart died on February 16, 1884. For another sketch of her life see Augustus J. Hare, "Mrs. Duncan Stewart," *Biographical Sketches* (London, 1885), pp. 137–82. Hare, one of her close friends, relates that when questioned about death, Mrs. Stewart replied: "I think that I believe all the promises of Scripture, yet, when I think of death, I hesitate to wish to leave the certainty here for what is— yes, must be—the uncertainty beyond." She is also reported to have affirmed, when a book appeared entitled *Is Life Worth Living?*,—"Ay, to the very dregs."

18. Other stories of Mrs. Oliphant's that treat of the return of the dead are the novel *The Lady's Walk,* first published in *Longman's Magazine,* December 1882, then revised and enlarged and published in book form by Methuen in 1897; and a short story, "The Portrait," first published in *Maga,* January 1885. In *The Lady's Walk* the spirit of a deceased relative tries in vain to forestall the death of a profligate youth but succeeds in saving the boy's family from financial ruin; in "The Portrait" a young man is influenced by the spirit of his mother to marry a girl cousin who had been treated unjustly by his father.

19. It was begun in *Macmillan's Magazine* as an Easter story (May 1882), concluded the following autumn, then issued as a New Year's gift book. The story was written, incidentally, while Mrs. Oliphant was in bed with the mumps!

20. Macmillan MSS., December 7 [1885], December 5 [1887]. "The Land of Darkness" was published in *Maga,* January 1887; "On the Dark Mountains" was published in *Maga,* November 1888. The different parts of the Little Pilgrim series were published separately and in various combinations in America, but were all brought together in a compact volume entitled *A Little Pilgrim and Further Experiences of a Little Pilgrim* (Boston: Little Brown and Co., n.d.).

21. Margaret Maison, *The Victorian Vision* (New York, 1961), pp. 325–26.

22. "The Fancies of a Believer," *Maga,* February 1895, pp. 237, 251, 255.

23. *Movements of Religious Thought in Britain during the Nineteenth Century* (New York, 1885), p. 167. Principal Tulloch dedicated this book to Mrs. Oliphant.

CHAPTER IV

1. *Annals,* III, 337.
2. Macmillan MSS., n. d.
3. *A & L,* p. 193.
4. "Count Charles de Montalembert," *Maga,* April 1870, p. 524.
5. *Ibid.,* p. 525.
6. Macmillan MSS.

7. Blackwood MSS. 4202 [1865].

8. Blackwood MSS. 4202, n. d.

9. He contributed a chapter, "Life among the Oppidans," to *Everyday Life in our Public Schools: Sketched by Head-Scholars of Eton, Winchester, Shrewsbury, Harrow, Rugby, Charterhouse*, edited by C. E. Pascoe (London, 1881). Cecco's contribution is signed T. R. Oliphant instead of F. R. He writes: "We think, at Eton, that no other school ever had so many sources of enjoyment, and, at least, we may be sure that no school got more out of its hours of play than Eton" (p. 62). See also Mrs. Oliphant's article "Eton College," *Maga*, March 1876, pp. 314–31, an essay-review of *A History of Eton College* by H. C. Maxwell-Lyte, in which she contrasts the hardships of student life with the present comfortable existence—"which makes his time at Eton the happiest of a boy's life."

10. Blackwood MSS., 4202, n. d.

11. "Mrs. Oliphant," *Fortnightly Review* (N. S.), August 1897, pp. 277–85.

12. *Memories and Friends* (New York and London, 1924), pp. 83–84, 90.

13. "A Sketch from Memory," *Temple Bar,* September-December 1899, p. 238.

14. Blackwood MSS. 4213. Mrs. Oliphant had more than a casual interest in fashion. In 1878 Macmillan published her book *Dress* in their "Art at Home" series. A chatty volume, it is nevertheless distinguished from the other works in the series by its graceful writing and its numerous literary references, including allusions to *Sartor Resartus* and a chapter on "Dress in the Poets."

15. The biography was published posthumously by Cassell, *Queen Victoria: A Personal Sketch* (London, 1900). The poem, "22nd June 1897," appeared in *Maga*, June 1897, pp. 887–88.

16. Blackwood MSS. 4225.

17. Blackwood MSS. 4238, January 6 [1868].

18. Blackwood MSS. 4238, October 3 [1868]. Mrs. Coghill printed part of this letter (mistakenly marked as addressed to Mrs. Tulloch), *A & L,* p. 220, but discreetly omitted the last three sentences quoted here.

19. Blackwood MSS. 4238, n. d. [1868]. The letter to Isabella Blackwood is, unfortunately, not extant.

20. CXC (1899), 261.

21. Blackwood MSS. 4238, n. d.

22. She wrote to George Lillie Craik to explain a delay in the delivery of her manuscript of *The Makers of Florence:* "My brother who has been living with me for some time has had an attack of very serious illness and is lying between life and death so that I have the confusion of watching and anxiety to hinder my work" (Macmillan MSS., July 12 [1875]).

23. Blackwood MSS. 4462, n. d. [1884].

24. Blackwood MSS. 4424, May 4 [1881].

25. Macmillan MSS., February 22 [1875]. See also her comments on writing fiction in the "Old Saloon," *Maga*, June 1888, pp. 831–52. Here she discusses Henry James' essay on the art of fiction and Charles Reade's habit of collecting material for his books from incidents reported in the newspapers: "For our own part, we have no faith at all in facts, nor in study, nor in conscious observation of your neighbour's follies or peculiarities. A trifle here and there catches the creative eye —broken lights from this and that, gleams of comprehension, a sudden sight of how minds are working, of how feelings arise. Anything more than this, definite and formal studies, are very unproductive" (p. 841).

26. There is an anticipation of this type of heroine in *Lucy Crofton* (1860) in which a flirtatious young fortune hunter jilts a noble-hearted suitor for a much richer man. She is not punished, and the jilted young man recovers sufficiently in the novel's sequel, *Heart and Cross* (1863), to win the Victoria Cross in the Indian army and to marry a sweet girl who has loved him all along.

27. See her *Maga* (May 1862) article "Sensation Novels," discussed above, Ch. II, pp. 50–52 Mrs. Oliphant touches—very gingerly—on the related subject of the "fallen woman" only once, in *A Country Gentleman and his Family* (1886) where she introduces a "kept woman" who comes from America (where, she implies, moral standards are generally lax). Her treatment of the character is sympathetic, but she predicts a dire future for her—" 'She'll fall lower and lower . . . and then she'll die, perhaps in the hospital.' "

28. "London Notes, August 1897," *Notes on Novelists* (London, 1914), pp. 357–60.

29. *A & L,* p. 313.

30. This novel is another example of how Mrs. Oliphant's melodrama often spoiled an otherwise good novel. Set in a remote Scottish village, it offers a fascinating portrait of the religious fanaticism of the Irvingite movement—the evangelical revival meetings, the mystic "prophetess" who speaks with the gift of tongues. Unfortunately, for her main plot Mrs. Oliphant uses a lurid, melodramatic murder mystery.

31. This novel was first published serially in America in the *Atlantic Monthly* from January 1887 to February 1888, and the name of Thomas Bailey Aldrich, the *Atlantic's* editor, is listed as joint author in the American editions. In a letter to George Lillie Craik she explained: "Mr. T. B. Aldrich's name is joined to me as joint author, but what he has done to it is nominal, a touch here and there throughout the book, which seemed to me profitable in the present state of the American copyright" (Macmillan MSS., July 26 [1888]). In a letter in November of the same year she suggests that Macmillan put Aldrich's name in brackets on the title page: "He has made various

small alterations all through which I have restored in the English proof." In the English editions Mrs. Oliphant's name appears alone on the title page, but Aldrich's name is printed below hers on the half-title page.

32. *Notes on Novelists*, p. 359.

CHAPTER V

1. *Annals,* III, 352–54. See also Waldo Hillary Dunn, *R. D. Blackmore* (London, 1956), pp. 176–77.

2. Mrs. Oliphant appears to have worked with a literary agent only once. He was A. P. Watt, whose services Walter Besant praised so highly in his *Autobiography*. On May 11, 1886, Mrs. Oliphant wrote a short testimonial note to Watt: "I have much pleasure in saying that in the as yet very slight business you have been so kind as to manage for me, all has been most promptly, kindly, and pleasantly done, and I hope I may have further experience of the same friendly services" (*Letters Addressed to A. P. Watt* [London, 1898], p. 90). Watt handled American publication rights for many of his clients, and this was probably the nature of his business with Mrs. Oliphant.

3. Blackwood MSS. 4540, April 25. A similar complication is discussed in the Macmillan MSS. In 1887 she wrote to George Lillie Craik:

> I am extremely startled by the account you send me. My impression was that I was a hundred pounds in your debt and no more (the little items of £10 and £5 I had forgotten). I think there is one mistake. When I returned from the Continent in July '84 we had some talk about the Little Pilgrim, and you wrote saying that an allowance of £100 or £150 could be made up to that time and the royalty begin after. Am I dreaming about this? I don't think so. If you have copies of your business letters you will no doubt have them in better order than I have mine—but I think I have all your letters and will look if I can find this. It must have been written (the letter, I mean) in the end of July or August '84. If I am correct this will reduce the balance against me either to the £100 (and the trifles) which I was aware of or to £150. The arrangement of the Venice book was for £450 so that may count on the credit side. I have been accustomed to keep my accounts in my head only, but I seldom make any great error. However, this will rest upon your letter to which I refer. If I am wrong in respect to it, I can only say that the error has been quite involuntary.
>
> (December 3 [1887])

4. Blackwood MSS. 4540, May 31, June 4, September 19 [1889].

5. Blackwood MSS. 4490, March 20.

6. Blackwood MSS. 4225, n.d. [1867].

7. Blackwood MSS. 4309, October 16.

8. Blackwood MSS. 4323, October 30 [1874]. She repeated this request in letters of December 2 and December 14, raising it now to a thousand guineas: "which is a pretty sum and picturesque as well as agreeable."

9. Blackwood MSS. 4380, June 5.

10. Blackwood MSS. 4424, May 4, October 27.

11. Blackwood MSS. 4507, November 3 and 16. Scribbled in pencil, probably by Blackwood, on the November 3 letter is the comment, "More of a study than a story."

12. Blackwood MSS. 4523, October 8 and 11.

13. Blackwood MSS. 4225, n. d. [November 1867].

14. Blackwood MSS. 4410, February 18.

15. Blackwood MSS. 4621, July 27.

16. Blackwood MSS. 4119, n. d.

17. Blackwood MSS. 4163, n. d.

18. *A & L,* pp. 203, 432.

19. Blackwood MSS. 4266, n. d.

20. Blackwood MSS. 4280, August 1.

21. Blackwood MSS. 4295, December 4.

22. *A & L,* pp. 288–9.

23. Blackwood MSS. 4280, n.d.

24. Blackwood MSS. 4449, February 6 and 12.

25. Blackwood MSS. 4337, June 29.

26. Blackwood MSS. 4396.

27. See above, Ch. I, p. 23.

28. Blackwood MSS. 4119, n. d.

29. Blackwood MSS. 4126, n. d.; August 12, September 10.

30. Blackwood MSS. 4424, August 4 [1881].

31. Blackwood MSS. 4437, December 1 [1882].

32. Blackwood MSS. 4184, n. d.

33. *A & L,* pp. 215–16.

34. Blackwood MSS. 4238, January 6.

35. Blackwood MSS. 4410, July 3.

36. Blackwood MSS. 4462, November 13.

37. Blackwood MSS. 4476, March 14, May 20.

38. Blackwood MSS. 4578, March 23.

39. Blackwood MSS. 4507, March 18. Mrs. Oliphant apparently did not join the Society of Authors, but many writers she knew and respected were members—Sir Theodore Martin, Friedrich Max Müller, R. D. Blackmore, Charles Reade. Several of these, it should be noted, were Blackwood authors. See *Autobiography of Sir Walter Besant* (London, 1902), pp. 216–34.

40. Blackwood MSS. 4323, August 25.

41. Blackwood MSS. 4349, October 23.

42. Blackwood MSS. 4364, November 5.

43. Mrs. Oliphant may not have had complete faith in her friend's

abilities as critic and literary historian, but she valued her name: "Annie Thackeray's book will sell whether it is good or not," she wrote Blackwood (MSS. 4410, February 18 [1880]). Earlier, in drawing up the list of contributors she had observed of her: "I do not know how to put her in the list. Mrs. Ritchie means nothing. Will you put this in the advertisement?" (Blackwood MSS. 4396, May 2 [1879]). The book was advertised and published under the better-known name of Miss Thackeray.

44. Blackwood MSS. 4410, February 18 [1880]. The Blackwood files for 1879 (MSS. 4396) contain a record of the payment she received that year for the series.

45. Blackwood MSS. 4396, July 2 [1879].

46. Blackwood MSS. 4364.

47. February 11, 1880. The letter is published in *Letters of Anthony Trollope*, edited by Bradford A. Booth (New York and London, 1951), pp. 432–33.

48. Blackwood MSS. 4413, January 29 [1880].

49. Blackwood MSS. 4410, January 31, November 17 [1880].

50. Blackwood MSS. 4490, April 11 [1886].

51. *A & L*, p. 337.

52. Blackwood MSS. 4523, June 28, November 20.

53. Blackwood MSS. 4540, December 4.

54. Blackwood MSS. 4578, November 30.

55. Blackwood MSS. 4578, February 1 [1891].

56. Blackwood MSS. 4578, March 8, July 14.

57. *A & L*, pp. 321–22, 338–39.

58. Blackwood MSS. 4507, June 8, July 15, July 20.

59. Blackwood MSS. 4540, March 10.

60. Blackwood MSS. 4592, September 21, October 28.

61. The letter is not dated. It is published in F. D. Tredrey's *The House of Blackwood, 1804–1954*, (Edinburgh, 1954), pp. 173–74.

62. Blackwood MSS. 4592.

63. Frederick Greenwood, publisher of the *Pall Mall Gazette*, continued the column from January 1898 to November 1899. See J. W. Robertson-Scott's *The Story of the Pall Mall Gazette* (London and New York, 1950), p. 279.

64. Blackwood MSS. 4621, November 3 [1894]. On December 7 she wrote: "I wished you to pay me five hundred a year for the two years. I do not speak of this as a definite price for the book, which could be settled when it is further on."

65. *A & L*, p. 409.

66. *A & L*, p. 421.

67. *A & L*, p. 414.

68. Blackwood MSS. 4635, January 1, February 1, and n. d.

69. *A & L*, p. 426.

70. Tredrey, *The House of Blackwood*, p. 178.

71. *A & L,* p. 316.

72. *A & L,* p. 291.

73. Macmillan MSS., July 3. Mrs. Oliphant sought eagerly for a magazine editorship that would provide steady, secure income. About a year earlier she had written to William Isbister: "Did the idea of setting up a child's magazine like Scribner's St. Nicholas ever cross your mind? I had a kind of notion that it did. If so, and you want an editor, I should be very glad to offer myself" (Isbister MSS., March 6 [1877?]).

74. *A & L,* p. 294.

75. Macmillan MSS., October 10 [1883].

76. Macmillan MSS., April 29 [1883].

77. Blackwood MSS. 4476, May 20 [1885].

78. Macmillan MSS., April 17, written from Beaulieu.

79. Macmillan MSS., n. d. [1889].

80. One of the few records of her experiences with American publishers appears in J. Henry Harper's *The House of Harper: A Century of Publishing in Franklin Square* (New York, 1912), pp. 357–59. Harper prints an answer from the company to a complaint received from Mrs. Oliphant in 1873, apparently for inadequate compensation for American editions of her works. The company acknowledged printing some of these from sheets sent by her English publishers or their agents and paying for these at the standard prices which, in view of the competition from "a perhaps irresponsible rival," were admittedly low, especially when the sales were moderate. They conclude, with a rather personal thrust, "we venture the assertion that successful English authors cannot justly complain of unfairness or illiberality on the part of American publishers."

81. Blackwood MSS. 4202, March 16.

82. Blackwood MSS. 4476, n. d.

83. Blackwood MSS. 4163, n. d., and November 6 [1861].

84. Blackwood MSS. 4337, September 8. On September 16 she acknowledged receipt of the loan from Blackwood.

85. Blackwood MSS. 4437, July 2.

86. Isbister MSS., May 25 and January 17 [1879?]. The months and days are given on these letters, but the years can only be conjectured from the contents.

87. August 8, November 3, January 26. All written from Windsor, year uncertain.

88. For a dark picture of the exploitation of Victorian authors by publishers, see Walter Besant's *Autobiography* (pp. 233–34). Besant, to be sure, was defending his establishment of the Society of Authors. The situation he describes and the rapidly growing membership lists of the Society suggest, however, that he was not exaggerating the seriousness of the unprotected writer's plight.

CHAPTER VI

1. *A & L,* p. 176.
2. Blackwood MSS. 4650, May 4 [1896].
3. "New Books: Biographies," *Maga,* February 1877, p. 175.
4. *A & L,* p. 357.
5. "Mrs. Oliphant as a Biographer," *Maga,* April 1898, p. 510.
6. "The Old Saloon," *Maga,* August 1891, p. 291. See also, "Norman Macleod," *Maga,* April 1876, p. 508; "New Books," *Maga,* December 1872, p. 746; "Men and Women," *Maga,* April 1895, pp. 637–38.
7. "New Books," *Maga,* April 1871, pp. 440–41.
8. "New Books," *Maga,* August 1872. For other citations see list of Mrs. Oliphant's contributions to *Maga* in *A & L,* pp. 445–51.
9. "The Opium Eater," *Maga,* December 1877, p. 718; *Literary History of England* (New York, 1883), I, 335; "Miss Austen and Miss Mitford," *Maga,* March 1870, p. 294; "The Old Saloon," *Maga,* June 1887, p. 757.
10. "A Century of Great Poets, No. III, William Wordsworth," *Maga,* September 1871, p. 325; *Literary History of England,* II, 285, and II, 226–27; "Charles Dickens," *Maga,* June 1871, p. 673; "Mr. Thackeray's Sketches," *Maga,* February 1876, p. 235.
11. One of Mrs. Oliphant's last publications was a long essay, "The Sisters Brontë," in a volume of appreciations published by Hurst and Blackett, called *Women Novelists of Queen Victoria's Reign* (London, 1897). The essay is interesting for its retrospective viewpoint as well as for its reflection of Mrs. Oliphant's anti-sentimental and anti-romantic predilections in fiction. She also expresses a characteristic revulsion against the family gossip spread by Mrs. Gaskell and Clement Shorter.
12. Although she found the plot of *Tess* repulsive and thought Angel Clare silly, she enjoyed the country scene depicted in the novel: "We feel inclined to embrace Mr. Hardy, though we are not fond of him, in pure satisfaction with the good brown soil and substantial labour of the fields—which he makes us smell and see" ("The Old Saloon," *Maga,* March 1892, pp. 464–65). She had just discussed Mrs. Humphry Ward's *The History of David Grieve,* after which *Tess* came to her as a breath of fresh air. *Jude the Obscure,* however, was to her full of "grossness, indecency and horror." She found the characterization of Jude effective with his self-education and noble aspirations, but the book on the whole seemed to her to teach one lesson— that the whole institution of marriage was bad. This was a trend she noted with alarm in many other novels of the day. ("The Anti-Marriage League," *Maga,* January 1896, pp. 137–42.)
13. "Modern Novelists," *Maga,* May 1855, p. 565.
14. *Maga,* August 1863, pp. 168–69.

15. "New Books," *Maga,* October 1871, p. 477.

16. *Athenaeum,* May 27, 1882, pp. 659–60.

17. *Fraser's Magazine,* October 1882, p. 511. Commissioned in 1880, the book engrossed Mrs. Oliphant for an unusual amount of time. The generous payment of £1,000 Macmillan gave her seems to have left her relatively unencumbered with other work, to judge by the comparatively few novels she produced during this two-year period.

18. May 27, 1882, p. 660.

19. J. H. Millar, *A Literary History of Scotland* (New York, 1903), p. 493.

20. July 1897, p. 161.

21. For attribution of her *Spectator* articles we are indebted to Robert H. Tener. See his unpublished dissertation "Richard Holt Hutton: Criticism of Five Nineteenth Century Poets . . ." (Birkbeck College, University of London, 1960).

22. January 25, 1890, pp. 116–17; February 1, 1890, p. 164.

23. *Spectator,* September 6, 1890, pp. 307–8.

24. *Spectator,* January 11, 1890, pp. 49–50.

25. "Mrs. Oliphant," *The Bookman,* August 1897, p. 113.

26. "The Latest Lawgiver," *Maga,* June 1868, p. 678.

27. "J. M. W. Turner, R. A.," *Maga,* January 1862, p. 34.

28. "Michelangelo," *Maga,* October 1875, p. 467.

29. "The Royal Academy," *Maga,* June 1876, p. 757.

30. *Ibid.,* p. 758.

31. "The Looker-on," *Maga,* August 1894, pp. 301–2.

32. *The Victorian Age of English Literature* (New York, 1892), II, 510.

33. Macmillan MSS., October 4 [1882].

34. *Spectator,* July 12, 1890, pp. 49–50.

35. See her letter to William Blackwood: "I am going on a regular round of theatres this week. I quite agree with you about actors and acting—the one going up (temporarily), the others going down. I am trying (but this is a great secret) to dramatize a story of my own with hopes of the Kendals taking it. Please however keep this venture entirely to yourself as it may come to nothing" (Blackwood MSS. 4476, April 5 [1885]).

36. Blackwood MSS. 4380, February 11 [1878].

37. "In London," *Maga,* February 1873, p. 233; "Three Days in Paris," *Maga,* October 1878, p. 472; "Hamlet," *Maga,* April 1879, p. 463; "The Looker-on," *Maga,* June 1895, p. 916.

38. June 28, 1897, p. 10, cols. 1–2.

CHAPTER VII

1. Blackwood MSS. 4462, July 1 [1884].

2. Blackwood MSS. 4280, n. d. [1871–72].

3. *A & L*, p. 128. The novel which she sold *The Graphic* was not the one she had on hand but one she immediately dashed off—*Innocent*.

4. Macmillan MSS., April 11 [1877].

5. Lady Ritchie (Anne Isabella Thackeray), *From the Porch* (New York, 1913), p. 22.

6. Blackwood MSS. 4280; 4295 (January 2 [1872]); 4323 (March 20).

7. *A & L*, pp. 249, 283.

8. *A & L*, p. 242.

9. Blackwood MSS. 4337, September 20 [1875]. But in a letter the following month to Miss Blackwood, she says that the scholarship is worth about £50 a year for three years (*A & L*, p. 251).

10. *A & L*, pp. 254, 262.

11. *A & L*, pp. 265–66.

12. *A & L*, p. 268.

13. Blackwood MSS. 4396, August 4; 4437, January 31.

14. A later novel treating of the same problem is the absurdly melodramatic *Who Was Lost and Is Found* (1894). Here the scapegrace son has run away from his home in Scotland and his loving widowed mother. He returns after fifteen years of life as an outlaw in the American Far West. Sullen and cowardly, the son is cold to his mother until she is accidentally shot by the villain, the son's former companion in crime who has pursued him from America. Shocked at last into decency and respectability, the son settles down and marries. But he remains an idle, useless fellow: "Robbie never became a model man. He never did anything, notwithstanding the fulness of his life and strength. He had no impulse to work—rather the reverse: his impulses were all the way of idleness. He lounged about and occupied himself with trifles, and gardened a little, and carpentered a little, and was never weary."

15. Blackwood MSS. 4462.

16. *A & L*, p. 319.

17. Blackwood MSS. 4507, August 23, October 18; 4523.

18. On March 15 [1890] Cyril wrote William Blackwood to request payment for the volume. The publisher scribbled in the margin of his letter: "I thought this cub had been paid in full. Please look up what was paid." He received £30 on April 9 and the additional £30 some time later. On August 9 he completed the manuscript: "I send you herewith the last bit of 'de Musset' revised by my mother and myself." His mother apparently kept a vigilant eye on the book. On July 6 [1890] she wrote Blackwood: "By the way, why is not his name put in the advertisement of the de Musset volume? It cannot surely be a disadvantage to have the name of Oliphant attached to it" (MSS. 4558).

19. Blackwood MSS. 4540.

20. *A & L*, pp. 376, 148.

21. Howard Overing Sturgis remembered him as having "a curious air of age about him, though scarcely thirty. He was very shy and reserved. No doubt it was due to his ill-health, but I used to feel as if his mother and I were people of ordinary middle age and normal condition of life, who had somehow to modulate and hush our talk when he was by, as one does for a much older person who must not be disturbed or worried" (*Temple Bar*, September-December 1899, p. 245).

22. *A & L*, pp. 252, 336–37.

23. Blackwood MSS. 4380, December 20; Macmillan MSS., April 16 [1878].

24. *A & L*, p. 291.

25. *A & L*, p. 277.

26. Quoted in a review of *A & L* in *Quarterly Review*, CXC (1899), 264.

27. *A & L*, p. 325.

28. Blackwood MSS. 4540, March 7. The story appeared in *Maga*, January 1890.

29. Blackwood MSS. 4725, n. d.; 4558, May 28 [1890]. Mrs. Oliphant sent the Henryson article to *Maga* without his knowledge, because he had been discouraged by their rejection of an earlier article. The Henryson article was published in October 1890, the Dunbar in September 1893.

30. *A & L*, p. 402.

31. *A & L*, p. 342.

32. *A & L*, pp. 379, 400, 407.

33. *A & L*, p. 352.

34. Blackwood MSS. 4238, April 8, and 4449, June 10 [1883].

35. "The Library Window" is anthologized in two of Dorothy Sayers' collections, *Great Short Stories of Detection, Mystery and Horror*, 2nd Series (1931), and *The Second Omnibus of Crime* (1932). It was translated into French by Marguerite Faguer as "La Fenêtre de la Bibliothèque" In *Les Oeuvres Libres*, Janvier 1957, pp. 67–120.

36. Blackwood MSS. 4650, December 11 [1896]; 4664, n.d. [1897]. This letter was addressed to Craik offering Macmillan the story to publish in book form as a continuation of *Stories of the Seen and the Unseen*.

37. Blackwood MSS. 4280, March 18. Part of this letter is printed in *A & L*, p. 229.

38. *A & L*, p. 237.

39. Blackwood MSS. 4364, March 28; 4490, March 30; 4337, October 30 [1875]; 4507, February 13 [1887].

40. Blackwood MSS. 4540, August 29 [1889].

41. Blackwood MSS. 4621, July 24 and December 19.

42. Blackwood MSS. 4650. The urgency of this letter is indicated by the fact that she wrote him again on May 13 to ask if he had received it; on May 14 she wrote to Archie Smith asking if Mr. Blackwood was away and mentioning that she had had no reply to a letter sent a fortnight before. We have no record of Blackwood's reply, but she obviously did not receive the position.

43. Blackwood MSS. 4643, September 2 [1896].

44. Blackwood MSS. 4664, March 19 [1897]. Part of this letter, but not her request for the loan, is printed in *A & L*, pp. 432–33.

45. "A Commentary from my Chair," *Spectator*, December 7, 1889, pp. 804–5.

46. *Memoirs of J. M. Dent, 1849–1926*. With some Additions by Hugh R. Dent (London and Toronto, 1928), pp. 79–80.

47. Introduction to Mrs. Oliphant's *A Widow's Tale, and other Stories* (Edinburgh and London, 1898), p. vi.

48. *A & L*, p. 238.

49. Blackwood MSS. 4621, n. d.

50. "Mrs. Oliphant," by "One Who Knew her," *The Academy*, July 3, 1897, pp. 15–16.

51. *Quarterly Review*, CXC (1899), p. 263. Mrs. Oliphant's critical judgment on the Queen's literary efforts did not soften at the same pace as her more personal judgments. On February 16, 1884 she wrote to Blackwood of *Leaves from the Highland Journal:* "What a pity that the Queen should print such rubbish! It must be most distressing for the elder members of her family at least—and I don't wonder that the ladies were in a ferment. If she had wanted to give a little vraisemblance to all the vulgar stories about John Brown she could not have done more. It was her innocence I suppose. But one should not be so innocent at her age" (Blackwood MSS. 4462).

52. *A & L*, p. 333.

53. Blackwood MSS. 4621, n. d.

54. *A & L*, p. 4.

55. Blackwood MSS. 4337, May 8.

56. *A & L*, pp. 385, 400.

57. Blackwood MSS. 4664.

58. *A & L*, p. 410; Blackwood MSS. 4621, December 31 [1894]; 4650, October 15. After Mrs. Oliphant's death, Denny worked with Mrs. Coghill collecting and arranging the letters for the *Autobiography*, but Mrs. Coghill complained to Blackwood that "by dilatoriness and inaccuracy she has greatly added to my labours" (Blackwood MSS. 4686, March 13 [1899]). Thanks to the influence of George Lillie Craik and Blackwood she was granted an annual Civil List pension of £75 (Blackwood MSS. 4664, December 14 [1897]). Late in 1897 her married sister Madge Valentine died following the birth of her third child. Denny wrote to Blackwood: "My brother-in-law Mr. Valentine is anxious I should stay at Elmwood [Lochee, Forfarshire] and

make it my home and look after the children, which indeed is the only thing left for me to do—so my life is settled so far" (Blackwood MSS. 4664, n. d.).

59. Blackwood MSS. 4650, April 16 and 23.

60. *A & L*, p. 425.

61. Blackwood MSS. 4664. Macmillan published a collection of her stories posthumously in 1898—*That Little Cutty and Two other Stories*.

62. The text of this letter is published in Tredrey's *The House of Blackwood, 1804–1954*, pp. 78–79.

63. *Letters of Anne Thackeray Ritchie*, edited by Hester Ritchie (London, 1924), p. 242. The Tennyson poem referred to is his "Ode to the Duke of Clarence." Lady Ritchie recalled to a friend some words Mrs. Oliphant said shortly before her death: "If you revisit this spot (a very lovely one) and see the sunshine come suddenly through the green leaves, believe it is my spirit that is with you." Quoted by Mackenzie Bell, *Representative Novelists of the Nineteenth Century* (New York, 1927), III, 337–8.

64. *Memoir of Robert Herbert Story*, p. 44.

65. Blackwood MSS. 4664, June 26 [1897]. According to the *Times*, November 6, 1897, Mrs. Oliphant left a personal estate of which the gross value was £4,932 and the net value £804. Her most pressing financial affairs were settled quickly. Immediately after the funeral Denny and Madge packed up all the papers and letters relating to the Blackwood history and returned them to the publisher. The books and furniture were sold within less than a month so that the house could be put up for sale unfurnished. Enough life insurance had been left to pay off the mortgage, and the house was sold on August 5 (Blackwood MSS. 4664, July 21 and 25 [1897]). Mrs. Coghill took over Mrs. Oliphant's private papers to prepare the *A & L*. Unfortunately she withheld almost all of her personal letters; those to Mrs. Duncan Stewart, Miss FitzMaurice, and other very close friends, all of whom had died before Mrs. Oliphant, had been destroyed by their families, and Mrs. Coghill regarded many of her own as "too intimate for printing" (Blackwood MSS. 4672, n. d. [1898]). The posthumous publication of several collections of her stories and of the *A & L* (which went into three editions) apparently settled her principal obligations to her publishers Blackwood and Macmillan. Mrs. Coghill, whose husband had died in 1897, was a wealthy woman and did not press for payment for her work on the *A & L*. Blackwood finally settled with her in 1899. She wrote him: "I know of course about my cousin's debt to you, and it was because of this that I said nothing of payment for my work. As you wish to send me an acknowledgment of it now, I will willingly accept what you propose—fifty guineas and nine guineas typewriting expenses" (Blackwood MSS. 4686, June 9 [1899]).

66. Blackwood MSS. 4657, July 5, July 21 [1897].

67. *Memorial to Mrs. Oliphant: An Account of the Inaugural Ceremony in St. Giles Cathedral, Edinburgh, July 16, 1908* (pamphlet), (Edinburgh, 1908). The text of Barrie's speech is in *McConnachie and J. M. B.: Speeches by J. M. Barrie* (New York, 1939), pp. 21–26.

Index

271